ZANZIBAR
BACKGROUND TO REVOLUTION

ZANZIBAR:

BACKGROUND TO REVOLUTION

BY MICHAEL F. LOFCHIE

PRINCETON UNIVERSITY PRESS
PRINCETON, NEW JERSEY
1965

FOR KAY

ACKNOWLEDGMENTS

Rapid and far-reaching change has become the central feature of political life in contemporary Africa. Despite this, revolution has been a rare phenomenon; successful revolution, still rarer. Zanzibar's recent past, therefore, is unique, and any effort to examine the causes of the Zanzibar revolution can be at best only tentative and exploratory. This volume claims no more than to set out certain factors which may be important in understanding why Zanzibar's multi-party parliamentary system collapsed in a violent episode of political transformation.

The list of those to whom the author feels a sense of indebtedness is practically endless, and it is impossible to think by name more than a tiny fraction. Because so much of the information presented here was obtained in interviews and informal discussions with Zanzibaris, a special thanks is owed to the people of Zanzibar for their generosity and hospitality. Leaders of all political parties cooperated with this study. Among them, the author would like to acknowledge the indispensable assistance of the following: *Afro-Shirazi Party* leaders Abeid Karume, Aboud Jumbe, Othman and Ali Sharif, Rastom Sidhwa, Jamal Ramadhan and Khamis Masoud; *Zanzibar Nationalist Party* leaders Ali Muhsin, Abdulrazak Musa, Ali Serboko, Muhsin Abeid, Vuai Kiteweo, Hilal Muhammed, Ibuni Saleh and Ahmed Baalawy; *Zanzibar and Pemba People's Party* leaders Mohammed Shamte, Abdulla Suleiman, and Bakari Mohammed. Of the British colonial officials working in Zanzibar during my stay there, I owe special thanks to Messrs. M. V. Smithyman, A. L. Pennington and Clarence Buxton.

A large number of scholars have read the manuscript or listened patiently to an exposition of its contents. I am especially indebted to Professors David Apter, Seymour Lipset and Gwendolyn Carter for their useful comments, criticism and advice.

To the Foreign Area Fellowship Program (formerly administered by the Ford Foundation) I am grateful for several years of generous and unstinting financial support which enabled me to pursue a program of African studies at the University of California, Berkeley; to undertake language training in Swahili and to engage in eighteen months of field research in Zanzibar during 1962-1963. To the African Studies Center at UCLA and to its Director, Professor James Coleman, I am indebted for a faculty research fellowship which provided additional free time for completion and revision of the manuscript. Although all of these friends, colleagues and institutions have made this study possible, they are by no means responsible for any errors of fact or limitations of interpretation. For these, the author assumes full responsibility.

Finally, there are two individuals but for whose immeasurable contributions this study could never have been undertaken or completed. To Professor Carl G. Rosberg, Jr. of the University of California, Berkeley, I owe the deepest and most profound thanks. His penetrating and stimulating analysis of modern Africa and his close personal friendship and encouragement have been among the greatest rewards of a career in African studies. My wife, Kay Lynn Lofchie, to whom this book is dedicated, deserves an acknowledgment that could only be properly indicated if this book were to appear under our joint authorship. Typing the entire manuscript through its innumerable draft stages, compiling and organizing the tables, assuming the heavy burden of editing and preparing the final index were the least of her contributions.

Los Angeles   Michael F. Lofchie
June, 1965

☬ CONTENTS

LIST OF TABLES AND MAPS

TABLES

MAPS

ZANZIBAR
BACKGROUND TO REVOLUTION

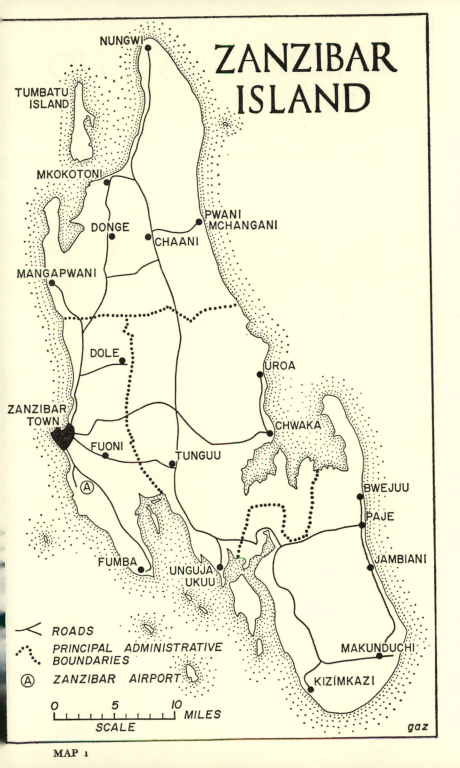

ZANZIBAR ISLAND

NUNGWI

TUMBATU
ISLAND

MKOKOTONI

DONGE

PWANI
MCHANGANI

CHAANI

MANGAPWANI

DOLE

UROA

ZANZIBAR
TOWN

CHWAKA

FUONI

TUNGUU

Ⓐ

BWEJUU

PAJE

JAMBIANI

FUMBA

UNGUJA
UKUU

MAKUNDUCHI

⟨ ROADS

•••• PRINCIPAL ADMINISTRATIVE
      BOUNDARIES

Ⓐ ZANZIBAR AIRPORT

KIZIMKAZI

0   5   10
|__|__|__|__|__|__| MILES
      SCALE

gaz

MAP 1

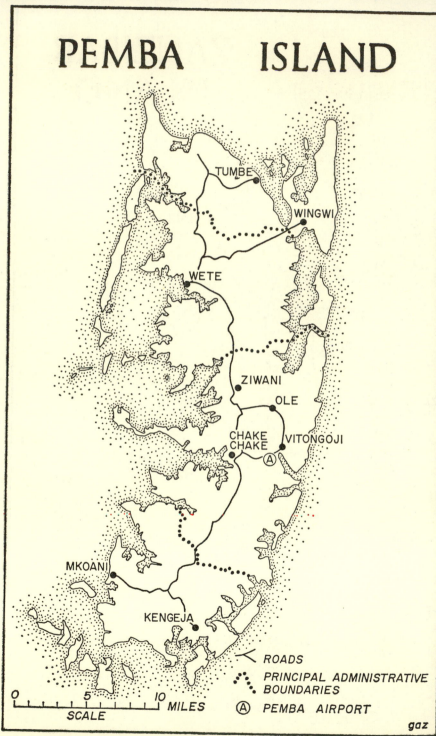

PEMBA ISLAND

TUMBE

WINGWI

WETE

ZIWANI

OLE

CHAKE
CHAKE

VITONGOJI

(A)

MKOANI

KENGEJA

ROADS

PRINCIPAL ADMINISTRATIVE
BOUNDARIES

(A) PEMBA AIRPORT

0   5   10 MILES
SCALE

gaz

MAP 2

ॐ INTRODUCTION

The Character of Zanzibar Politics[1]

As a small island country, Zanzibar's history has been profoundly affected by geographical factors. An unusually mild tropical climate, exceptionally favorable soil conditions, and a pattern of prevailing winds which place it directly on the Indian Ocean trade routes have, since ancient times, made Zanzibar both attractive and accessible to travelers and colonists from the Arabian peninsula, the sub-continent of Asia and the continental African mainland. Despite Zanzibar's equatorial position, it does not experience the grueling, enervating heat of many other similarly located areas. Year-round temperatures, cooled by almost continuous ocean breezes, rarely exceed 90° F. and the mean maximum temperature of Zanzibar Island is less than 85° F. Pemba Island, somewhat closer to the equator, has a mean maximum temperature only a degree or two warmer. Nor is there great seasonal variation. Both islands have mean minimum temperatures in the mid- to upper 70's. Moreover, Zanzibar and Pemba Islands both benefit from a moderate annual rainfall, 61″ and 76″ respectively, which, while quite adequate for nearly all forms of cultivation, does not foster the jungle-like growth characteristic of certain

[1] On April 24, 1964, Zanzibar merged with the neighboring country of Tanganyika and thereby ceased, in formal constitutional terms, to be an independent nation. As a sovereign country, Zanzibar had comprised the two large islands of Zanzibar and Pemba and a small number of adjacent islands off the coast of East Africa. Zanzibar Island is approximately 53 miles long by 24 miles wide (maximum measurements) with an area of 640 square miles. Its geographical coordinates are Latitude 6° South, Longitude 39° East. It is separated from the African continent by a channel about 22½ miles across at its narrowest point. Pemba lies about 25 miles to the northeast of Zanzibar and is approximately 42 miles long, 14 miles wide (maximum measurements) with an area of 380 square miles.

Introduction

West African countries or the Amazon River valley in Brazil.

Remarkably fertile soil conditions exist on both islands and, together with the relatively mild climate and moderate rainfall, make possible the intensive year-round cultivation of a wide variety of export and food crops. On Pemba, arable soil is ubiquitous and only in a few remote areas does the quality of the land deteriorate and become unsuitable for heavy commercial farming. Zanzibar Island differs significantly in this regard. Here, good land is to be found predominantly only in the western portion of the island. A ridge running irregularly north and south bisects the island and, in the area east of this ridge, soil conditions are much poorer and visibly unsuitable for intensive cultivation. This geographical division has had extreme historical importance. Colonial immigrant communities gradually came to possess almost monopolistic occupancy of the fertile western area and, by the end of the nineteenth century, the indigenous population had come to reside almost entirely in the eastern section.

Zanzibar and Pemba also differ enormously in respect of their overall topography. Pemba has an extremely irregular coastline indented by an almost infinite number of creeks and inlets. Within a mile of the coast, the island ascends in a series of separate steppes to an altitude of about two hundred feet above sea level. The most striking feature of Pemba is the extremely hilly quality of the interior. Though the highest point on the island is only slightly more than three hundred feet above sea level, the visual impression created by the interior terrain is one of precipitous valleys, steep ravines and hillside terraces with almost no areas of plain or flatland. This gives the island an erratic and meandering system of inland drainage. There are numerous small streams, many of which flow in opposite directions towards the eastern and western shores, while others end in marshes or swamps on the valley bottoms. Despite the obvious difficulties such a terrain places in the way of efficient cultivation, Pemba possesses an extremely productive agriculture. Tree crops such as coconuts, cloves and bananas are grown on the hillsides; groundcrops such as rice, cassava and other vegetables are raised on the valley floors.

Zanzibar, in marked contrast to Pemba, has both a fairly even unindented coastline and a relatively flat terrain. Though the highest point on the island, located on the central ridge, is more than four hundred feet above sea level, and though Zanzibar also has a steppe-like configuration near the coast, the interior terrain is relatively flat. The land ascends gradually from the coastal terrace to the central ridge and the general visual impression, on both sides of the ridge, is of flatlands and rolling plains. Due to the clear demarcation of areas of good and bad soil, the rural ecology of Zanzibar Island has far greater variation than that of Pemba. West of the ridge there are intensely cultivated clove and coconut plantations; the countryside is green, richly productive and heavily settled. East of the ridge, where the soil is rocky and poor, cultivation is sparse and the countryside largely consists of wild brush vegetation or unsettled forest. Here, the principal areas of human habitation are coastal villages where fishing is an important supplement to agriculture.

Zanzibar's most important crop is cloves and the clove industry is the basic mainstay of the domestic economy. The fortunate combination of mild climate, arable soil and moderate rainfall has furnished an almost ideal environment for clove cultivation and, in the past, gave Zanzibar a near monopoly of world clove production. Though coconuts, limes, tobacco and several other agricultural commodities are also grown for overseas sale, cloves alone have, in recent years, accounted for about three-fourths of the country's total export revenue. Approximately four-fifths of Zanzibar's cloves are grown on Pemba Island due to the wider and more even distribution of fertile land. But the economies of the two islands are closely interlocked through the migration of labor and the fact that Zanzibar Island has become the country's processing and shipping center.

Since the Second World War, Zanzibar has had to face increased competition from new clove producers such as the Malagache Republic. This competition, together with a series of other difficulties, has created a severe and chronic depression in Zanzibar's clove-based economy. Over-concentration on the production of cloves to the detriment of food crops, for example, has forced Zanzibar, though an agricultural country, to become a heavy importer of agricultural products while, in bumper years, Zanzibar's clove farmers harvest and process more cloves than are purchased by the entire world market. Moreover, the two principal world markets for cloves, Indonesia and India, are experiencing critical foreign exchange difficulties and have drastically reduced their clove purchases in order to conserve currency. Since these two countries often accounted for more than three-fifths of Zanzibar's total overseas sales, their cutbacks have had an enormous impact. As a result of all these factors, the world price of cloves has plummeted to a small fraction of what it was in the early 1950's, Zanzibar has been consistently unable to sell its entire crop, and the Government has been faced with rapidly declining revenue due to a loss of clove duty.

The heart of Zanzibar's economic and political life is Zanzibar Town, located on a triangular peninsula at about mid-point on the western coast of Zanzibar Island. The town is divided into two sections: Stonetown, at the extremity of the peninsula, and the Ngambo

(African Quarter), by far the larger of the two sections and adjacent to the main part of the island. These two sections have differed fundamentally in their racial composition, physical appearance and economic development. The Ngambo has been populated almost entirely by Africans living in slum conditions either in mud huts or small, poorly built houses. Practically the only businesses in the Ngambo are the numerous retail shops and stalls which service the day-to-day needs of the African population. The physical appearance of the Ngambo has thus been one of extreme poverty, and in this respect the African area of Zanzibar Town does not visibly differ from the African slum areas of Dar es Salaam, Nairobi, or other large African cities.

The Stonetown area has become internationally known for its Middle Eastern appearance, its massive white stone buildings in an Arab architectural style, its narrow winding streets and its endless labyrinth of alleys. The Stonetown area also contains a spacious, well-protected, deep-water harbor. Indeed, a major reason for the development of this site as the contemporary capital of Zanzibar was its ability to offer safe accommodation to large ocean-going vessels. In addition to the Middle Eastern character of its architectural style, Stonetown also differs from Ngambo in creating an image of economic prosperity. Zanzibar's largest business concerns, its banks, insurance firms and overseas trading companies are all located here; its retail shops do not serve the day-to-day needs of the residents, but cater to the expensive tastes of the international tourist trade. Perhaps most important, the population of Stonetown has been almost entirely non-African and composed of immigrant ethnic groups from the sub-continent of Asia and the Arabian peninsula.

The present government of Zanzibar is currently seeking to equalize the economic and material conditions of

Introduction

Stonetown and Ngambo but, until recently, the physical differences between these two areas of the city graphically symbolized the basic feature of social stratification in Zanzibar, the impoverishment and subordinate status of the African community. This pattern of stratification was the basic factor shaping Zanzibar's contemporary pattern of political development.

Immigrant non-African minorities have frequently sought to preserve a privileged position in societies where there are African majorities. The Union of South Africa, Southern Rhodesia, the Portuguese African territories and, until recently, Kenya are the most obvious examples of this type of situation. In Zanzibar, too, the central feature of contemporary political development has been the persistent effort of a powerful alien oligarchy to retain its position of political and economic supremacy. The Arab minority of Zanzibar constituted in proportion to the total population the second largest alien elite in all the countries of Africa south of the Sahara. It may be assumed that, out of a present population of more than 300,000, the Arab minority numbers about 50,000. Only in South Africa, where a minority of European descent comprises more than 20 per cent of the total population, is there a proportionately larger minority of alien origin than in Zanzibar.

The basic political technique of dominant immigrant minorities in Africa has usually been to avoid any liberalization of the institutions of government, so as to deprive the African majorities of access to political power. For in practically every country where African nationalism has led to the introduction of democratic institutions, the result has been to bring to power chosen representatives of the majority population. In this respect, Zanzibar's recent political history is unique for, unlike the Europeans of South Africa, Southern Rhodesia, the Portuguese territories or Kenya, the Arabs of Zanzibar did not seek to entrench themselves as a ruling caste through systematic and repressive subordination of the African community. Instead, they attempted to gain voluntary acceptance among Africans by fostering a multi-racial concept of national community and by championing the cause of representative self-government. Arabs, who had formed an autocratic ruling group since early in the nineteenth century, were not only the first to initiate a nationalist movement, but of all the communities in Zanzibar were the most vociferous in demanding that British colonial rule be replaced by fully democratic parliamentary institutions. Zanzibar nationalsim was thus—at its inception and for a considerable period thereafter—the creation of the Arab oligarchy and not of the African majority population.

Arab political leaders started Zanzibar nationalism in 1954, partially in an effort to remove the British before the African community could become politically organized. In June, the Arab Association began to boycott the Zanzibar Legislative Council and demanded immediate progress towards self-government and a national common roll election. The boycott lasted for more than a year and a half, until early 1956 when the British Government agreed to these demands. During this period a nationalistic political party, the Zanzibar Nationalist Party (ZNP), was formed and Arabs began to take such an active part in organizing and leading it that throughout the pre-independence era, the ZNP sought to live down a reputation as an Arab-dominated party. By means of intensive organization, militant nationalism and a strong appeal to Muslim unity, it did succeed in attracting numerous non-Arab supporters and most of its members were African.

The nationalistic political activities of the Arab elite stimulated the formation of an African political party, the Afro-Shirazi Party (ASP). The ASP was an attempt to unite two historically and ethnically distinct African communities, an immigrant mainland African community numbering about 60,000 and a Shirazi or indigenous African community of about 200,000. From the very beginning of their party in February, 1957, ASP leaders were motivated principally by resentment of the social and political preeminence of the Arab oligarchy, resentment which expressed itself in virulently anti-Arab propaganda and in the publicly expressed desire of ASP leadership to transform Zanzibar into an African-ruled nation.

A third political party, the Zanzibar and Pemba People's Party (ZPPP), was formed in late 1959. It began as a splinter group from the ASP after a long conflict between mainland African and Shirazi African leaders. Initially the ZPPP hoped to be an independent third force in Zanzibar politics, one which would avoid the racism of the ASP yet remain essentially an African party devoted to African interests. Gradually, its antipathy towards the militantly anti-Arab views of the ASP and a sympathy for the multi-racial concepts being articulated by Arab leadership brought the ZPPP closer and closer to the ZNP; in June, 1961, after a bitterly contested election, a ZNP/ZPPP coalition government was formed. The formation of this coalition dramatized the deep division within the African community over the issue of Arab rule in Zanzibar and revealed the willingness of large numbers of Africans to accept Arab leadership.

The vast majority of Zanzibar Africans, however, regarded the ZNP and, by association, the ZNP/ZPPP coalition as well, as dedicated to preserving the political and economic supremacy of the Arab community. Their growing conviction that the coalition government operated in Arab interests was clearly revealed in Zanzibar's last general election held in July, 1963. The ASP polled more than 54 per cent of the popular vote and received over 13,000 votes more than the coalition parties combined. Because the ASP's popular support tended to be concentrated in a relatively small number of constituencies, however, it gained only 13 out of 31 seats in the National Assembly. The two coalition parties won 18 seats and were able to remain in power.

The results of the July, 1963, election meant that the Arab oligarchy had, at least temporarily, succeeded in preserving its political supremacy after the introduction of democratic institutions. The establishment of complete representative democracy with universal suffrage and freely contested elections did not end Arab domination over Zanzibar's African majority because the African community was by no means solidly opposed to Arab hegemony. The Arab-led ZNP was able to gain sufficient African support to do extremely well in several constituencies where there were overwhelming African majorities and, in coalition with the ZPPP, formed the Government of Zanzibar during the final stages of constitutional development. In more than two and one-half years of ZNP/ZPPP coalition government, ZPPP leaders publicly supported the ZNP and accepted its views on practically every major issue of national policy. Thus, when independence occurred in December, 1963, the most salient feature of Zanzibar politics was the strong likelihood that, despite a representative constitutional framework, the Arab oligarchy would be able to use the ZNP to strengthen its domination of state and society in Zanzibar.

This book seeks to explain the Arab oligarchy's success in establishing a popular basis of support within the African community, and hence why democratic constitutional arrangements failed to reverse the traditional political relationship between the Arab minority and the African majority. This was, in a sense, the fundamental cause of the African community's violent seizure of power in January, 1964; force had become the only method by which African leaders could oust the Arab ruling caste from its historic position of political and economic supremacy and create an African-ruled state. The following analysis of the African revolution and of the unique pattern of political development which preceded it emphasizes three related factors: first, an inherent ambivalence in Zanzibar's political culture—a powerful impetus toward multi-racial unity based upon common adherence to Islam, and a strain toward extreme disunity based on economic differences between the races; second, major regional differences in Arab-African race relations between Zanzibar and Pemba; and third, the special role of the British colonial government in helping the Arab community to preserve its dominant position.

The strains toward and against multi-racial unity were the basic political forces which operated in Zanzibar society. They had existed in continual opposition to one another since Zanzibar became an Arab colony early in the nineteenth century. Islam furnished a powerful impetus towards inter-ethnic solidarity among a racially stratified population and was conducive to widespread African support for the nationalist movement sponsored and led by the Arabs. But, at the same time, economic differences which operated along racial lines accentuated ethnic divisions and caused them to become an alternative and divisive basis of political loyalty.

Islam in Zanzibar created a pervasive religious environment highly favorable to inter-racial political solidarities. This environment furnished Arab leaders with the basic ingredient of an effective appeal for African political support: a common faith. Arab and African Zanzibaris shared not only the same theology, but all the various institutions and practices which accompanied it such as mosques, Koranic schools and a host of identical holidays, rituals and ceremonies. These made Islam a highly visible symbol of the common religious identity of Zanzibaris of all races.

The explicit social teachings of Islam provided forceful impetus to cordial and cooperative relations between races. Islam endows racial diversity with sacred status as a divine creation: "Among His signs is the creation of the heavens and the earth, and the diversity of your tongues and complections (sic). This is surely a sign for all those who possess knowledge."[2] The Koran is, in fact, quite explicit in making harmonious race relations a religious duty: "Men, we have created you from a male and female and divided you into nations and tribes so that you might get to know one another."[3] Arab leadership employed these precepts to foster a widespread conviction among Africans that the Faith enjoined multiracial unity upon all believers as a holy obligation.

The political theory of Islam contributed, as well, to the ease with which Arab political leaders, though members of an immigrant oligarchy, were able to find political support among Africans. The Koran lacks a clear concept of the State, but one important passage reads: "Obey God and His Apostle and those who have authority over you."[4] Thus, obedience to those in power is, like racial harmony, a divinely imposed duty. Since Arabs constituted Zanzibar's closest approximation to a traditional ruling class, the Koranic insistence on deference to established leadership in effect gave religious legitimacy to their political role and their status as a dominant elite.

The highly integrative potential of Islam suggests that some explanation is necessary for the absence of a uni-

[2] Koran: 30, 31.
[3] Koran: 49, 13.
[4] Koran: 4, 62.

fied political culture in Zanzibar for, despite the social and political teachings of the Koran and despite the assertive structural visibility of common Muslim institutions, Zanzibar politics have been bitterly divided along racial lines.

The explanation is to be found largely in the pronounced tendency for race to coincide with economic class. Arabs constituted a privileged political and economic elite until the African revolution; they were the owners of the largest coconut and clove plantations and occupied many of the highest administrative positions in the Zanzibar civil service. Asians (persons of Indo-Pakistani descent) formed Zanzibar's commercial and middle class; they dominated wholesale and retail trade, import and export businesses and enjoyed nearly exclusive occupancy of the middle tiers of the civil service. Africans were historically the broad underprivileged mass of the Zanzibar population; they were the unskilled manual and agricultural laborers, tenant farmers and petty agriculturists. Each racial group possessed a separate social and economic sub-culture, and most social relations were carried on within ethnic boundaries. With few exceptions, the only extensive inter-ethnic contact was in the marketplace, and here race relations were conducted in the idiom of economic superior to economic inferior: employer-employee, master-servant, or landowner-laborer. This made race an extremely important part of the life of every individual, and caused it to become an important basis of loyalty and group solidarity.

There have been other societies in which race and class were overlapping categories and in which interracial violence was not a characteristic phenomenon. The caste structure of classical India is an example. Here, and in other comparable areas, stability resulted largely from a basic congruence between the prevailing social ethos and the existing social arrangements. Usually the religious beliefs performed a legitimizing function, and explained the class structure in sacred terms to make it acceptable.

Zanzibar never possessed a fully-developed caste system, for Islam did not lend itself to buttressing a racial pattern of stratification. If anything, Islam contained strongly implied egalitarian strains in its liberal racial doctrines and in its principle that the only differences between men are those of piety.[5] In addition, Zanzibar, like other African territories in recent times, experienced a wholesale infusion of overtly and explicitly egalitarian political norms and social values. These, too, made its class structure appear increasingly illegitimate to the African majority.

As egalitarian ideas gave rise to a pattern of aspirations deeply at variance with the economic relations between ethnic groups, some Africans organized separate racial associations in order to seek rapid social and political changes. A basic division arose during the era of nationalism between these Africans and a large number of Africans who felt that such separate racial political organization was against Islamic multi-racial precepts. The latter joined in common cause with Arabs to give an Arab-led political party a parliamentary majority. The former, frustrated in their attempt to gain political power by constitutional means, participated in the African revolution which overthrew the Government of Zanzibar shortly after Independence.

Despite the ubiquitous economic differences between Arabs and Africans, however, there were large areas of Zanzibar where the African population did not resent the Arabs. A powerful sense of racial grievance and resentment emerged, on the whole, only among the Africans of Zanzibar Island. Pemba Africans were far less

[5] Koran: 49, 13.

motivated to end the Arab community's status as a dominant elite. Their implicit willingness to continue the traditional relationship between the races was critical in enabling the Arab oligarchy to retain political hegemony within a representative institutional framework. Pemba Africans were consistent supporters of the ZNP, and their support alone gave that party about one-half of its National Assembly seats.

The fundamental differences in attitude between Zanzibar and Pemba Africans can, in part, be explained historically. Zanzibar's African population suffered massive social upheavals under the impact of Arab settlement in the nineteenth century. Here, the Arab immigrants quickly imposed their authority over the local tribes and created an autocratic colonial regime. Though the Arab colonists sought to administer the indigenous population through a form of indirect rule, the traditional African political institutions collapsed as a result of their sudden forced subordination to alien government. In the course of the century, the Arab settler colony indulged in wholesale alienation of the best land and the African population was confined to remote coastal areas of poor quality soil. The principal form of social contact between Arabs and Africans on Zanzibar was the forced labor which Africans were compelled to perform on some Arab plantations. This experience and the racial friction it had created led Zanzibar Africans in recent years to join eagerly in political movements seeking to establish an African government.

Arab contact with Pemba Africans has been altogether different. The Arab incursion into Pemba was much later than that into Zanzibar, and was undertaken only after the consent of the local African rulers. Since this consent made it comparatively unnecessary for Arabs to employ repressive measures to ensure social control, the autocratic nature of Arab colonialism was not nearly so visible in Pemba as it was in Zanzibar. Moreover, Arab land alienation in Pemba did not result in widespread disruption of indigenous social life. Though a certain amount of land alienation did occur, there was no wholesale expropriation by Arab settlers of the best land. Fertile soils abound in Pemba, and the local African communities continued to retain possession of highly cultivable areas. Thus, the creation of an Arab colonial community in Pemba did not involve serious hardships for the indigenous African communities, either through forced administrative subordination or through land acquisition, and for this reason Pemba Africans were far less disposed than Zanzibar Africans during the era of competitive party politics to enter into anti-Arab political movements.

Unevenness in the incidence of modernization may also help to explain the vast differences between the contemporary political attitudes and behavior of Zanzibar and Pemba Africans. Zanzibar Island has been the scene of far-reaching development in the introduction of western educational, economic and technological institutions. Most of these have been concentrated in Zanzibar Town, which is the center of its administration, commerce and trade, and the matrix of an extensive infrastructural network. Nearly one-fourth of the African population of Zanzibar has been fully urbanized and resides in the town on a fairly permanent basis. Thousands of Africans have thus been absorbed into the modern occupational sector of the Zanzibar economy and brought into intense contact with a new, secular political culture. Uprooted from traditional ties and affiliations, and alerted to the full meaning of the concept of representative government, they were available for recruitment into African mass movements seeking a major political reconstruction of Zanzibar society.

Pemba, on the other hand, has had relatively little social change during this century; there is little urbanization, and the island remains a predominately rural and agrarian society. Pemba Africans have been both geographically and culturally remote from the forces of secular modernization which mobilized the Africans of Zanzibar. An Islamic religious culture and traditional forms of social organization remain the paramount commitment of most Pemba Africans, and African mass movements have had little success in attracting their support.

British colonial policy in Zanzibar helped to perpetuate the dominant status of the Arab oligarchy. Great Britain first established its political hegemony over Zanzibar in 1890 by signing a protectoral treaty with Zanzibar's Arab Sultan, and consistently thereafter interpreted its rule as protecting power as one which involved a special obligation to protect Arab interests. The colonial administration believed firmly that Zanzibar was, in constitutional terms, an Arab state. This belief was reflected in the vastly disproportionate representation awarded Arabs on legislative and advisory bodies; in the heavy recruitment of Arabs into top positions in the administration, the judiciary and the educational system; and in a pattern of close cooperation and consultation between top British officials and leaders of the Arab community. These policies, in effect, preserved the Arab colonial state intact within the overarching framework of British imperial rule.

The British administration virtually ignored the political interests of the African majority throughout this century. No African was nominated to Zanzibar's Legislative Council until after World War II and, until the revolution, very few Africans ever managed to gain important administrative positions. The British colonial administration may also be held ultimately accountable for the heavily discriminatory nature of Zanzibar's educational system which strongly favored Arabs and Asians against Africans, particularly at the secondary school level. This grave racial imbalance in access to higher education contributed directly to the static quality of Zanzibar's race-class system. Britain's unwillingness to undertake major educational reform may well indicate an unspoken assumption that the African community would remain permanently in a subordinate economic and political condition.

Britain's long-range desire to introduce parliamentary institutions and to transform the Sultanate into a constitutional monarchy did not basically qualify the assumption of permanent Arab paramountcy. Administrators in the country saw no tension between their desire to create a democratic majoritarian state and the strong sense of obligation to respect and preserve the special position of the Arab community. The process of evolution of representative government was regarded, somewhat ethnocentrically, as a changing relationship between Protector and Protected rather than as a development having enormous bearing on the character of race relations within Zanzibar society. It was perhaps more important, however, that the full institutionalization of parliamentary democracy was viewed as an extremely long-range enterprise in political tutelage, and one in which the Arab community could play an important role.

The notion that democratic self-government could occur only after many generations of careful instruction characterized British attitudes in many colonies. Throughout the period during which Britain was seeking to establish parliamentary institutions in Zanzibar, there was an implicit assumption that once representative government occurred, other problems would sort themselves out; and not until recently was any serious attention paid to the political consequences of enfranchising an overwhelming African majority. Moreover,

Introduction

the massive enfranchisement of Africans after 1957 was
not accompanied by a corresponding effort to undertake
the other reforms necessary to place Africans education-
ally and economically on a competitive basis with Arabs
in the electoral arena.

PART I

HISTORICAL AND SOCIAL
BACKGROUND

CHAPTER I

The Establishment of the Arab State

Autonomous African communities have existed in Zanzibar since ancient times.[1] The first settlements in Zanzibar were established by immigrants from numerous sections of the African mainland. Having entered the islands of Zanzibar and Pemba at a number of different points, they created separate village communities whose characteristic form of government was a monarchy or chieftainship. There was no coalescence into broader polities until comparatively recent times. The largest historical unit of political organization was either a single settlement or a loose association comprising a small number of neighboring settlements.

The absence of any overall unity among these village communities, the vulnerability of their fragmented political culture and their exposed and indefensible insular position left them unable either to resist alien settlement or to protect themselves against sporadic colonial invasions. They have thus been subjected to a succession

[1] There is an abundant secondary literature on the history of Zanzibar and the East African coast. This chapter, therefore, is intended as an interpretive essay which emphasizes those aspects of Zanzibar's historical development relevant to the contemporary political scene, rather than as an orthodox historical narrative. The principal works consulted in the preparation of the chapter were: R. Coupland, *East Africa and Its Invaders* (Oxford: The Clarendon Press, 1961); R. Coupland, *The Exploitation of East Africa, 1856-1890* (London: Faber & Faber Ltd., 1939); Sir John Gray, *History of Zanzibar from the Middle Ages to 1856* (London: Oxford University Press, 1962); L. W. Hollingsworth, *Zanzibar Under the Foreign Office, 1890-1913* (London: Macmillan & Co. Ltd., 1953); Kenneth Ingham, *A History of East Africa* (London: Longmans, 1962); W. H. Ingrams, *Zanzibar Its History and Its People* (London: H. F. & G. Witherby, 1931); Roland Oliver and Gervase Mathew, eds., *History of East Africa* (Oxford: The Clarendon Press, 1963). A more extensive list of works on this subject may be found in the bibliography.

of occupations by a variety of European and Asiatic nations. This has afforded them continuous and intense inter-ethnic contact with a rich assortment of peoples and cultures, and in the ensuing process of cultural exchange they have absorbed many of the economic, political and social practices of the immigrant communities.

Despite the influx of traders, immigrants and invaders throughout the centuries, the indigenous African communities were able to survive and absorb such intruders. However, when Arab colonists arrived in the nineteenth century they found the African population politically vulnerable and unable to resist the establishment of an Arab colonial state. This situation existed partially because the previous centuries of contact with Persia and Arabia had acculturated the African communities in the customs and traditions of the Middle East, and also because they had become accustomed to accepting alien settlement without resistance. But the major source of vulnerability was the absence of political unity among the local African groups.

Among the first immigrants to arrive continuously and to live and intermarry with the local African population in large numbers were the Persians, who began to land in Zanzibar in about the tenth century.[2] Unlike other early travelers and traders in the Indian Ocean, these Persians severed ties with their own homeland, the

[2] Sir John Gray argues that intermarriage with the local African population did not begin to take place for some time after the initial Persian settlement on Zanzibar. In his words, ". . . the impression that one gets is that generally speaking these early immigrants at first kept themselves aloof from the local inhabitants and that a constant influx of fresh immigrants enabled them to keep their stock more or less pure. But later, when the stream of immigrants became little more than a trickle, and when for purposes of self-defense the colonists had to have recourse to alliances with the local African tribes, racial barriers began to break down and miscegenation became fairly widespread." Gray, p. 19.

principality of Shiraz in Persia, and planned to settle permanently in Africa. The Persian immigrants became absorbed into the local population and gradually disappeared as a separate group, but their influence on the native village communities was considerable. The Persians began to unify the hitherto disparate native villages into slightly more consolidated political communities. Ruling dynasties of mixed Persian-African descent gradually emerged. These provided focal points of identity leading to the gradual formation of two contemporary African tribes—the Hadimu and the Tumbatu. The African population converted to Islam and adopted numerous ceremonies and traditions from Persian culture. Indeed, Persian impact was so great that today the vast majority of Zanzibar's indigenous African population calls itself "Shirazi."

In spite of its long-range effect, Persian immigration to Zanzibar actually occurred during only a very short period. The most persistant relationship between Zanzibar's African communities and any immigrant race has been with Arabs. Arab traders and explorers came to Zanzibar centuries before the Christian era, for even at this early date the Indian Ocean slave trade was well established.[3] Though Zanzibar lacked a large enough population to warrant slaving expeditions, its proximity to the East African coast and the safety it offered from warlike coastal tribes made the island an ideal stopping point in the ocean-going commerce. After the founding

[3] The great antiquity of Arab contact with the coast of East Africa is largely a result of geographic factors. Between December and early February a north, northeast monsoon blows steadily across the Indian Ocean from the Arabian peninsula and the western coast of India; in April, this trade wind reverses itself and a south, southwest monsoon blows away from eastern Africa towards the Persian Gulf countries. This remarkable pattern of prevailing winds promoted a continuous annual ocean-going trade between Arabia and Africa long before any overland commerce would have been possible. See Coupland, *East Africa,* p. 15.

of Islam in the seventh century, there was a marked intensification of Arab contact with Zanzibar and the East
African coast. Exiles from religious wars and persecu-
tions and from internal dynastic conflicts joined traders
in the stream of immigration. Those from Oman became
particularly important, for they began to establish colonies where before they had only traded.

Zanzibar offered ample inducement to these early settlers. It had neither ivory nor slaves, but it did possess a
spacious protected harbor and an unlimited supply of
fresh water, timber and coconut palms. Numerous Arab-
sponsored settlements grew up along the entire East
African coastline, and the most prosperous of these colonies—Magadishu, Mombasa and Malindi as well as Zanzibar—developed extensive trade relations with inland
tribes. Each one, however, remained a more or less self-
contained urban polity and not a part of an integrated
Arab empire.

Nevertheless, the colonies did develop a distinct, com-
monly-shared civilization. This civilization, usually referred to as Swahili, was a mixture of African and Arab
cultural elements. Its principal components were Arab
architecture, art and dress, the Muslim religion and the
Swahili language which gives this culture its name. This
language is African in grammar and essentially African
in vocabulary, but is heavily infused with Arabic.[4]

[4] Coupland points out that Swahili civilization attained a high
level of material abundance but the Arab colonists failed to bring to
East Africa the literary and artistic achievements of the medieval
Arab world. In his words, ". . . by the end of the fifteenth century
the Arab colonists in East Africa attained a high level of material
civilization. . . . But it was not, it seems, a cultured life. In other
countries, the Arabs not only preserved and passed on to their
Christian enemies the legacy of Hellenism; they made their own
contribution to the literature, art, and science of the world. In the
tenth and eleventh centuries the centres of Arab learning at Cor-
dova, Toledo and Seville illumined the darkness of medieval
Europe. . . . But in East Africa, no trace of this higher life appears."
Ibid., p. 39.

Throughout the entire period of Arab immigration and colonization there was also a heavy influx of Asians, largely from the region of Bombay, Surat and Cutch on the northwest coast of India. The Asians were almost exclusively traders and businessmen, rather than colonists. They never made it a practice to establish even temporary residence in East Africa but preferred to return to India once their commercial affairs had been completed. Even after they had created a permanently settled community in Zanzibar they did not enter into a close cultural relationship with the local African population. For this reason, the indigenous Africans of Zanzibar (and of other East African countries) have adopted practically nothing of Asian culture for their own.

Though the Asian immigrants remained culturally aloof, they entered into close business relations with the resident Arab colonists, and by the fifteenth and sixteenth centuries they had emerged as the dominant economic force of the entire Indian Ocean. Asians became the most powerful financiers and brokers, controlled a considerable portion of the shipping, and conducted most of the trade and commerce either as private businessmen or as managers for wealthy land-owning Arab magnates. Gradually the Arabs lost their economic self-sufficiency and became dependent upon the financial and business skills of the Asian trader-class. Eventually they became a leisured aristocracy which maintained itself solely through ownership of land and a monopoly of political power.[5]

Arab domination of the colonial scene in East Africa was interrupted early in the sixteenth century by the arrival of the Portuguese. Within the first decade of the century the Portuguese captured and subdued all the colonies along the coast and established themselves as

[5] *Ibid.,* pp. 27ff.

the supreme political power in the Indian Ocean. They conquered Mombasa (then the most powerful seaport on the East African coast) as early as 1505, and shortly thereafter completely eliminated any remaining Arab resistance. Their motives, however, were primarily economic and to a degree missionary. For Portugal intended to use its power to establish a national monopoly of the Indian Ocean trade and to convert the local population to Christianity. In pursuit of this objective, Portugal rapidly expanded its effective occupation to India and Arabia and by 1580 had even succeeded in capturing Muscat, the capital of Oman. The Portuguese managed to retain their influence in varying degrees for nearly two centuries.

Although Portugal was the commanding force in East Africa for so long a period, it exercised little lasting influence on the entire area north of present-day Mozambique. Its civilizing and Christianizing mission was as much a failure as its effort to take over the Arab trading empire. Today few traces remain of its former presence in the art, architecture, dress or language of East Africa. There are several reasons for this failure. Portugal made no attempt to use its control as a basis for introducing efficient and systematic administrative machinery or viable political institutions, nor did Portugal employ intensive colonization as a mechanism for the transmission of its culture. At the peak, the Portuguese establishment in East Africa never totaled a thousand men, and thus its effort to introduce a new culture lacked the sustained impact of a resident colonial population. In contrast, the Swahili culture had become firmly embedded—the outgrowth of many centuries of contact between the Arab world and African society—and was an integral feature of East African life. The only significant effect of the Portuguese presence in East Africa was that it temporarily interrupted the development of an Arab colonial empire.[6]

The Arabs of Oman succeeded in ousting the Portuguese from their capital, Muscat, in 1650 and immediately afterwards began a determined reassertion of their colonial policy in the Indian Ocean. Among their earliest successes was a subjugation of the Portuguese settlement in Zanzibar, although for the Omanis Zanzibar had little intrinsic importance at that time. Their primary objective was the recapture of Mombasa, and this was accomplished in 1699 after a siege that lasted nearly three years.

By their expulsion of the Portuguese, the Omani Arabs clearly established their military and naval supremacy in the Indian Ocean, and regained at least formal sovereignty over the coastal colonies. It was far more difficult for Oman to reestablish firm political control within the newly liberated settlements. Strict supervision of colonial affairs had never been a salient feature of Omani colonialism before the arrival of the Portuguese and, under the Portuguese, colonial local government had been of the loosest sort. Many of the coastal settlements wanted to continue to manage their own affairs, and during the century or so after the recapture of Mombasa, Oman was continually preoccupied with the problem of local separatism and the difficulty of translating its formal sovereignty into a commanding role in the administration of the East African towns.

Mombasa, the most powerful and important of the coastal cities, was the most assertive in pressing its claim to self-rule, and in 1741 seized upon a moment of instability in Oman to declare itself fully independent. The

[6] For a fuller discussion of the Portuguese period in East Africa and of Portuguese-Arab relations, see G. S. P. Freeman-Grenville, "The Coast, 1498-1840," *History of East Africa,* ed. Roland Oliver and Gervase Mathew (Oxford: The Clarendon Press, 1963), pp. 129-168; also Gray, pp. 31-81 and Coupland, *East Africa,* pp. 41-72.

instigator of Mombasa separatism was the governor of the city, Muhammad Uthman al-Mazrui, who had been appointed to his position by the ruling family of Oman, the Yarubi. The occasion of his assertion of independence was a dynastic struggle in Oman, as a result of which a new dynasty under the headship of Ahmed Said al-Busaidi assumed power. Mazrui claimed that the change of dynasty had released him of responsibility to the Sovereign of Oman.

For some time the Busaidi dynasty was too preoccupied with consolidating and establishing its own position to act against the Mazrui. The Mazrui family took advantage of this opportunity and entrenched itself as a local autonomous dynasty within Mombasa. Later, the Busaidi lacked the power to invade Mombasa and evict the Mazrui, a weakness which had enormous bearing on the subsequent history of Zanzibar. For the Busaidi, failing to gain control of Mombasa, turned to Zanzibar as an alternative seaport from which to conduct their maritime activities in the Indian Ocean. A century later, they established the capital of their realm there.

During this intervening century, domestic and international difficulties in the Arab world prevented the Busaidi family from extending its influence actively along the East African coast; Oman, in fact, did not begin to recover from these troubles until the first quarter of the nineteenth century. In 1806 the Busaidi throne was assumed by Seyyid Said Sultan (al-Busaidi), a grandson of the founder of the royal Busaidi line. Seyyid Said ruled for fifty years and during his reign he overcame local resistance to the Busaidi dynasty, defeated the Mazrui family, and established a Sultanate in Zanzibar. In the course of these events, Seyyid Said enlisted the help of Great Britain. Britain was anxious to develop cordial relations with the Busaidi largely because its colony in India gave it a considerable interest in keeping the friendship of Indian Ocean states. Thus began a relationship of cooperation between the Busaidi and Great Britain which eventually resulted in the establishment of a British Protectorate over the Busaidi Sultanate in Zanzibar.

After his success in Oman, Seyyid Said immediately began to reassert his authority in East Africa. With the aid of the al-Harthi family who held the office of governor in Zanzibar, he retook Pemba in 1822 and prepared to launch an assault against the center of Mazrui power itself. Seyyid Said assumed that nothing less than the complete subjugation of Mombasa would give Oman full control over Indian Ocean commerce, for Mombasa possessed the best harbor, the most impregnable defenses, and a key position on the coast.

Seyyid Said's first military expedition to recapture Mombasa arrived late in 1827. Though he resorted alternately to diplomatic treachery and bombardment of the city, he was able to gain only a rather inconclusive submission. Afterwards, Seyyid Said visited Zanzibar. His visit there is of extreme importance, for he seems to have been quite taken with its beauty and potential richness. Some historians date from this time his decision to place the new East African capital of his Sultanate there instead of at Mombasa. Even if this be so, uncontested sovereignty over Mombasa remained the primary objective of Oman's Indian Ocean policy.

A year after the treaty was signed Mombasa revolted, and Seyyid Said determined to seize control and to defeat the Mazrui once and for all. He sent ships and an army and this time instructed them to carry out a head-on assault. After a series of costly attacks his military expedition failed, and once again Seyyid Said accepted the course of diplomatic negotiation; he had to acquiesce in a treaty with terms less favorable than previous ones. This defeat was probably the determinative factor in

Seyyid Said's decision to create a new capital for his regime on Zanzibar. It had become obvious that Mombasa was militarily impregnable and that its defenses could resist any armed assault Oman was capable of launching against it. This meant, in effect, that recapture of the city and full control of its domestic affairs were impossible objectives. Oman did, however, possess a vastly superior fleet which accorded it easy mastery over the seas. There remained only to find a suitable port at which to station the fleet, and Seyyid Said could isolate Mombasa economically. He did recapture Mombasa in 1837, but it was an empty victory. His fleet easily controlled the sea from Zanzibar and this would in any case have made Zanzibar the new cultural, political and economic center of the Indian Ocean.

Seyyid Said's decision to locate his capital on Zanzibar was an abrupt departure from Oman's long-standing disinterest in the island. The recapture of Zanzibar from the Portuguese in the middle of the seventeenth century had been only one step in a planned reconquest of all the Indian Ocean colonies and no separate importance was attached to it. Oman, absorbed in problems on the Arabian peninsula, had neglected Zanzibar along with the rest of the coastal towns. During the entire period between the defeat of the Portuguese and the final subjugation of the Mazrui, Mombasa had assumed an overriding importance in Oman's strategies and policies.

Seyyid Said's choice of Zanzibar was not entirely whimsical. There had been a rapid expansion in the volume of the slave trade, caused in part by a demand for slaves in the colonies of the New World, and Zanzibar was central to most of the trade routes into the interior whereas Mombasa was far up the coast and inaccessible to the most important ivory and slave caravans. The Arab families of Zanzibar had gained a comparatively solid reputation for loyalty to Oman. As an island,

Zanzibar would be insulated from the inter-urban rivalries of the coast and from the depredations of warring inland tribes. There were in addition some significant natural resources—timber, coconuts and money cowries, to mention a few. Seyyid Said realized the immense fertility of the island and understood the economic potential of cloves.

In sum, about 1830, Zanzibar entered the first phase of its contemporary constitutional development, and became an independent Arab state under an Arab sovereign off the coast of East Africa. It was also an imperial state, since the Sultan of Zanzibar exercised at least nominal sovereignty over a number of towns and trading centers along the coast of the nearby mainland. Zanzibar remained an independent Arab state for sixty years until Great Britain, extending its own empire in East Africa, made Zanzibar its Protectorate.

The initial problem confronting Seyyid Said on Zanzibar was to establish the paramount authority of his dynasty. Among the older Arab families on the island there was considerable resistance to the transfer of the Busaidi regime from Oman to Zanzibar; though loyal to the Sultan, these families had previously enjoyed considerable political freedom and were unaccustomed to Omani interference in their local affairs. Many of the resident Arab families were active in the slave trade, and this created additional apprehension about the Busaidi intrusion. They feared that Seyyid Said's association with Great Britain and the abolition movement would lead to a restriction of their activities.

Some of the local Arab clan-families were extremely wealthy and powerful and were in a very strong position to resist any attempt by Seyyid Said to establish centralized governmental authority. Their potential military strength, for example, was considerable, since on their plantations and estates they frequently employed hundreds of workers and slaves who could be armed. The al-Harthi clan was reputed to possess more than 1,500 such armed slaves. A few of the families themselves numbered hundreds of persons, and several even employed mercenary soldiers. The dynastic clans also enjoyed a viable economic basis for their separatism; their estates grew cash crops for export in the Indian Ocean trade and they participated directly in the trade as merchants and exporters. Though the Sultan had a larger army than any of the Arab lords, a military standoff existed because the lords were sufficiently strong to engage in a prolonged armed conflict which would be ruinous to the economy.

The political situation may be compared to European feudalism. The Arab magnates behaved very much like semi-autonomous barons in their efforts to resist the Busaidi. They recognized the formal sovereignty of the Busaidi family, but they viewed the Sultan himself as merely a *primus inter pares* whose position did not entitle him to special authority. They took advantage of the military impasse between themselves and Seyyid Said and sought through tactical politics to maximize their autonomy and influence. Despite formal acknowledgment of Busaidi suzerainty there was a continual thrust by local Arab leaders to usurp the position of political preeminence.

The Busaidi, however, enjoyed several decisive advantages in this struggle. As the Sultan of Oman, Seyyid Said controlled military and financial resources far greater than any of the local Arab lords. His established administration in Oman and his political contacts with the other coastal cities enabled him to recruit a force of administrators, civil servants and personal followers who were known to be loyal to him and his family. By encouraging and assisting immigration from Oman he built up a large popular following within the Arab community. Seyyid Said quickly became the largest and most powerful of all the Arabs on Zanzibar, and as the opposition was disunited, he was soon able to enforce obedience to his regime.[7]

A basis of accommodation existed in the fact that Seyyid Said's fundamental objective was not simply to overwhelm all Arab resistance or to establish a unitary society but to build a stable effective government. This held advantages for both sides. For the Arab lords, it meant that the Sultan's army would be available to help maintain social control over the large and rapidly expanding slave population. A slave rebellion in 1840 had proven impossible for local Arab forces to control and had continued for six months until military reinforcements could be brought from Arabia. There was the additional problem that Arab settlement was extending further and further into the lands of the indigenous African population, another situation, which might imminently demand a sizeable trained defense force.

Aside from problems of social control, the merchant-exporters of Zanzibar saw economic benefit in the presence of the Sultanate. They were still in competition with their counterparts in the other coastal cities, and anything which strengthened Zanzibar's overall competitive position redounded to their advantage. The presence of the Sultan with his large and powerful navy and his extensive international contacts could prove a valuable asset.

For Seyyid Said, a peaceful—if uneasy—relationship with the local Arab community meant that he could turn

---

[7] For an extended discussion of Seyyid Said's attempt to consolidate his regime on Zanzibar, see Gray, pp. 135-138, and Sir John Gray, "Zanzibar and the Coast, 1840-1884," *History of East Africa,* ed. Roland Oliver and Gervase Mathew (Oxford: The Clarendon Press, 1963), pp. 216ff.

his attention to other objectives, principally to placing the Sultanate on a sound financial footing. He organized a customs and revenue service, staffed with Asians recruited from the local Asian business community. Thus began a practice which characterized the entire subsequent development of Zanzibar's administrative apparatus: the reliance on Asians in the clerical, auditing and staff positions of the civil service.

The Sultan also attempted to organize a judicial system, but his success in this (and for that matter, in the effort to create a sound revenue department as well) was very limited. Seyyid Said's rule was of far too personal a nature to allow much scope for the successful long-term operation of bureaucratic institutions. He preferred to govern directly, delegating specific responsibilities on a piecemeal basis to trusted advisers and friends rather than relying on formal structures. Under Seyyid Said, the office of the Sultan combined the legislative, administrative and judicial functions of government. He promulgated laws by royal decree, asked members of his family or private staff to see that they were carried out, and sat as sole and final judge on any important cases that might arise under them.[8]

Personal government along these lines gave the Busaidi regime its distinctive quality as an extremely limited governmental enterprise. The functions of the state were strictly confined to those which the Busaidi family and its most trusted advisers could supervise directly, and the range of domestic state activities was consequently very small. There was no system of education and welfare, very little public works, and only intermittent activity in keeping law and order. On a geographical basis, national political life existed only in Zanzibar Town and the immediately surrounding area; on a group basis, political participation was the exclusive pre-

[8] Gray, *History of Zanzibar,* pp. 144-147.

rogative of the Sultanate and of a few influential Arab families.

The Busaidi state thus achieved very little structural penetration of Zanzibar's African society. There was practically no assertive thrust of national political institutions into the daily lives of the African population, and political contact of almost any sort between the indigenous African communities and their new rulers was sparse. The Busaidi began by exercising loose supervision over the indigenous population through a kind of indirect rule—which was gradually tightened into direct control. But the important point is that there was never any real institutional bond between the African majority and the Arab state. Africans remained culturally and politically differentiated, and although there was a national government, it did not accomplish national integration.

As early as the first half of the nineteenth century, the Busaidi state contained the basic structural features of contemporary political conflict. These were an Arab elite stratum which monopolized political power and progressively intensified its domination over a differentiated African majority, an Asian commercial and middle class increasingly recruited into the administration, and an African majority more and more deprived of economic and social status. Much of Zanzibar's subsequent political history can be understood as an interplay of these three forces.

By the time Seyyid Said moved his capital to Zanzibar, the African inhabitants of Zanzibar and Pemba had coalesced into three tribal groupings: the Pemba, the Tumbatu and the Hadimu.[9] The names of the first two

---

[9] There are two major ethnographic studies dealing with the indigenous African population: John Middleton, *Land Tenure in Zanzibar* (London: Her Majesty's Stationery Office, 1961), and A. H. J. Prins, *The Swahili Speaking Peoples of Zanzibar and the*

are drawn from the places where they reside. The Pemba are the original African inhabitants of Pemba Island to the north of Zanzibar. The Tumbatu are the original inhabitants of Tumbatu Island, a very small island immediately off the northwest coast of Zanzibar. For centuries, the Tumbatu made it a practice to emigrate from Tumbatu to Zanzibar and in the nineteenth century they already inhabited a large number of villages throughout the northern area of the island. Hadimu is an Arabic word meaning "slaves," the nickname by which the Arab settlers called the Africans who inhabited most of Zanzibar Island. Among all three tribes were people who claimed a greater degree of Persian ancestry, and these often referred to themselves as "Shirazi."

Each of these three tribes had evolved out of a mixture of peoples—the aboriginal or earliest Africans, who came from a wide variety of tribes and places on the mainland, and the Persian immigrants who arrived most heavily between the tenth and twelfth centuries. Gradually these heterogeneous communities grew to share a common culture made up of a common religion (Islam), a common language (Swahili), and a pattern of social ties which grew out of intermarriage, geographical proximity, and a mutual economy. Similarly, all three tribal groupings were in the process of evolving articulated political institutions and a centralized system of authority. There is even some evidence of overall integration, an embryonic pattern of political merger between the Tumbatu and the Hadimu.

Of the three, the Hadimu had gone farthest towards centralized government and were ruled by a monarchical figure known as the "Mwinyi Mkuu" or "Great Ruler." The dynasty of the Mwinyi Mkuu was Shirazi and there had probably been in recent generations frequent inter-

East Coast: Arabs, Shirazi and Swahili (London: International African Institute, 1961).

marriage between the ruling family and Arab immigrants. Political relations between the Hadimu king and the village communities were carried on through a series of intermediary institutions. Immediately beneath the king in authority were administrators called "Masheha" whose position was comparable to that of district commissioner. Each of the districts into which the Hadimu realm was divided contained a number of villages, the smallest unit in the administrative structure, in which there were wide variations in political practices. At this level of government the diverse traditions and backgrounds of the various people who composed the Hadimu tribe probably came into play to create a multiplicity of styles of village organization. The basic format was a council of elders, usually four men representing the oldest families in the village.

Within the Hadimu system of government there was a trend towards the concentration of greater and greater power in the hands of the Mwinyi Mkuu. The principal example of this development was in the office of Sheha (singular). The Masheha were probably at one time chosen by the people of the districts over which they presided and the role of the Mwinyi Mkuu was limited to giving formal approval of the popular choice. By the nineteenth century, however, the Hadimu king had begun to exercise considerable influence over the choice of Sheha. The Mwinyi Mkuu generally made his own personal choice known beforehand so that the outward trappings of selection from below could be maintained. But as the result of his interference there was latent tension in Hadimu society between a Sheha chosen by the king and a group composed of the person who would have been the popular choice and his supporters.

Neither the Pemba nor the Tumbatu possessed such elaborate political institutions. The Tumbatu had a form of centralized authority, an institution similar to the Sheha of the Hadimu. The Tumbatu Sheha could be a woman, an unusual occurrence in Muslim societies, and during the first half of the nineteenth century one Sheha was married to the Mwinyi Mkuu. The marriage, however, did not lead to an extension of the authority of the Hadimu throne over the Tumbatu. Pemba society, on the other hand, was politically pluralistic and there was no one in even nominal sovereignty over the entire island. The highest figure of authority was a local chief, known as the Diwani, who exercised loose supervision over a small number of local chiefs. The Diwani and the local chiefs governed in consultation with committees of elders in the villages.

There was no real problem of race relations between Arab colonials and the African population of Zanzibar until the transfer of the capital of the Sultanate. Previously the Arab population had been very small (about three hundred at the end of the eighteenth century), its contact with the indigenous Africans was limited and, the fact of most importance, the Arab colonials had not attempted to establish administrative domination. When Seyyid Said decided to create a new capital at Zanzibar, he set off a sprint of emigration from Oman. He immediately summoned to Zanzibar an entourage of officials and administrators to put the new government into operation and to staff its customs and taxation departments. These were followed by a wave of immigrants seeking free land and other opportunities in agriculture. Like colonials everywhere, these immigrants came as the bearers of a civilization which was superior in its military power—and hence in its capacity to enforce its will upon the local inhabitants.

Of the native inhabitants, the Hadimu alone sustained the full impact of the Arab immigration. The Pemba, on their island to the north, and the Tumbatu in the northernmost areas of Zanzibar Island were remote from the areas of Arab settlement. The Hadimu occupied exactly that portion of Zanzibar Island in the path of the Arab intrusion. In the ensuing process of interethnic contact, the Africans were ill-equipped to prevent the Arabs from asserting a proprietary relationship over their polity and over their lands.

As early as 1828 Seyyid Said sought to gain from the Hadimu their explicit acknowledgment of his colonial claim to their island, and negotiated with the Mwinyi Mkuu for this purpose. He wanted to achieve Hadimu recognition and formal acceptance of a dual sovereignty over Zanzibar and thereby to gain legitimacy for the presence of his regime alongside an independent African society. In addition Seyyid Said wanted exclusive authority over Zanzibar's external economic affairs, such as trade relations and the levying and collecting of duties. An agreement was reached and the Sultan undertook a financial obligation to compensate the Hadimu chief for the partial abdication of his authority.

A variety of factors cast doubt on the legality of the agreement between the Sultan and the Mwinyi Mkuu and hence on whether it furnished a constitutional basis for Arab rule on Zanzibar. The circumstances of the discussions hardly indicate that the covenant was consented to freely by the Hadimu ruler. During the bargaining, Seyyid Said positioned his entire fleet (including numerous ships of war and transport carriers for several thousand soldiers) directly offshore. The implication that Seyyid Said was prepared to achieve his objective by force, if necessary, could not have been clearer, and must have dispelled any lingering thoughts that the Mwinyi Mkuu might have had about the possibility of resistance.

There is serious doubt as well that the two men were bargaining, *ad idem*, for the same thing. Seyyid Said's principal objective was to gain legitimacy for his regime among the Hadimu, but the terms of his agreement with the Mwinyi Mkuu covered a number of topics including arrangements for a labor supply and a head tax. Since the goodwill of the population was an important factor in the success of his entire venture, African recognition of the legitimacy of his position was doubtless uppermost in Seyyid Said's mind. There is a good case to be made for the position that the Mwinyi Mkuu was thinking along altogether different lines, perhaps about personal compensation for his services to the Sultan with respect to the labor supply and head tax.

Even the limited division of sovereignty implied by Seyyid Said's desire to assume exclusive control over foreign affairs would require that the Hadimu conceive their political authority as an alienable item. There is authoritative anthropological evidence that the Hadimu did not regard their property in land as a permanently alienable commodity. It is even less likely that they viewed so abstract a possession as authority as a saleable good. In all probability the cultural vocabulary of the Hadimu simply did not contain any conceptual provision for commercial transaction over these important areas of human relations.

The final outcome of the negotiations between Seyyid Said and the Mwinyi Mkuu was a kind of indirect rule under which the Sultan could govern the Hadimu through their traditional institutions. The Arab monarch sought to make it a firm point of his native policy to conduct his relations with the Hadimu through their traditional leaders. The Mwinyi Mkuu was allowed to continue as paramount tribal authority; Seyyid Said intentionally made no effort to replace the system of Masheha and village councils with Arab administrative officials, for he hoped in this way to maintain the goodwill of the Hadimu and to prevent the emergence of a hostile population near the seat of his government.

Seyyid Said's native policy could have succeeded in avoiding racial tensions between the Arab immigrants and the Hadimu only if he had been able to minimize contact between the communities, for the relationship was inherently unequal. The emergent Arab community in Zanzibar was the most powerful political and military force in the Indian Ocean. Within two centuries it had defeated Portugal, created an empire and embarked upon a policy of aggressive economic expansion. Hadimu society formed an essentially closed, self-contained unit based on a local subsistence economy. Politically the Hadimu were moving gradually towards a form of centralized authority, but their polity lacked military strength and possessed no means to resist a colonial intrusion. This inequality meant that as a pattern of inter-ethnic contacts between Arabs and Hadimu emerged, it would be conducted along the lines of ruler-subject or master-servant relations.

Exactly this occurred during the nineteenth century. The Arab community built an expanding and flourishing agricultural economy which first enveloped and then reduced the Hadimu to a subordinate economic status. This development was of momentous importance for it led to the emergence of a landed Arab aristocracy. Without it the Arab colonials might have remained a dominantly urban elite composed of government officials and merchants, and only remotely in touch with the native population. But as a rural plantation-owning class, the Arabs began to impose heavy demands on Hadimu society.

Seyyid Said's treaty with the Hadimu provided for corvée, the temporary recruitment of forced labor. Initially the Hadimu were required to furnish work gangs simply for clearing the forest and cutting timber for building purposes; later, as the plantations began to produce crops, the Hadimu were also compelled to work during harvest seasons. During the entire nineteenth century, the institution of corvée was the principal medium through which the indigenous African population came into contact with the emergent Arab oligarchy. The cumulative effect of generations of forced labor was to dramatize to the entire Hadimu population that they had been made the subjects of an alien government.

Land alienation became another dominant pattern of social contact between Arab and Hadimu. Even before the arrival of Seyyid Said and his followers the Arab community on Zanzibar had begun to acquire fairly extensive landholdings north of where Zanzibar Town now stands. But not until the arrival of Seyyid Said and the initiation of wholesale efforts to make Zanzibar the largest producer of cloves for the Indian Ocean spice trade did land alienation assume serious proportions. Previous acquisition involved little change in the character of land usage or in the historic pattern of settlement and, in total, probably did not represent a large quantity of land. Later on, under the impetus of a high world demand for cloves, alienation of the land proceeded at a staggering rate and involved not only deforestation and the introduction of an intensive, plantation type of cultivation, but also the systematic eviction of the local inhabitants.

There is serious debate over the question of how heavily settled the plantation areas of Zanzibar were before the nineteenth century and over the nature of the alienation process. The anthropologist John Middleton has argued that the clove areas were virtually uninhabited before the Arabs came, and that the Omani colonists basically took over unoccupied land where dense tropical forest heavily infested with malaria had prevented

African settlement.[10] This position is supported by an absence of archeological or anthropological evidence of indigenous African village life in the plantation area previous to its occupation by Arabs. There are presently African villages in the area but they are of comparatively recent origin, subsequent to the growth of the clove industry.

The historian Sir John Gray has argued that a great deal of the acquisition of fertile land by Arabs was brought about by various forms of expropriation of the original landowners. Gray has described the alienation process as a very human one, involving intense contact between the indigenous African inhabitants and the intruding colonial population: "Whilst there may have been cases in which a Hadimu landowner was evicted by an Arab with a strong hand and a multitude of people, and that in other cases expropriation was procured by means of fraud, the general impression is that many of these changes of ownership were brought about by means which would have borne scrutiny by a court of law. . . . In other cases, a Hadimu might be induced to relinquish or abandon his land by a species of cold war waged by Arab neighbors in such a manner that continued occupation to which the Hadimu was entitled, became intolerable."[11] In balance, the available evi-

---

[10] Middleton, pp. 10-13. The core of Middleton's argument is that the present pattern of indigenous African settlement on Zanzibar Island does not differ from that which existed when Seyyid Said first arrived. Of the fertile areas of the island, Middleton says "formerly they seem to have supported a dense forest little utilized by the indigenous peoples before the coming of the Omani Arabs and the planting of cloves by slave labor in the early nineteenth century" (p. 10). And of the African population, Middleton argues "the indigenous inhabitants lived mainly in the coral areas and in small fishing villages around the coasts. Much of the western [fertile] part of the island was covered with forest . . . and was not used except as a source of wood and other forest products and probably for hunting" (p. 11).

[11] Gray, *History of Zanzibar*, pp. 167-168.

dence points to the use of a certain amount of violence in the process of land acquisition. Middleton concedes that there must have been some cases of forcible eviction, and there is abundant testimony of this in the oral tradition of the Hadimu.

Even if there were no use of force, and even if those areas taken over by Arabs had been scarcely used, Arab claims of legitimate occupancy are dubious. Seyyid Said's treaty with the Hadimu did not transfer to him territorial sovereignty over the Hadimu lands; ultimate ownership therefore remained with the Hadimu rulers and the Hadimu tribe. The Hadimu had no concept of private ownership but regarded all their land as the permanent and inalienable property of the community: according to their custom, land could be held by a person during his lifetime as long as he made use of it, but it never became his private possession. It must be presumed that even in those cases where Hadimu received financial compensation in a land transaction, they had no intention of surrendering permanent freehold ownership.

By far the most pernicious consequence of the alienation of the Hadimu lands was that in the end it created a rigid pattern of geographic segregation between the Arabs and the Hadimu. Since fertile soil is found only west of the ridge bisecting Zanzibar Island (see Map 1 on page 246),[12] geological and soil conditions meant that

[12] This fertile area forms an irregular quadrangle to the north, east and south of Zanzibar Town. The quadrangle extends north of the town about fifteen miles, inland about six or eight miles, and south of the town about six miles. Largely as a result of this close proximity between Zanzibar Town (which acts as the center of government, administration, trade and commerce for the entire country) and the fertile area where the Arab population concentrated, the Arab community of Zanzibar Island became highly urbanized. Most of the larger plantation owners took up urban residence, leaving their plantations in the hands of managers. The rate of urbanization among the Arabs here was well over 50 per cent. By

the alienation process left the Arabs in possession of roughly the western half of the island, and the Hadimu of the eastern half. This geographic segregation had profound economic meaning. Since the Arabs came to enjoy nearly exclusive occupancy of the most fertile soil, they possessed a virtual monopoly of intensive clove and coconut cultivation. The steady exodus of the Hadimu from the fertile area and their removal to the eastern portion of the island created a *de facto* native reserve where fishing and labor migration were necessary to supplement the meager existence eked out in agriculture.

The expropriation of their lands, incessant demands for labor, and at times a tendency for Arab sovereigns to interfere in the succession of the Mwinyi Mkuu proved more of a strain than the traditional political institutions of the Hadimu could withstand. The office of Mwinyi Mkuu passed into eclipse by the third quarter of the century, and the absence of a central source of authority weakened the system of Masheha. By the end of the century the Masheha were replaced by Arab district administrators appointed by the central government.

The extension of Arab paramountcy into Pemba did not generate latent political hostility towards Arab rule among the local African communities. Rather, there tended to develop among Pemba Africans a widespread acceptance of the concept that Arabs were the legitimate rulers of Zanzibar society. This belief may be largely accounted for in terms of the wide difference between the historical pattern of Arab-African relations in Pemba and that in Zanzibar. The Arab colonial regime did not

---

contrast, the Arab community of Pemba, though more than twice as large as that of Zanzibar, formed less than one-fourth of the town population of that island because it was under 25 per cent urbanized.

initially establish its authority over the Pemba population by force, but by voluntary agreement with a group
of local African rulers.[13] This had enormous long-term
significance. It endowed Arab hegemony with a basis in
popular consent which it did not enjoy in Zanzibar, and
thereby made it unnecessary for the Pemba Arabs to
employ harsh and autocratic methods to ensure political
stability.

Land relations between Arabs and Africans in Pemba
also became a basis for inter-ethnic solidarity rather than
a source of intense racial friction. Arable land in Pemba
is far more plentiful and widely distributed than in
Zanzibar. For this reason, Arab land alienation did not
deprive the African community of nearly all the best
land, nor did it result in a rigid pattern of racial segregation based on land ownership. Arab and African farmers lived side by side or in areas of roughly comparable
fertility and, when the Arabs introduced cloves to
Pemba, many African landowners, as well, prospered
from this source of income. During the nineteenth and
early twentieth centuries, these African plantation owners and the Arab settlers suffered or prospered together
as a result of falling or rising world clove prices. This
integrative pattern of land relations, together with the
consensual validation for Arab political supremacy,
tended to keep Arab-African relations in Pemba from
invidious connotations of superiority-inferiority.

In sharp contrast to the impoverishment and political
disintegration of the Hadimu tribe was the prosperity
of the Arab community. The major factor in this prosperity was the success of Seyyid Said's policy of expanding the Indian Ocean trade. This policy assumed various
forms, one of which was the creation of a specialized
plantation economy devoted to intensive clove cultivation. Arabs had introduced cloves to Zanzibar from

[13] Gray, *History of Zanzibar,* p. 172.

Reunion in 1818 and were growing them successfully for some time before the transfer of the capital of the Sultanate. Seyyid Said realized that the clove had enormous economic potential for several reasons. First, there was a high demand for cloves in the world market; second, the sensitive clove plant thrived only under exactly those climatic and soil conditions that Zanzibar had to offer; Zanzibar thus possessed a potential natural monopoly. Seyyid Said fostered extensive clove cultivation both by force and by distributing land to his followers on condition that a fixed percentage of cloves be grown. The clove industry grew with prodigious rapidity. According to the historian Coupland: "The plantations which . . . in 1834 were still in their infancy were producing by the end of Seyyid Said's reign an average annual crop of about seven million pounds, and the value of the cloves exported every year came next to that of the ivory and the slaves."[14]

In the final analysis, however, an increase in the slave trade more than any other single factor elevated Zanzibar to the position of major economic center of the Indian Ocean. This trade expanded greatly after Oman's expulsion of the Portuguese. In addition to the old markets at Muscat, Persia and India, two more markets had developed, the East African colonies themselves and the colonies of the New World. One early explorer calculated that during the first quarter of the nineteenth century slaves accounted for three-fourths of the total Zanzibar population.[15] The volume of the slave trade

[14] Coupland, *East Africa*, p. 314.

[15] There were several nineteenth century attempts to estimate the population of Zanzibar. The first was that of a Captain Smee of the Indian Navy in 1811. He believed that the population of Zanzibar was about 200,000, of whom between two-thirds and three-fourths were slaves. Towards the middle of the century, the explorer Sir Richard Burton estimated the combined population of Pemba and Zanzibar as 400,000, of whom about two-thirds were slaves. And in 1895, the British Consul, Sir Lloyd Mathews, gave the total popula-

in Zanzibar during the first half of the century has been estimated at between ten and fifteen thousand per year.

This prosperity completely transformed the character of the Arab settlement. From a limited colonial community, it became a rich and powerful state. The royal government received tax duty on every item in the stream of goods passing through, and its revenue was sufficient to support the most expensive appurtenances of national sovereignty such as an army and navy. Zanzibar also featured an extensive bureaucratic apparatus (including a judiciary), conducted a foreign policy, and before the end of the century developed a system of native administration for the African inhabitants.

Trading caravans from Zanzibar bearing the Sultan's flag penetrated deep into the East African interior, beyond the Great Lakes. Arab traders long preceded European explorers as the first visitors to most upland regions. The larger caravans were usually well-protected and possessed clear military superiority over the upland tribes whom they met. This prompted the explorer Burton to comment that Zanzibar's trading caravans constituted the first real invasion of the area.[16]

Zanzibar's contact with the East African interior was, in some ways, more than simply an invasion and constituted in effect a kind of occupation. The large armed caravans normally traveled about for months on end and, as their routes were well established and they followed one another in rapid succession, their presence became a per-

---

tion of the Sultanate as only slightly over 200,000, of whom about two-thirds were slaves. All these estimates (and others made during the nineteenth century), however, were based only on visual reckoning and are thus liable to gross inaccuracies. In any case, the nineteenth century population must have been several hundreds of thousands and well over half of the population consisted of slaves. See Zanzibar Protectorate, *Report on Proposals for a Social Survey of Zanzibar*, by Edward Batson (Zanzibar: Government Printing Press, 1948), p. 8.

[16] Coupland, *East Africa,* p. 308.

manent and salient feature of the interior areas. Furthermore, Arab merchants who were associated with the caravans and who also enjoyed the protection and nationality of Zanzibar set up trading centers along the caravan routes, and settled more or less permanently in the interior.

On the basis of these towns and of the continuous presence of the caravans, the Sultan claimed to exercise sovereignty over most of contemporary East Africa. It is doubtful that the Sultan's military power extended beyond the borders of the towns and there was never a continuous effective Arab occupation of the vast areas outside the towns. But the fact remains that for more than a generation Zanzibar was the imperial power dominant over hundreds of thousands of square miles of East African territory.

CHAPTER II

British Colonial Policy in Zanzibar

The essentially autocratic nature of British colonial rule had much to do with enabling the Arab oligarchy to preserve its dominant political status. Zanzibar became, like other colonial territories during the era of British overlordship, an administrative state with ultimate control in the hands of British officials. The basic functions of government—the formulation and execution of policy, and the maintenance of law and order—were conducted by a disinterested efficient bureaucracy, unanswerable to local opinion. Since this sort of administration did not allow for the free competitive play of opposed political forces, there was very little opportunity for Africans to challenge either the overall framework of colonial rule or the special political position of the Arab elite. Moreover, by systematically according Arabs preferential treatment for legislative and administrative positions as well as by preventing other communities from effectively challenging the Arabs' preeminent position, the colonial government had an extremely conservative stabilizing effect on the political and social structure of the country. Thus, British colonial policies not only preserved the Arab community's status as an economic and political elite, but they also endowed the entire racial pattern of stratification with a remarkable degree of continuity. The highly differentiated system of racially identifiable economic and social classes which existed when the British Protectorate was first established in 1890 remained virtually intact until the revolution.

At the pinnacle of its importance in the mid-nineteenth century, Zanzibar was the most powerful political force in the Indian Ocean. This preeminence was shortlived, however, for within a quarter of a century Zanzibar's national destiny had become subject to the political ambitions of European powers.[1] Toward the end of the century, the surge of European imperialism dramatically reversed power relations in the Indian Ocean, and the competition for East African colonies between Great Britain and Germany threatened Zanzibar's very existence. By 1884, for example, Britain and Germany concluded a bilateral agreement which deprived the Sultan of the entire East African hinterland and reduced his possessions to a narrow strip of territory along the coast. The most significant feature of this treaty was that the Sultan and his government had had no voice in its arrangement, and were powerless to resist its implementation.

Numerous factors help account for this sudden change in power relations, among them the economic, scientific and technological revolutions of Western Europe. Of all the impulses towards European expansion into Africa, one in particular—the anti-slavery movement—operated with special intensity in Great Britain. Great Britain's determination to abolish slavery in East Africa led it to attempt to assert its influence over the Busaidi dynasty and the Zanzibar Government. Britain's military and technological superiority made it practically inevitable that it should quickly come to occupy a position of decisive ascendancy over all areas of state policy in the Sultan's realms.

Britain's first important contact with the Busaidi dynasty had been as an ally in Oman's wars against a powerful pirate fleet in the Middle East. The principal motive at that time was to clear the Indian Ocean and the Arabian sea for shipping going to its colony in

---

[1] For the classic study of the rise of European influence in East Africa, see R. Coupland, *The Exploitation of East Africa, 1856-1890* (London: Faber & Faber Ltd., 1939).

India, but there was already considerable domestic pressure on the British government to take active measures against the slave trade. During the early nineteenth century, Britain did not have legal jurisdiction over the citizens of European countries involved in the trade; furthermore, it needed the friendship of the Busaidi Government, which controlled much of the slave trade, in its effort to prevent Napoleon from occupying the Middle East. For these reasons, gradualism in the elimination of slavery became a cardinal principle of British policy in the Indian Ocean throughout the nineteenth century. In 1822, Britain signed the first of a series of anti-slavery treaties with the Busaidi Government. The Moresby Treaty, as it was called, did not interfere with the status of slavery or with commerce in slaves in the areas of East Africa and Arabia under the sovereignty of the Sultan of Oman.[2] Its most important provisions merely allowed Great Britain to attempt to interrupt the slave trade between East Africa and European countries, mainly France and Portugal. With only minor modifications, the terms of the Moresby Treaty describe British Indian Ocean policy until the late 1840's. During this period Britain's anti-slavery activity was confined to minimizing the sale of slaves from Moslem to Christian countries, but the conclusion of an additional treaty in 1845 marked the beginning of a new phase of policy. Britain persuaded Seyyid Said to attempt to halt the trade between his East African dominions and the Persian Gulf countries (Arabia, Persia and India). This treaty went far beyond what Seyyid Said could reasonably expect most of his subjects to support, and their resistance made it extremely difficult to enforce. More important, however, was the fact that Seyyid Said's personal complicity in the treaty and the unpopularity

[2] R. Coupland, *East Africa and Its Invaders* (Oxford: The Clarendon Press, 1961), pp. 214-216.

which followed it tended to weaken the authority of his regime. He was forced to use Britain's presence and support as an implied sanction behind his throne. Thus, in effect, the 1845 treaty engendered a subtle pattern of dependency linking the royal dynasty to Great Britain.

The extent of Britain's involvement in the political affairs of the royal family soon became apparent. After Seyyid Said's death in 1856 there was a dispute among his sons over the succession and also over the constitutional relationship between the new capital at Zanzibar and the former capital at Muscat. The Governor-General of India, Lord Canning, was asked to intervene and in effect resolved the problem by declaring Zanzibar and Muscat independent of one another. In constitutional terms, this judgment confirmed the legal status of the Sultan at Zanzibar as an autonomous monarch and also confirmed his exclusive claim to sovereignty over the East African dominions. But politically, it made the position of the Sultan at Zanzibar more than ever dependent upon the presence of Great Britain.[3]

Britain's role as guarantor and sponsor of the Sultanate gave it extraordinary power over the Sultan and his government, and this power was used to achieve the final abolition of the slave trade. In 1873 the Sultan, Seyyid Barghash, was coerced to promulgate decrees forbidding altogether the sale and transportation of slaves in his dominions, an act which climaxed the intrusion of British influence on Zanzibar's domestic affairs since it radically alienated the Sultan's followers and forced him to rely completely on Great Britain for protection.

In 1890 the Government of Great Britain reached an agreement with the Sultan legally creating a Protectorate relationship between itself and Zanzibar.[4] The es-

---

[3] Kenneth Ingham, *A History of East Africa* (London: Longmans, 1962), pp. 83-84.

[4] For an intensive study of the establishment of the Protectorate

tablishment of a Protectorate was, in a sense, purely a matter of lending official solemnification to Britain's informal acquisition of paramount influence in Zanzibar politics. In world politics, the Protectorate relationship gave international meaning to the Sultan's dependence upon Great Britain, for it prevented the annexation of Zanzibar by other European powers. Germany had made a strong bid for control over Zanzibar as well as Tanganyika during the partition of East Africa. As it was not a principle of German colonial policy to preserve local political institutions in its colonies, it may well be that Britain's assumption of the status of protecting power enabled the Sultanate to survive. At any rate, the Sultanate gained immeasurably in stature during the era of British protection.

In strict constitutional terms the concept of a Protectorate implies a limited domestic role on the part of the protecting government. The Protectorate treaty is conceived of as an agreement with a sovereign and independent nation whose consent to the treaty both defines and limits the role of the Protector. There was no doubt of Zanzibar's status as a sovereign nation. As the historian Coupland has commented: "Zanzibar had now acquired by time and usage its recognized place as an independent state in the society of states. It had concluded treaties with several other states on a footing of equality, and if it had accepted one particular treaty under duress it had yielded as sovereign states have often yielded to *force majeure* without losing its independence."[5]

The initial terms of Britain's agreement with the Sultan were consistent with the principle that, as a Pro-

---

relationship between Great Britain and Zanzibar, see L. W. Hollingsworth, *Zanzibar Under the Foreign Office, 1890-1913* (London: Macmillan Co. Ltd., 1953).

[5] Coupland, *The Exploitation,* p. 266.

tectorate, Zanzibar must continue to exercise an important degree of control over its own affairs. Britain was to assume exclusive powers only in the area of foreign relations. Succession to the throne and control over internal affairs were to remain royal prerogatives—subject, in the case of the latter, to Britain's advice. There was thus created what has been called a "dual mandate"—two governments sharing sovereignty over a single people.

The practical realities of Britain's relationship to the Sultanate scarcely coincided with any notion of a sustained division of authority. Through usage, concession and agreement, Britain assumed control over the entire apparatus of government, staffing most of the key posts with Englishmen. The final result was that Britain's position in Zanzibar was the same as in those African territories which had been made full colonies. By the beginning of World War II, Britain had achieved a position of such dominance that it was able, when it wished, to govern without regard for local opinion.

Britain used this power to establish complete authority over the Sultan and his government. Within half a dozen years after the formation of the Protectorate, Britain had asserted the prerogative of acting as final arbiter on succession to the Sultanate, a matter of policy specifically beyond the terms of the Protectorate treaty. On the death of Sultan Seyyid Ali in 1893, several eligible candidates contended for the throne. Britain chose the least intractable among them and secured his succession by force. In return for its support, Britain demanded a series of political concessions which profoundly altered the character of its constitutional relationship to Zanzibar, and provided at least a quasi-constitutional basis for future intervention in matters of succession and internal affairs. The new Sultan was compelled to accept the paramount Suzerainty of the Queen of England—a fundamental abrogation of the "dual mandate" concept but a definition of Britain's political position more in keeping with its actual power over the land and people of Zanzibar.

The new Sultan was also forced to agree to a series of other important concessions of sovereignty, such as acceptance of British control over the executive, administrative, and financial branches of the government. One important concession at that time was an agreement to abolish domestic slavery. Since slavery was an important basis of Zanzibar's plantation agriculture, and hence a ubiquitous practice, Britain's right to abolish it became, in effect, the liberty to exercise police and judicial powers throughout the country. For all practical purposes, this gave Britain full direct legal jurisdiction over His Highness' subjects: the Sultan's final area of effective sovereignty, an exclusive legal jurisdiction over Zanzibar's Arab and African population, had been removed.

Not until 1914, however, did Britain abandon the final lingering pretense that the Sultan's Government was a constitutional equal and that the Sultan continued to exercise a degree of sovereignty over Zanzibar. In the twenty-four years since the creation of the Protectorate, the fiction of dual sovereignty had been maintained by conducting Zanzibar affairs through the Foreign Office and by stationing a Consul-General in the country, arrangements customarily associated with relations between Britain and another independent state. Lest these practices be construed as an effort to give institutional meaning to the concept of dual sovereignty, Britain now transferred control over Zanzibar affairs from the Foreign Office to the Colonial Office, and replaced the position of Consul-General with that of British Resident. To provide a final symbol of Britain's paramountcy, the Governor of Kenya Colony and Protectorate was designated as High Commissioner to Zanzibar.

Despite Great Britain's unassailable power position,

Zanzibar's constitutional status as an Arab Sultanate under British protection exercised considerable long-range influence on the colonial government. Local British officials continued to view Zanzibar as an Arab nation and their political and social relations with the local population were confined almost exclusively to Arabs. Even while the pretense of constitutional equality was being abandoned, British administration in Zanzibar demonstrated a persistent attachment to the concept of Arab rule. This attachment was clearly reflected not only in a continued official display of deference to certain Arab institutions, especially the Sultanate, but in the consistent preference given Arabs for top Government positions and overseas scholarships, and in the willingness of the administration to consult closely with Arabs over major areas of policy. Both symbolically and in actual practice, Britain enabled the Arab community to play the major role in its administration of Zanzibar society.

British colonial policy in Zanzibar passed through three fairly distinguishable phases. The first, the abolition of slavery in the Protectorate, required about twenty or twenty-five years. The second phase, a period of establishing a sound and efficient administrative framework, began just before World War I and was completed by the mid-1920's.[6] After this, the effort to provide a viable administrative basis for government continued, but the major emphasis of colonial policy shifted to the task of introducing parliamentary representative institutions. The growth of parliamentary government occupied the period from 1926 until independence— thirty-eight years—and most of this last policy phase was characterized by administrative and political stability.

[6] For a detailed discussion of the creation of an effective administrative system in Zanzibar, see Hollingsworth, pp. 57-72 and pp. 191-206. See also Lord Malcolm Hailey, *Native Administration in the British African Territories* (London: His Majesty's Stationery Office, 1950), Part II, pp. 1-15.

None of these phases had specific official status as such; nevertheless, they represent a pattern of shifting emphasis in the colonial activities of the British Government in Zanzibar.

The willingness of the local British administration in Zanzibar to pay special attention to the interests of the Arab community was particularly discernible during the abolition of slavery in the Protectorate. Although early British colonial policy placed primary emphasis on the termination of slavery, the British authorities in Zanzibar took a far more conservative attitude towards abolition than did the Foreign Office authorities in London.[7] Local administrators were receptive to Arab arguments about the economic importance of slavery in the Protectorate and became deeply concerned about the economically disruptive consequences of abolition. They grew far less convinced of the virtue of immediate action than were officials in England, and argued for a continuation of the historic policy of gradualism in order to avoid undermining Zanzibar's economy. Local officials also insisted that there should be financial compensation to Arabs who suffered a heavy loss in giving up their slaves.

The necessity for gradualism was accepted eventually by the British Government. A decree abolishing the legal status of slavery was promulgated in 1897, but it exempted certain categories of slaves (concubines, for example) and laid the burden of obtaining freedom on the slaves themselves. They had to apply to rural Arab officials to obtain freedom, and because of this requirement the abolition decree operated quite slowly. The local Arab officials proved reluctant abolitionists, partially because many of them were slave owners. Another reason for the protracted quality of the abolition process was that there was no concerted effort by the govern-

[7] Hollingsworth, p. 135.

ment to provide freed slaves with an alternative means of livelihood. As a result, only about ten thousand persons petitioned for release from slavery during the years immediately following the abolition decree, although slaves had been estimated as roughly two-thirds of a total population greater than 200,000.

A second anti-slavery law was passed in 1909,[8] declaring financial compensation at an end after 1911, and hastening the emancipation process since it gave slave owners an incentive to cooperate with the government. Various forms of hidden slavery and semi-slavery continued to exist in Zanzibar for some time, and unpaid labor on a more or less voluntary basis remained a prevalent social institution. The British accomplishment was the elimination of involuntary servitude and the many cruelties and abuses associated with it, but Britain failed to accompany abolition with a systematic effort to equip freed slaves for any but the most menial economic status.

After abolition, the principal emphasis of British rule in Zanzibar was on providing the Protectorate with an efficient administrative system. The earliest British officials had found the Sultan's bureaucracy in abominable condition—ridden with nepotism, corruption and inefficiency, and inadequately financed to provide the country with the minimum services necessary to health and cleanliness. The historian L. W. Hollingsworth, who spent more than twenty years as an administrator in Zanzibar, has recorded his impression: "There was a complete lack of even the most elementary sanitary arrangements. Heaps of rubbish and filth were allowed to litter the streets and alleys. . . . Buildings were hastily erected anyhow and anywhere without any government control. At nighttime the entire town was in darkness . . . the approaches to the harbor were inadequately lighted and the entrance buoys were uncared for and

[8] *Ibid.,* p. 157.

inadequate. Steamers were allowed to anchor where they pleased, while Arab dhows came and went without any papers or supervision of their crews."[9]

Britain undertook a thorough reorganization and expansion of the Sultan's Government. The most significant areas of reform were finance, social services and public works. British administrators helped provide Zanzibar with systematic taxing, budgeting and accounting bureaus, medical and educational facilities, and a system of roads and communication throughout the Protectorate.[10]

The massive expansion of the Zanzibar bureaucracy resulted in a wholesale recruitment of Arabs into the Government and in the creation of a sizeable class of Arab administrators, teachers and technicians. Since the total size of the British establishment in Zanzibar was never very large, and even at its height (after World War II) did not total more than a few hundred persons, Britain was forced to draw heavily for administrative personnel on the local population. Largely because of the continuing official constitutional view of Zanzibar as an Arab state, members of the Arab community were systematically given preference for the top bureaucratic

[9] *Ibid.*, p. 59.

[10] The widely respected proposition that such an integrative national infrastructure has much to do with the emergence of nationalism would appear to indicate that these bureaucratic and communications institutions were an important contribution to Zanzibar's subsequent political development. In terms of their effect, this may well be the case. In the official British view, however, administrative reform was simply the necessary prerequisite of any well-governed society. If anything, bureaucracy was widely considered as a conservative or politically neutral institution, an impersonal instrument of effective authority, and the prime mechanism through which government policy was transmitted throughout society —not as the essential structural stimulus of a massive popular demand for democratization. The most elaborately developed version of an infrastructural theory of nationalism is Karl Deutsch, *Nationalism and Social Communication* (New York: Wiley and Sons, 1953).

positions; and, through a variety of devices such as overseas scholarships and differential salary scales, Arabs were actively encouraged by the British to enter the administration. Thus, the Arab regime, which previous to the arrival of Great Britain had consisted of little more than the Sultan and a limited circle of personal officers and agents, grew into a sizeable bureaucratic structure composed of trained and skilled Arab professionals.

The introduction of parliamentary democratic institutions and the creation of a constitutional monarchy were the ultimate objectives of British policy in Zanzibar. The first tentative step in this direction was taken in 1914 when Great Britain established a Protectorate Council, consisting of His Highness the Sultan as President, the British Resident as Vice-President, three other official members, and four representatives of the Arab and Asian communities. The Council was a purely advisory body, analogous in its function to an extraparliamentary cabinet. It had no autonomous powers of legislation; its purpose was simply to provide the Sultan and high British officials with some formal mechanism for consulting with leaders of local opinion. The Council represented at best a very small step towards the ultimate introduction of a fully representative body.

No further constitutional progress was initiated until the mid-1920's. The office of High Commissioner was abolished in 1925 and a limited degree of legal jurisdiction over the non-European population was restored to Arab and native courts. In 1926, Executive and Legislative Councils were established, the former presided over by His Highness the Sultan. The Legislative Council (Legco) was principally an advisory body but, unlike the Protectorate Council, it did possess limited lawmaking authority, provided its decrees were signed by the British Resident. The Legislative Council was not, however, truly representative since the majority of its members were British officials, and the others, who represented the different racial communities, were carefully chosen by the British colonial administration.

Despite these initial limitations, the Legislative Council was of enormous importance in subsequent constitutional evolution. For in Zanzibar, as elsewhere in British colonial territories, it was gradually adapted into a fully representative parliamentary body. Though not initially conceived or planned as an embryonic parliament, the Legislative Council proved uniquely suitable to this course of evolution because of its inherent flexibility. It enabled the colonial authorities gradually to increase the "representativeness" of governmental institutions while at the same time retaining ultimate control over public policy.[11] Thus, except for certain minor bureaucratic and administrative changes required during the final stages of constitutional advance, the Legislative Council was the center of the entire process of constitutional development.

Piecemeal modification of the composition and character of representation in the Legislative Council, timed in most cases to coincide with educational and social advance, was the principal technique through which British colonial policy transformed oligarchic colonial rule into parliamentary democracy.[12] The dominant, if not exclusive, focus of attention in this process was the balance existing at any given time between leaders of local opinion and representatives of British officialdom. In

[11] For a full study of the historical evolution of the Legislative Council and its development in other British colonial territories, see Martin Wight, *The Development of the Legislative Council* (London: Faber & Faber Ltd., 1947).

[12] The most fertile source of information about the development of Zanzibar's Legislative Council is: Zanzibar Protectorate, *The Debates of the Legislative Council* (Zanzibar: Government Printing Press). These are bound in annual or biennial volumes and available for the entire period between 1926 and 1960 (with the exception of the war years).

the theory of constitutional development behind the Legislative Council system, progress was defined as a gradual increase in the share of representation awarded to leaders of local communities.[13]

Britain's view that Zanzibar was constitutionally an Arab state was nowhere more clearly reflected than in its treatment of local representation in the Legislative Council. For thirty of the thirty-eight years between the establishment of the Legco and independence (1926 to 1956), it was standard British policy to give Arabs the largest representation of any racial community. During much of this period, the Arabs enjoyed representation equal to that of the other local communities combined. Moreover, it was also a frequent practice of the colonial administration to consult informally with the Arab representatives on major policy questions. This enabled Arab leaders to exercise considerable influence, both on the initial formulation of the Government's legislative programs and on their implementation once legislative consideration was completed. The Arab community con-

---

[13] See Wight, p. 72. British constitutional theory as applied to the evolution of the Legislative Council led to a particular sequence of changes in the pattern of representation. The terminology of this theory distinguished between "official" members—usually British administrators, but occasionally specially selected local persons— committed to support Government policy, and "unofficial" members—leaders of local ethnic communities—whose function was to represent the interests of their respective groups. The first stage of constitutional development was commonly referred to as the "official majority" because British administrators retained a flat voting majority. The second stage, "responsible government," occurred when an unofficial majority was brought into being and when local leaders were allowed to control specified areas of public policy. The third and final pre-independence stage of constitutional development, "internal self-government," was distinguished from the second in that a vastly increased amount of policy responsibility was transferred into local hands. As initially constituted, the Zanzibar Legislative Council contained eleven British officials and six unofficial members composed of three Arabs, two Asians and one European. The African community was unrepresented until 1946.

tinued to enjoy this decisive advantage throughout the entire period that the British Government remained in Zanzibar.

The principal effect of this system was that it deprived non-Arab Zanzibaris of any meaningful participation in their country's political affairs; neither Africans nor Asians ever achieved a degree of political influence comparable to that of the Arab community. They had practically no share in the formulation of domestic policy, nor could they influence the administration in its day-to-day conduct of governmental activities. Non-Arab participation in government was confined to criticizing policies decided upon in British offices, either in London or in Zanzibar. The African community was denied even this limited role until after World War II, since without legislative representation African leaders had no effective voice in Protectorate politics.

The emergence of militant nationalist movements in the early 1950's led Great Britain to initiate a course of constitutional evolution leading toward a more formally representative political system. The colonial government began to expand the unofficial side of the Legislative Council and in 1956 agreed to add a small number of members chosen by popular election.[14] In July, 1957, six elected members, five of whom were Africans, joined Legco and increased the total number of unofficial members to twelve. This marked the first occasion on which African representatives to Zanzibar's legislature outnum-

[14] Until the election of 1957, unofficial Legco members were nominated by the British Resident. For purposes of nomination, different racial associations were given official governmental recognition. These associations designated a certain number of persons acceptable to their membership, and the British Resident chose from among these. As a result, the common tendency was for nominated unofficial members to be conservative or moderate in their views, and to remain loyal to Great Britain in their speeches.

bered Arabs and were the largest single group of local leaders. As there were thirteen official members, however, Zanzibar remained under full British control and the African community's substantially increased legislative strength did not signify any basic change in political relations between the colonial regime and the local communities.

The second major period of Zanzibar's contemporary constitutional development began in 1961 when locally elected representatives were allowed to constitute a legislative majority. The first phase of this period has usually been referred to as the "responsible government" era, because local leaders were invited to accept ministerial portfolios in the Executive Council (Cabinet) and for the first time assumed responsibility for the formulation and implementation of major areas of policy. Among the most important ministries controlled by Zanzibaris were agriculture, health and education. British officials in the Legislative Council, however, continued to control the more sensitive ministries such as finance, defense and internal security, and the British Resident retained a veto over all public policy.

Zanzibar remained at the "responsible government" stage for only two years, then entered the terminal phase of colonial status, internal self-government. During internal self-government, British officials no longer sat in the Legislative Council, now renamed the National Assembly, and the distinction between official and unofficial members became irrelevant. Government nomination was eliminated as a method of selecting National Assembly members; all representatives were chosen by popular election. The British administration surrendered unlimited executive and legislative power to the Zanzibar Government, with three exceptions: defense, foreign affairs, and internal security remained colonial prerogatives until independence.

Historical and Social Background

The most important political feature of this period was that after June, 1961, Arabs (with the help of a few African leaders sympathetic to the interests of the Arab community) gained a majority of the Legislative Council seats and formed a coalition government in which Arabs assumed control of nearly all the important ministerial positions. Africans opposed to Arab political hegemony were in the minority and had to form an opposition. This situation, which lasted until the African revolution, meant that Arab rule had not only survived the introduction of representative institutions, but had acquired a degree of legitimacy under constitutional democracy. In effect, Britain's concept of Zanzibar as an Arab-state was a self-fulfilling prophecy, for it led to colonial policies and practices which facilitated a continuation of Arab oligarchic rule.

CHAPTER III

Social Structure of Zanzibar

The single most important feature of Zanzibar's contemporary political development has been the failure of nationalism to unify the population. Widespread antipathy toward colonial rule, a common desire to attain self-government, and participation in an extended struggle to achieve these objectives did not produce a significant degree of solidarity among Zanzibaris. In fact, nationalism was accompanied by a radical breakdown of the social order.

The conditions under which external conflict (in Zanzibar's case, British colonialism) may intensify rather than ameliorate latent internal disunity within a society have been carefully studied by the sociologist Lewis Coser. His conclusion is that: "The usual relation between outer conflict and inner cohesion does not hold true where internal cohesion before the outbreak is so low that the group members have ceased to regard preservation of the group as worthwhile, or actually see the outside threat to concern 'them' rather than 'us.' In such cases, disintegration of the group rather than increase of cohesion, will be the result of outside conflict."[1] Coser's analysis was specifically concerned with the consequences of Nazi imperialism in pre-war France, but his central proposition—that external conflict cannot unify a society unless there is already a strong basis for solidarity—may be applied to the modern political condition of Zanzibar. *Nationalism did not generate increased internal cohesion because Zanzibar lacked a basis for solidarity viable enough to overcome the nu-*

[1] Lewis Coser, *The Functions of Social Conflict* (Glencoe: The Free Press, 1956), p. 93.

merous and extreme ethnic, cultural and economic disparities inherent in its society.

The most persistent and acute source of political disunity in Zanzibar has been its extreme racial diversity. Centuries of immigration from the Arab and Persian Middle East, the sub-continent of Asia and the African mainland have given Zanzibar an ethnically heterogeneous population which now numbers more than 300,000.[2] It is difficult, if not impossible, to enumerate the racial composition of the population with exact reference to ancestry. The various races have frequently intermarried and intermingled throughout Zanzibar's history, producing numerous mixed strains. Furthermore, concepts of racial identity have become highly charged with political meaning and are thus subject to further imprecision.

The most fruitful method of differentiating the racial groups, one which was employed in most of Zanzibar's past censuses, has been to use variables which are behavioral rather than genealogical. Those used with the greatest success have included self identification, common acceptance and general pattern of conduct. The 1948 Zanzibar census was the last to use these variables

[2] The most recent official census of Zanzibar was conducted in 1958 and gave the total population as 299,111. See Zanzibar Protectorate, *Report on the Census of the Population of Zanzibar Protectorate taken on the Night of the 19th and 20th March, 1958* (Zanzibar: Government Printing Press, 1960), p. 17. The density of Zanzibar's population contrasts strikingly with that of nearby mainland African countries. With more than 300,000 people crowded onto only slightly more than 1,020 square miles, Zanzibar has a mean population density of about 300 persons per square mile. The two islands differ in this respect. Pemba, with only slightly more than one-third of the total area of the country, has a population almost equal to that of Zanzibar (134,000 and 165,000 respectively). Its population density is about 352 per square miles whereas that of Zanzibar is less than 260. By comparison, it may be noted that the mean population densities of Kenya and Tanganyika are only about 30 per square mile, and that of Portuguese East Africa about 20 per square mile.

and gives the following figures for the Zanzibar population (see Table 1).[3]

TABLE 1

Distribution of Population by Ethnic Community in 1948

RACE	Zanzibar Island		Pemba Island		Total	
	No.	Per cent	No.	Per cent	No.	Per cent
African[4]	118,652	79.3	81,208	70.9	199,860	75.7
Arab	13,977	9.3	30,583	26.7	44,560	16.9
Asian	13,107	8.8	2,104	1.8	15,211	5.8
Comorian[5]	2,764	1.8	503	0.4	3,267	1.1
Goan	598	0.4	83	—	681	0.3
European	256	0.2	40	—	296	0.1
Other	221	0.2	66	—	287	0.1
Total	149,575	100.0	114,587	100.0	264,162	100.0

The only potential basis of solidarity among these
ethnic groups has been the Islamic Faith. The entire
population is overwhelmingly Muslim in religion; well
over 95 per cent of all Zanzibaris adhere to one or another Islamic sect. There is even considerable unity on
a denominational basis, since Sunni Muslims account

[3] Zanzibar Protectorate, *Notes on the Census of the Zanzibar Protectorate, 1948* (Zanzibar: Government Printing Press, 1953), p. 2.
The 1958 census does not differentiate the principal ethnic groups
of the country sufficiently well to be used here. Its utility in this
respect was seriously diminished when one of the major political
parties refused to allow the inclusion of separate categories for
Arabs and Africans. The result was an all-encompassing category
"Afro-Arab." See the 1958 Census, pp. 9, 17.

[4] The African population listed in this table includes the three
indigenous African tribes and the mainland African population.
The 1948 census gives the following figures for each of these: Hadimu, 41,750; Tumbatu, 46,000; Pemba, 59,750; mainland African,
51,000.

[5] The Comorians are an immigrant group in Zanzibar from the
Comores Islands, a small archipelago in the Indian Ocean just
south of Zanzibar. The Comores are under French administration.
The Comorians in Zanzibar have formed a distinct ethnic group
both because they were, until recently, French subjects and because
they possessed a high degree of self-consciousness of a separate

for more than four-fifths of the total population and nearly 90 per cent of all Muslims. Practically all of the Africans and a substantial majority of the Arab community are Sunni. This nearly unanimous adherence to a common religious persuasion has furnished Arabs and Africans with a powerful motive for political unity.

TABLE 2

Population by Religion

RELIGION	Mainland African	Indigenous African	Arab	Asian	Comorian	Total
Muslim	54,060	142,535	44,600	10,945	3,470	255,510
Sunni	52,815	141,775	25,520	4,640	3,365	228,115
Ibadhi	1,220	435	18,665	25	5	20,350
Shia	10	5[a]	345	6,275	100	6,735
Other	15	320[a]	70	5[a]	—	410
Christian	1,995[b]	410	—	920	65	3,390
Hindu	—	—	—	3,800	—	3,800
Other[c]	1,410	30	5	225	80	1,750

[a] Estimate only.

[b] Professor John Middleton has suggested that the Mainland African communit may have included a larger number of Christians than was revealed by the censu: Many of the census takers were Arabs, and there might have been a certain amount fear among the Mainlanders about revealing adherence to the Christian faith to member of the Arab community.

[c] Includes those who did not report, Parsee Asians, practitioners of tradition: African religions and members of small sect groups.

Religious differences do exist in Zanzibar (see Table 2).[6] There is a clear religious division between Arabs and Asians, for example. Arabs are either Sunni or

---

identity. Racially, the Comorians are a mixture of Arab and African strains; their socio-economic position is comparable to that of the Asian community in that they are a predominantly middle-class group.

[6] This table has been prepared on the basis of information which appears in: Edward Batson, *Religion*, Vol. III: *The Social Survey of Zanzibar*, Department of Social Studies, University of Capetown (Capetown, by the direction of the Zanzibar Government, n.d.). The reliability of this survey of Zanzibar society is fully discussed in the text of this chapter.

Ibadhi Muslims, whereas Asians are generally Shias or members of non-Muslim religious groups. Similarly, the Arab elite is religiously differentiated from the bulk of the population in that most wealthy Arabs are Ibadhi, not Sunni. But the political importance of these divisions has been extremely limited, and practically all Zanzibaris are keenly aware of the religious unity of their society. Indeed, had it not been for the glaring class differences between the racial groups, religion might well have provided a basis of solidarity around which local leadership could have built a unified national community.

The basic cause of inter-ethnic disunity in Zanzibar has been the economic and social differences between the races. From the end of the nineteenth century until just before the beginning of modern politics (1954), the social and political structure of the country could be likened to a three-tiered pyramid. At the base was an African majority which comprised the vast bulk of Zanzibar's agricultural and manual laborers, but which was essentially politically mute. In the middle was a small Asian class of clerks and shopkeepers, possessing a disproportionate quantity of the nation's wealth, but politically neutral. At the top, the Arab elite possessed considerable wealth in land, played an important role in governmental affairs, and was both respected and protected by the British as in some sense the rightful and legitimate rulers of Zanzibar society.

The Arab minority, comprising about one-sixth of the total population, has been described as Sub-Saharan Africa's second largest alien oligarchic minority, following in proportional size only the white community of South Africa. Those identifying themselves as Arabs have not always constituted so large a proportion of the population. Comparative census data for the last forty years indicates that until fairly recently their percentage of the total population was only half the present figure (see Table 3).[7]

TABLE 3

Population of the Arab Community
1924-1948

Census	1924		1931		1948	
	Pop.	*Per Cent*	*Pop.*	*Per Cent*	*Pop.*	*Per Cent*
Arabs	18,884	8.7	33,401	14.2	44,560	16.9

The remarkable aspect of this surge in persons considering themselves Arabs is that the bulk of the shift occurred in the brief period between 1924 and 1931; afterwards, the increase in the proportion of Arabs to the total population leveled off abruptly.

The question suggests itself, from where did the new Arabs come? A small proportion may have come from immigration or from natural increase. The total population of Zanzibar, including immigration from all sources, grew by about 17,000 during this same period from 202,665 in 1924 to 219,867 in 1931. A small fraction of this increase was doubtless Arab. But the vast bulk of the increase in the Arab population had to come from within Zanzibar society, from among segments of the population which had previously opted for categories of self-description other than Arab. Between 1924 and 1931 large numbers of former non-Arabs changed their minds, as it were, about the ethnic category most suited to their own descent and decided to "join" the Arab community.

By far the overwhelming majority of the Arab converts came from the tribal community known as Swahili. The Swahili people, who had numbered 33,944 in 1924 and were the largest single corporate group in Zanzibar, had virtually ceased to exist as such by 1931

[7] Zanzibar, *1948 Census,* p. 4.

when only 2,066 persons identified themselves as Swahili.

The tendency for large numbers of Swahilis to abandon this identity and to assimilate into other tribal communities was basically a result of the invidious connotations that had come to be associated with being Swahili. The ethnographer A. H. J. Prins has commented that: "The term [Swahili] seems to imply for those who live within the orbit of Swahili culture a number of characteristics of negative value such as slave descent, lack of pedigree, low occupational position, and a general 'boorish' uncivilized behavior and outlook on life . . . people of higher social strata in any given community readily refer to their inferiors as Swahili . . . the term is essentially an epithet of reference."[8] Customarily, people identifying themselves as Swahili were unusually self-conscious that the origins of their ancestry lay in the slave trade and that they were of mixed Arab-African descent. The identity Swahili invoked considerable status deprivation, and if an alternative were available, it was, for this reason, to be preferred.

The dominant motivation behind the substantial Swahili immigration into the Arab community was achievement of an improved social status, one offering a more respected and approved identity. The rich admixture of Arab ancestry made it a relatively simple matter for Swahilis to pose as Arabs, especially since most Zanzibar Arabs were already of mixed African descent. Nor did Swahili tribal solidarity pose any obstacle to a large-scale exodus; for Swahilis were at most an extremely amorphous, atomistic body, united only by a vague consciousness of being Muslim Africans, of speaking the language for which they were named, and of having common an-

[8] A. H. J. Prins, *The Swahili Speaking Peoples of Zanzibar and the East African Coast: Arabs, Shirazi and Swahili* (London: The International African Institute, 1961), p. 11.

cestral origins along the East African coast. This fragile unity was not reinforced by any mutuality of socio-economic interest, by any distinguishing cultural traditions and practices, or by integrative political institutions. There were no clear boundaries differentiating the Swahilis from members of adjacent tribal communities. There was simply no outstanding reason for a Swahili to remain a Swahili.

This massive surge in identification with the Arab community is vivid testimony that by the second quarter of this century being Arab had come to symbolize possession of the highest qualities of Zanzibar civilization. The Swahili word for "civilized," *uarabu,* means, in effect, being like an Arab. As the founders and bearers of the faith, the owners of the soil and the rulers of the land, their position embodied and defined the aspirations of all Zanzibar society. Their presence as an alien oligarchy contributed further to the atmosphere of deference and admiration by which they were surrounded.

The possibility of social movement into the Arab community indicates that Zanzibar Arabs formed an open, rather than closed, elite group. Unlike South Africa where the entire legal, judicial and police establishment has geared itself to prevent trespass across racial boundaries, the elite structure of Zanzibar society has been open to penetration from below. This was not a deliberate policy but the natural consequence of a society whose racial boundaries are indeterminate. Important and considerable limitations on upward mobility existed, but they tended to operate flexibly and in such a way as to leave openings through which a few individuals could rise to the upper levels of society.

Despite a pattern of cross-racial assimilation, however, economics and skin color remained fundamental limitations on upward mobility. Most Africans lacked the economic means to assimilate into the dominant

Arab oligarchy, and skin color—though a flexible criterion—noticeably differentiated the Arab elite from the
broad African mass. Upward economic mobility by Africans was an important feature of Zanzibar society, but
it never attained dimensions which threatened the racial
balance of power. Political and economic stratification
continued to be a fundamentally racial phenomenon in
the sense that, with few exceptions, class and color
groupings coincided.

A small exclusive Arab elite, composed essentially of a
limited number of long-settled families which had historic ties to Oman and owned large clove and coconut
plantations, formed the dominant core of this oligarchy.
The descendants of these early Arab families became a
self-perpetuating elite group. Their decisive advantages
in wealth and style of life enabled succeeding generations to achieve superior education and thereby to qualify
more easily for the highest positions in government and
commerce. In recent years they exercised commanding influence over Zanzibarization of the civil service and, by
allowing Asians to fill the intermediate and clerical levels of the administration, they prevented the emergence
of an African elite. In this way and through nepotism,
favoritism and other forms of preferential treatment,
Arabs monopolized the strategic sectors of the administration and retained firm control over the entire state
apparatus, the educational system and the clove industry, regulating the pace of African advancement in
such a way that it did not threaten their own position.

A striking social and economic gap existed between
the small elite group and the broad mass of the Arab
community. The overwhelming majority of the Arabs in
Zanzibar have formed a kind of peasant class of small
farmers and rural shopkeepers, a class with at least three
distinct points of origin. Part of the Arab peasantry
emerged as the major social consequence of economic

indebtedness of the Omani Arabs to Asian financiers.[9]
This indebtedness impoverished a sizeable proportion
of the original colonial aristocracy and reduced many
landholdings to peasant scale. Intermarriage between
Omani Arabs and indigenous African tribes often occurred after this impoverishment since differences in
class, status and style of living between the two communities had been removed, and since native landholdings provided an attractive economic incentive to ruined
aristocrats. Thus, in succeeding generations, peasants
claiming Arab ancestry have often been of markedly
mixed descent. An unintended but very important consequence of intermarriage between poor Arabs and indigenous Africans was that it led to obvious color differences between them and the noticeably lighter-skinned
Arab oligarchic elite who intermarried far less frequently.

The presence of a sizeable Arab peasantry is also accounted for by the tendency of numerous Swahili petty
farmers to represent themselves as Arabs to census takers.
Though comparable to the "poor Arab" group in being
of mixed descent, the Swahilis are far less truly Arab in
the genealogical sense of the term since any actual trace
of Arab parentage is many generations removed. The
Swahilis probably form the largest of the three groups
comprising the Arab peasantry.

The third principal group are the recent immigrants
from Oman, often called *Manga* or *Wamanga* Arabs.
(Manga is the Swahili word for the region of Muscat in
Arabia.) The Manga Arabs differ considerably from the
older Omani settlers, not only in the recency of their
arrival but also in that they came with no capital and
often had no intention of settling permanently. They

[9] During the nineteenth and twentieth centuries, Arab landowners passed heavily into the debt of Asian bankers. For a full discussion of this indebtedness as a political issue, see Chapter IV, "Pre-
War Politics in Zanzibar."

tended to become petty shopkeepers and small landowners in the rural areas and, after accumulating some sav-
ings, they frequently returned to Arabia. The Manga
Arabs were perhaps the purest of the Zanzibar Arabs
since the average period of residence was less than a
generation, and their number was constantly being re-
plenished with new arrivals. In the past there was open
hostility between the Manga Arabs and the longer-
established Omani elite, largely because the latter tended
to remain aloof from the economic hardships of the new
immigrants.

Asians have formed Zanzibar's middle class since the
earliest years of Arab rule when Seyyid Said encouraged
their immigration for this purpose. By ancient tradition
the bankers and merchants of East Africa, they have
monopolized not only trade and commerce, but also the
intermediate and clerical levels of government service
and private business. Asians service the tourist industry,
dominate the importation and distribution of hard
goods, and control the marketing and exportation of
cloves. In recent years they have begun to acquire extensive landed properties and numerous Arab estates
have passed into their hands. Though only a tiny fraction of the total population, they possess an enormously
disproportionate share of the nation's wealth; some
Asians have long since superseded Arabs as the richest
Zanzibaris. And like the Arabs, the Asians' social and
economic advantages have given their class position a
self-perpetuating quality.

The Asian community has never exercised continuous
effective political influence, and though able to act successfully as a kind of interest group on rare occasions,
its dominant style of behavior is non-political. This has
partially been the result of a lack of solidarity among
Asians, for within the Asian community there exists a
congeries of religious and caste sub-groups, and these

sub-groups tend to command a far stronger loyalty than does the community as a whole. The most important division has been that between Muslim and non-Muslim Asians. Of Zanzibar's Asian community (numbering some 20,000), about three-fourths are Muslim. The historic antagonism between these groups has been intensified in recent times by the religious conflagrations in India and by the partition of India and Pakistan. Among the Asian Muslims, moreover, there are tensions between the numerous separate religious groups such as Ithnaasheries, Bohoras, Ismailis and Sunnis. This fragmentation of loyalties has made it difficult for Asian leaders to muster concerted political action by the community.

A pronounced tendency to remain culturally orientated toward India and Pakistan and hence to avoid full assimilation into Zanzibar society has also contributed to political non-involvement by the Asian community. This cultural separatism has been concretely reflected in a very low rate of intermarriage between Asians and other racial communities. It is also reflected in the Asians' preference for segregated living areas which minimize social contacts with non-Asian groups and permit a partial re-creation of Indian life. Many non-Muslim Asians until quite recent times have regarded Zanzibar and East Africa as a purely temporary domicile necessitated by business, and not as a permanent residence. Muslim Asians have been less reluctant to consider permanent settlement in Zanzibar, but cultural, social and residential segregation has been an equally persistent feature of their relationship to other communities. The Asians' legal status as British Protected Persons and the difficulties of naturalization may also have engendered a sense of alien nationality that reinforced existing predilections towards political non-involvement.

Perhaps the most significant cause of the Asians' political non-involvement in the past was the insecurity of their middle-class life. As government clerks and private traders, Asians were wholly dependent upon the good will of other racial communities. Asian civil servants lacked the independence which their Arab superiors derived from large landholdings or simply from occupying administrative positions which no one could challenge. Asian shopkeepers depended upon a broad mass of African consumers. The pressure of working in occupations where personal relations were critically important fostered an ethic of service and profit; in the terms of this ethic, other considerations—politics included—were regarded not simply as extraneous, but as potentially harmful.

Africans, comprising nearly four-fifths the total population, supply Zanzibar with the vast majority of its small farmers, fishermen and manual laborers. They constitute by and large the lowest paid workers in government and private business. A small African bourgeoisie has emerged during this century, composed basically of a few families which had achieved moderate success as clove or coconut growers, but most African agriculturalists have incomes far below those of their Arab counterparts. Upward mobility has been extremely difficult for Africans to achieve, largely because of an educational system which strongly favored the city at the expense of the countryside, and the well-to-do at the expense of the poverty-ridden. As a result, most students at the secondary schools come from urbanized non-African racial groups, especially from the Asian and Arab communities. And Africans have been unable to compete successfully for overseas scholarships or, until after the revolution, for top government posts.

A long-standing division has existed between those Africans who consider themselves the indigenous inhabitants of Zanzibar and those of more recent mainland origins. The former, who number about three-fourths of the total African population presently estimated at 240,000, prefer the term "Shirazi" to the term "African" as a generic appellation. The concept of a Shirazi or mixed Afro-Persian ancestry has thus come to embrace all three original African tribes of Zanzibar and Pemba, the Hadimu, the Tumbatu and the Pemba. Originally the notion of a Shirazi community was a separate one and referred specifically to those segments of the original population which claimed a particularly high admixture of Persian descent. It has now lost that meaning and is widely used simply to distinguish all indigenous Africans, in terms of descent and length of residence, from the relatively recent mainland arrivals.

The mainland African population of Zanzibar is composed of members of a huge variety of tribes from all the East African countries, as well as Nyasaland, Mozambique, and even the eastern Congo. Particularly numerous are the Nyamwezi, Nyasa, and Yao tribes. The mainland African community includes both the descendants of African slave workers brought to Zanzibar for the clove plantations and modern voluntary migrant laborers. In recent generations, many mainland Africans who have come to Zanzibar for seasonal clove picking have stayed as either squatter-farmers on the clove and coconut plantations or as workers in Zanzibar Town. Regardless of their widely differing reasons for being in Zanzibar, mainland Africans tend to feel a strong sense of common identity.

Social differentiation between Shirazis and Africans of mainland origin is generally clear and precise. Even in cases where an individual is of mixed mainland and Zanzibari background, his own self-description and common acceptance usually locate him in one group or the other. It is likely that differing patterns of residence and occupation may help to preserve and perpetuate a sense of social distance between Mainlanders and Shirazis. The former tend predominantly to be employed in the towns, either in domestic service or in manual work as government laborers; those engaged in agriculture are usually squatters on land to which they have no permanent rights. Shirazis are a more rural community and tend predominantly to be fishermen and farmers on privately owned or community-held land.

Zanzibar's socio-economic structure has increased racial frictions latent in a plural society.[10] Class boundaries did not usually cut across racial boundaries but coincided with them. This added to communal tensions always endemic when alien cultures meet, by estranging the various ethnic groups into opposed economic classes. Members of different racial groups did not come to share any common economic interests which might have stimulated a sense of mutuality or a pattern of association based on cooperation between them. Neither in the division of labor nor in the marketplace did a multi-racial identity of purpose become a meaningful part of the daily lives of Zanzibaris.

Three indices of social structure—land ownership, oc-

[10] The usage of the concept "plural society" employed here closely follows that developed by the colonial historian J. S. Furnivall. In his book, *Colonial Policy and Practice* (New York: New York University Press, 1956), Furnivall described a plural society in the following terms: "It is in the strictest sense a medley, for they (the different racial groups) mix but do not combine. Each group holds by its own religion, its own culture and language, its own ideas and ways. As individuals they meet, but only in the marketplace, in buying and selling. There is a plural society, with different sections of the community living side by side, but separately within the same political unit. Even in the economic sphere there is a division of labor along racial lines" (p. 304). See also pp. 305-312. A more restrictive interpretation of the concept is employed by the social anthropologist M. G. Smith in his article "Social and Cultural Pluralism," *Annals of the New York Academy of Sciences,* Vol. 83, art. 5, pp. 763-777. See also Martin Wight, *The Development of the Legislative Council* (London: Faber & Faber Ltd., 1947), pp. 85-90.

cupation and access to higher education—are perhaps best suited to verify the hypothesis that there is a tendency for racial community to coincide with social class, and hence for economic relations to aggravate race relations in Zanzibar. These three indices reflect both present income and style of living and future prospects for upward mobility. Together they furnish an exact portrait of the social structure of the country.

In any country with an economy based almost exclusively on primary agricultural production, land ownership is necessarily a major indicator of the social distribution of wealth. This is the case in Zanzibar, where income from clove cultivation alone accounts for more than one-fourth of the gross domestic product (the total value of all income, production, and expenditure). The preeminence of cloves has affected the manner in which Zanzibaris measure the value of their land. The worth of a parcel of land is calculated only on the basis of the number of trees on it, not on acreage or other accouterments. One government report has commented that: "We were astonished to find that land as such had little or no value and that when it changed ownership, practically the sole consideration for valuation purposes was the actual number of clove trees, coconut palms and sometimes coffee trees growing on it. *Neither the age of the trees, nor their condition appears to influence the valuation to any marked degree.* . . . Similarly, other attributes such as the area of the land . . . the quality of the soil, and permanent improvements are of no real consequence."[11] There is no other criterion which can analyze the social structure of Zanzibar's agricultural population as cogently as the "number of trees" index.

An early attempt to contrast Arab and non-Arab land-

---

[11] Zanzibar, *Report on the Economic Development of the Zanzibar Protectorate,* by P. Selwyn and T. Y. Watson, C.N.G. (Zanzibar: Government Printing Press, 1962), p. 35.

holdings in terms of number of trees was begun by the
Zanzibar Government in 1922. Its results are summarized in Table 4.[12]

TABLE 4
1931 Government Survey of Land Ownership

No. of trees on Plantations	Arab Owners	African Owners	Arabs as Per Cent of Total
1,000 & over	177	8	95.7
500—999	169	28	85.7
300—499	213	67	76.1
200—299	178	101	63.8
100—199	381	325	54.0
0— 99	1,236	5,880	17.4

Arabs were found to comprise over 95 per cent of owners of the very largest plantations and more than 85 per
cent in the next largest category. Indeed, Arabs registered more plantation owners in every classification of
size except the smallest, and more than two-thirds of all
Arab owners possessed plantations of over 200 trees. African owners of plantations with more than 200 trees
number less than one-fourth of the Arabs in a similar
position (194 to 837). Africans were the vast majority of
plantation owners but more than four-fifths possessed
only small, family-sized plots of less than 100 trees.

A more recent attempt to analyze the social structure
of Zanzibar, using land ownership and other indices as
well, has been made by Professor Edward Batson, Director of the School of Social Science and Social Administration of the University of Capetown in South Africa.
Professor Batson assembled a twenty-one volume statistical encyclopedia of Zanzibar society entitled *The Social
Survey of Zanzibar* (hereafter, *Survey*). Inasmuch as the

[12] Quoted in: Edward Batson, *Report on Proposals for a Social
Survey of Zanzibar* (Zanzibar: Government Printing Press, 1948), p.
36.

following tables have been composed from his quantitative data, it may be useful to discuss briefly the origin and reliability of Batson's work.

The idea of a comprehensive survey of Zanzibar society was first conceived and considered by the Zanzibar Government immediately after World War II. The intended purpose of the *Survey* was to provide the government with sufficient background material to enable it to plan an integrated and systematic development program. In 1946 Batson was commissioned to perform a pilot study on the feasibility and expense of such a project.[13]

Batson submitted a favorable report and a proposed plan for the *Survey* that year, but his negotiations with the government over details and costs delayed the start of the *Survey* for more than two years. The field poll was finally carried out on an area by area basis during a five-month period at the end of 1948 and in early 1949. The aggregate poll was nearly two per cent of the total population, an unusually high figure made possible by the small size of the country. The timing of the poll was propitious for several reasons. Batson was able to check the gross results of his own survey against the results of the just completed Government Census of 1948, and also to a degree to draw upon its trained staff. Political disputes had not yet begun to cloud patterns of racial identification and the overall response to Batson's questionnaires was probably an honest one. Several methods of verification were available to Batson and his co-workers, including simple direct comparison with visual observations of this small and enclosed society over an extended period. It was of more consequence, however, since this was a purely social survey dealing only with demographic and not attitudinal variables, that Batson was able to spot-check some of his more important tables

[13] *Ibid.,* pp. 1-2.

against government files in the Land Office, Labour Office and Education Department. In sum, the *Survey* was conducted in a manner thoroughly consistent with the standards of scholarship; subject only to the minimum caveat normally associated with survey data, its results may be accepted as a fundamentally authentic and reliable statistical portrait of Zanzibar society.

The *Survey* also employed the index "number of trees" as its method of clarifying land ownership. Its findings corroborated the earlier governmental report that Arabs owned a radically disproportionate amount of the land, although Africans had improved their position in the interim. The results of the *Survey* are summarized in Table 5.[14]

TABLE 5

1948 Batson Survey of Land Ownership

NUMBER OF TREES	*Arabs*	*Asians*	*All Africans*[a]	*Total*
3,000 trees or more	165	75	—	240
1,000 to 2,999 trees	320	35	215	570
250 to 999 trees	1,885	190	1,690	3,765
50 to 249 trees	1,990	35	11,675	13,700
0 to 49 trees	1,640	10	8,600	10,250

[a]Includes Comorians

Arabs had maintained their dominant position, owning the majority of the very largest plantations, although nearly a third of the largest ones had become Asian property despite many government efforts to prevent such a change. The striking feature of Zanzibar society indicated in Table 5 was the extremely limited number of wealthy Arab magnates (probably less than one hun-

[14] This table has been compiled on the basis of Batson, *Land Ownership*, Vol. xv; *Survey*.

dred families). This small group plus a few moderately wealthy families constituted the core of Zanzibar's oligarchic elite. The vast majority of the Arab population, however, were of middle and lower class status.

More than two-thirds of the plantations of over 1,000 trees remained in non-African possession, but there was a pronounced tendency for Africans to emerge as owners of larger than family-size plantations. In great part this upward African mobility was facilitated by the freehold system of land tenure existing in much of Zanzibar. Opportunity for private ownership and cultivation provided a certain degree of flexibility and openness, and enabled some Africans to acquire land comparatively easily, either on credit or on long-term lease from Asian bankers. During periods of prosperity in the clove industry, many African growers consolidated and expanded their holdings and, as landed farmers, became an additional segment of the African lower-middle class.

While the overwhelming majority of the population were wholly dependent upon agriculture, nearly 60,000 persons, slightly over one-fifth of the population at the time of the *Survey*, were enumerated in non-agricultural pursuits (see Table 6). These must be considered as a separate community, since economic differentiation among them is based on occupation rather than land ownership. Non-agriculturalists were divided into five principal occupational categories: 1) *upper level*—about 120 persons composed of top professional men, senior administrators, and owners of large commercial concerns; 2) *upper-middle level*—not quite 1,000 persons composed of auxiliary professional workers (i.e. secondary school teachers and retail store owners); 3) *middle level*—about 7,000 persons composed of non-manual uncertified professional workers, clerical personnel (both in government and in commercial firms), and manual skilled labor (i.e. cabinet makers); 4) *lower-*

middle level—about 36,000 persons composed of vendors, itinerant peddlers and semi-skilled workers; 5) *lower level*—about 15,000 persons composed of unskilled manual workers and agricultural laborers. In a table on the racial composition of these occupational categories, it may be useful to differentiate within the third category (*middle level* occupations) between manual and non-manual workers.[15]

TABLE 6
Urban Class Structure by Occupation

CLASS	Arabs		Asians		Indigenous Africans	
	No.	Per Cent	No.	Per Cent	No.	Per Cent
Upper	5	4.2	115	95.8	—	—
Upper-Middle	185	21.8	420	49.4	45	5.3
Middle (non-man.)	1,410	25.3	1,800	32.3	1,475	26.5
Middle (manual)	105	5.7	605	33.2	210	11.5
Lower-Middle	6,025	16.8	1,665	4.6	19,025	53.1
Lower	1,975	13.4	135	.9	5,400	36.5

CLASS	Mainland Africans		Comorian		Total	
	No.	Per Cent	No.	Per Cent	No.	Per Cent
Upper	—	—	—	—	120	100.0
Upper-Middle	60	7.1	140	16.5	850	100.0
Middle (non-man.)	715	12.8	165	2.8	5,565	100.0
Middle (manual)	815	44.7	90	4.8	1,825	100.0
Lower-Middle	8,445	23.6	650	1.8	35,810	100.0
Lower	7,125	48.2	155	1.0	14,790	100.0

The near monopoly of the highest category by Asians indicates the degree to which this community has traditionally supplied Zanzibar with both its wealthiest businessmen and its doctors, lawyers and architects. It does not indicate, as may offhand appear, that Asians possessed a decisive overall economic advantage over the

[15] Batson, *Occupations,* Vol. v; *Survey.*

Arabs, since their commercial wealth was at least partially balanced by Arab wealth in land. Just prior to independence, when Britain was pursuing a policy of rapid Zanzibarization of the upper civil service, Arabs were given highest priority for the very top positions. Arabs, Asians and a small number of Comorians comprised well over four-fifths of the membership of the two highest categories and more than three-fifths of the top three.

The large number of indigenous Africans in the third category (middle, non-manual occupations) is accounted for by the fact that numerous Shirazis were employed by the government as teachers in village primary schools or as policemen. The African middle class then was almost completely rural in character and lived, as well as worked, in the countryside. It is thus not at all comparable to the urban Arab-Asian middle class of clerks and minor officials, either in income or in style of living; and, scattered widely throughout the rural areas, this African middle class in no way constituted a cohesive or an effective elite group. Indeed, by the middle of this century, alien immigrant minorities had clearly dispossessed Zanzibar's indigenous African tribes of elite positions within their own society.

A more integrated view of the racial composition of the elite structure in Zanzibar society may be obtained by combining data on land ownership and occupational status. The utility of such a table is that it presents class structure as the outcome of a total social process, and does not imply a non-existent separation between agricultural and non-agricultural elites. The following system of socio-economic rankings was composed on the basis of *Survey* data (Table 7): 1) Rank A—includes both persons of upper level occupations and owners of very large plantations; 2) Rank B—includes both persons of upper-middle level occupations and large plantation owners; 3) Rank C—includes both persons of middle level occupations and medium-sized plantation owners; 4) Rank D—includes both persons of lower-middle level occupations and small plantation owners; and 5) Rank E—includes both persons of lower level occupations and those who own no plantations at all.[16] A rough balance existed at the highest level of society between Arabs and Asians, and, as would be expected from previous data, Table 7 confirms non-African domination of elite social groupings.

TABLE 7

Urban & Non-Urban National Class Structure

RANK	Arabs		Asians		Indigenous Africans	
	No.	Per Cent	No.	Per Cent	No.	Per Cent
Rank A	165	47.8	180	52.2	—	—
Rank B	515	36.3	480	30.3	160	11.3
Rank C	3,255	30.3	2,505	23.4	2,805	26.2
Rank D	11,865	13.9	1,565	1.8	47,765	55.8
Rank E	605	11.4	125	2.3	1,225	23.0

RANK	Mainland Africans		Comorians		Total	
	No.	Per Cent	No.	Per Cent	No.	Per Cent
Rank A	—	—	—	—	345	100.0
Rank B	165	11.6	150	10.6	1,420	100.0
Rank C	1,765	16.5	395	3.7	10,725	100.0
Rank D	23,520	27.5	895	1.0	85,610	100.0
Rank E	3,235	60.7	140	2.6	5,330	100.0

The situation of a radical economic imbalance between the various racial groups has been reflected in and perpetuated by an identical imbalance in Zanzibar's educational system. Table 8 indicates, for the year of the *Survey,* the number of students of each racial group

[16] Batson, *Personal Socio-Economic Rank,* Vol. XII; *Survey.*

at the different levels in the educational system.[17] Over four-fifths of the students at the highest grade levels were of non-African minority groups. Indigenous Africans were in much the worst position. Village primary schools teach only up to Standard VI, and the economic burden of sending a child to board at a higher school is simply beyond the financial resources of practically all Shirazi families. Mainland Africans have been

TABLE 8

Distribution of Secondary School Students by Ethnic Community

STANDARD	Arabs		Asians		Indigenous Africans	
	No.	Per Cent	No.	Per Cent	No.	Per Cent
Standards I–VI	3,715	29.2	955	7.5	4,905	38.5
Standards VII–IX	430	25.7	595	35.5	185	11.0
Standards X–XII	225	32.1	290	41.4	20	2.9

STANDARD	Mainland Africans		Comorians		Total	
	No.	Per Cent	No.	Per Cent	No.	Per Cent
Standards I–VI	2,630	20.7	520	4.1	12,725	100.0
Standards VII–IX	230	13.7	235	14.0	1,675	100.0
Standards X–XII	115	16.4	50	7.1	700	100.0

somewhat better off because they are an urban group and their children could easily commute from home to Zanzibar's only secondary school. The mainland community also includes a small number of Christians for whom education was provided by missionaries. Nonetheless, education has not been a means by which either Shirazi or mainland Africans might achieve upward mobility. Instead, Zanzibar's educational system has been, in a sense, simply a mechanism through which already

[17] Batson, *Educational Achievement,* Vol. x; *Survey.*

over-privileged racial groups increased their social and economic advantages.

No matter which index of social structure is employed—land ownership, occupation or education—the inescapable conclusion is that Zanzibar society was rigidly stratified along ethnic lines. Zanzibar was thus a radically plural society, wholly unsuited to the emergence of a unified nationalistic political movement. Each racial group possessed its own separate sub-culture with an internal gradation of status and wealth, a distinctive pattern of collective behavior and an intensely separatist group loyalty. Nor was there any indication that social integration would occur, for the most significant feature of this plural society was the stable character of the race-class system and the almost complete absence of upward mobility for the African population.

Upward African mobility could have occurred in at least three different ways: through intermarriage, the development of a more open elite structure, or the growth of economic opportunity for members of lower class racial communities. None of these, however, led to a significant leveling of the economic relations between the racial groups.

1). *Although intermarriage occurred, it was not sufficient to blur ethnic boundaries and fuse the different groups together.* In fact, this small degree of intermarriage helped to stabilize the dominant position of the Arab oligarchy. By providing a few Africans with means by which to join the Arab elite, it dramatized the absence of any hard and fast legal barriers between the races. This obscured the hopelessness of the African position in general, and thus delayed the emergence of a militant African protest.

2). *The closed, self-regenerating quality of Zanzibar's elite community inhibited any extensive upward social mobility for Africans.* Virtually all elite groups tend to perpetuate themselves but this is even more the case when the elite is ethnically differentiated from the broad mass of the population. The Arab-Asian monopoly of elite status in Zanzibar created, in effect, a kind of *de facto* ascriptive culture. These two groups carefully guarded their dominant position by conducting elite recruitment predominantly within their own communities. Thus, to be born an African was in itself—irrespective of education, landownership or family position—a handicap to upward mobility.

3). *Zanzibar's static agricultural economy also placed severe limitations on the upward mobility of the African population.*[18] As a simple agrarian society, it did not offer a wide range of economic opportunity, and the number of elite positions available was extremely small. Thus, even if Zanzibar had possessed an achievement ethic and recruited its elite on the basis of ability, there were so few channels of mobility that the total aggregate volume of upward movement by Africans would have remained extremely small.

The ethnic fragmentation of Zanzibar's social structure became even more pronounced in the decade prior to independence, the period of competitive party politics. Due in large measure to a severe economic depression, there was a rapid constriction of the existing economic channels of upward mobility. The world market price of cloves, Zanzibar's principal export, dropped abruptly after 1951 and led to a stagnation of the entire national economy. Whereas in the past, for example, land ownership had been a source of wealth for some Africans, this was now no longer the case. Moreover, due to the increased difficulty of maintaining their own

[18] The problem of achieving social equality in developing nations has been considered at length by the anthropologist Lloyd Fallers. See: Lloyd Fallers, "Equality, Modernity and Democracy in the New States," *Old Societies and New States,* ed. Clifford Geertz (Glencoe: The Free Press, 1963), pp. 158-219.

economic position, Arabs and Asians became more and more defensive in guarding their privileged status. In this way, economic crisis not only reinforced the pluralistic and ethnically fragmented quality of Zanzibar society, but it thereby forced Africans to turn increasingly towards political agitation as a means of resolving social inequality.

PART II

THE ORIGINS OF
POLITICAL CONFLICT

CHAPTER IV

Pre-War Politics in Zanzibar

Political groups during the pre-war period were organized principally along ethnic lines. This was largely the result of three factors. First, the approximate coincidence of race and class accentuated ethnicity and made it a salient aspect of day-to-day social relations. Second, the government's twin practices of nominating communal representatives in its conciliar bodies and of giving official recognition to racial groups created an institutional environment highly conducive to the formation of ethnically based associations. Third, under early colonial government almost all critical or sensitive problems were resolved by the British authorities without consulting the local communities. This left local politics with few issues, and there was thus no strong stimulus to political disagreement or organization along liberal-conservative lines.

The African community did not begin to become politically organized until comparatively late in the period between the wars. The African Association, composed of mainland Africans, was founded in 1934 but remained rather inactive politically for some time afterwards. The Shirazi Association was not formed until 1939 and did not begin to assert itself until after the war. Neither of these groups was given any legislative representation before World War II, and this sharply restricted the extent to which they could represent the interests of their communities before that time.

The most active political groups during the pre-World War II period were the Arab Association and the Indian National Association. The former was founded just after the turn of the century to fight for financial compensation for slave owners affected by abolition. Later, it began to represent the general interests of the Arab landowning community. The Indian National Association was formed just before World War I, and generally speaking it represented the interests of the Asian commercial and financial classes.

Overt political competition between these two associations stemmed from the socio-economic polarity between the Arab and Asian communities. Each communal association was controlled and led by persons whose individual position and role in Zanzibar's economy clearly epitomized the differences between the two groups. The Executive Committee of the Arab Association was nearly always composed of members of the wealthiest and longest established Arab families. The President, for example, was Abdulla Suleiman al-Harthi, a direct descendant of the al-Harthi family from which the governors of Zanzibar had been appointed before the establishment of the Sultanate. The Indian National Association was controlled by the largest merchants and exporters. Although the leadership groups in both these associations had the support of the rank and file membership of the community, they functioned very much in the interests of narrow, exclusively defined elites. This became very apparent during a dispute over the indebtedness of Zanzibar's agricultural classes, the major political controversy of the inter-war period and one which has been selected here for an intensive case study.

The need for a case study approach to the politics of this period is readily apparent. Because of the autocratic and restrictive character of British administration during the "official majority" era, there was very little overt social or political conflict among the local communities. For this reason there is little use in a comprehensive chronological exposition of political events and developments. It is far more informative of the nature of political and social life in Zanzibar at the time to select a single social and political problem and trace its development as a national political issue.

The indebtedness of the agricultural classes has been chosen for case study because it illuminates the character of political interaction among the local communities and between the communities and the colonial administration far more clearly than does any other problem. Indebtedness had always been a matter of concern to the British administration, but in the years immediately before World War II it became the most critical political issue in the Protectorate. The indebtedness issue strained race relations between the Arab and Asian communities to a point just short of violence; it threatened to wreck Zanzibar's agricultural economy, and created a parliamentary impasse. It offers an ideal example of the development of extreme social conflict within a political framework stabilized by British rule, and of the particular methods and objectives of political agitation necessitated by the presence of an only partially representative parliamentary body.

The following case study is intended to illustrate four basic propositions about the nature of Zanzibar's politics during the inter-war period. The essential purpose of these propositions is to illuminate the impact of colonial rule on the character of socio-political conflict in Zanzibar, and to illustrate the most salient features of the political life of the time. They establish and define the political background out of which nationalism emerged after the war, and in this respect form a sort of base-point against which to contrast all subsequent political change.

1). *British colonial rule was an extremely conservative political force. Its effect, if not its intention, was to freeze social and class relations in the pattern in which they had existed when the Protectorate began.* During the administration's involvement in the indebtedness controversy, this manifested itself in a tendency for the whole energy and attention of the colonial bureaucracy to become mobilized in a massive effort to preserve the Arab aristocracy in its fixed position at the top of the society. There was never, during Zanzibar's entire colonial history, a comparable output of official energy directed towards improving the broad mass of the African population.

2). *The Arab community was a declining aristocracy. The very presence of British colonialism cut Arabs off from the very highest levels of political power and prevented top Arab leadership from exercising authority on its own to preserve itself economically.* Indebtedness was reducing Arab landholdings and other property and thereby rapidly reducing the sheer numerical size of the Arab elite. Colonial policy slowed this process but did not stop it. The wholesale entry of Arabs into nationalistic politics after the war was not nearly as much an aristocratic movement as it was a movement of the petty bourgeois from families which had come down in the world. Their motivation was far less a sense of aristocratic *noblesse oblige* than it was a desire to resist further economic misfortune, and perhaps an ultimate desire to create a firm political basis from which to rebuild an ancient economic heritage.

3). *Pre-war politics were decidedly elite phenomena.* The politically participant and relevant groups were the middle and upper classes. The indebtedness controversy, the chief example of open political conflict during the pre-war era, was a struggle between a declining rural Arab aristocracy and a rising urban Asian bourgeoisie. The African community, which provided the agricultural and laboring mass of the population, was conspicuously absent not only from the indebtedness crisis, but from all other political agitation. It lacked any representation in the Legislative Council, which left it outside the realm of political affairs and, in effect, made it an "underlying population."[1] The process of political communication, the transmission and feedback of political messages and symbols such as values, aspirations and group interests, had not yet penetrated the African community. Because the mass of these people lacked any of the mechanisms through which adequate political communication might occur (an informed leadership body or a literate minority which was actively attentive to the mass media), it remained culturally remote from the stimuli of political action.

4). *Any strain toward solidarity in Zanzibar politics was along racial lines.* It became evident during the course of the indebtedness dispute that communal association was a far more powerful source of loyalty than economic or occupational class. Thus, for example, Asian plantation owners who might have been expected to side with Arab agriculturalists for reasons of economic interest tended to support the Indian National Association. Similarly, those few Arabs who were exporters or members of the Zanzibar Chamber of Commerce and therefore had economic ties to the Asian business group, tended to subscribe to the position of the Arab Association. For all but a very small number of members of each community, racial identity and occupational class did coincide; thus, the merchants and exporters were practically all Indians and the agriculturalists involved were practically all Arabs. The most salient feature of the entire conflict, however, was the nearly automatic tendency for all the contending parties to identify themselves and their opponents in racial terms

[1] The concept of an "underlying" or politically non-participant population was developed by the political scientist Karl Deutsch. He defines it as "that part of the population which is not mobilized for intensive communication." *Nationalism and Social Communication* (New York: John Wiley and Sons, 1953), p. 102.

and to view the conflict as a racial—not an economic—dispute. This tendency later became one of the most pronounced features of Zanzibar politics.

The indebtedness of Arab plantation owners to Asian financiers can be dated from the very beginning of the clove industry, when Arab colonials from Oman sought funds to develop their clove and coconut estates. It had led to open racial friction between Arabs and Asians long before the growth of British influence. The debtor-creditor relationship between an Arab landed gentry and an urban Asian business class was not a new phenomenon in East Africa; it was only an extension of the historic relationship of Arab dependence upon Asian business skill which had existed traditionally in the Arab coastal settlements. In Zanzibar, however, Arabs had ceased to be purely a political elite and trading community and had become in part a rural agricultural class. In so doing, they became vulnerable to more extreme forms of economic dependence.

The situation in Zanzibar was the same as in many other areas of the world. Under free market conditions, unprotected primary producers have nearly always experienced economic difficulty in their associations with middlemen, and in a number of countries this difficulty has elicited remedial and supportive legislation to help the agriculturalists. In Zanzibar, however, the authority to provide such legislation was in the hands of an alien colonial government.[2]

[2] There are a large number of Zanzibar Government documents which deal with the problem of agricultural indebtedness. The most important of these are (in chronological order): V. H. Kirkham, *Memorandum on the Functions of a Department of Agriculture with Special Reference to Zanzibar* (Zanzibar: Government Printer, 1931); R. S. Troup, *Report on Clove Cultivation in the Zanzibar Protectorate* (Zanzibar: Government Printer, 1931); C. F. Strickland, C.I.E., *Report on Cooperation and Certain Aspects of the Economic Condition of Agriculture in Zanzibar* (London: Crown Agents for

The degree of Arab indebtedness grew steadily during the nineteenth century and began to assume considerable proportions just before the establishment of a Protectorate. It has been estimated that by the 1880's about two-thirds of all the clove plantations were fully mortgaged to Asians. In the 1913 Annual Report on Zanzibar sent to the Colonial Office, local British officials called the seriousness of Arab indebtedness to the attention of London authorities: "The large plantations are chiefly owned by Arabs, a few being held by Indians. . . . The Arabs are heavily involved financially, their properties being mortgaged to Indians who are, as a rule, in a position to foreclose, but prefer to allow the Arab to remain on in a more or less dependent position. The Arab has been unable to accommodate himself to the changed conditions of labour arising from the abolition of slavery in 1897, while the Indian prefers the business of shop-keeper, merchant or money-lender to that of farmer."[3] Thus there had already emerged among resident colonial authorities a strong desire to use their policy-making powers as a means of alleviating Arab distress.

There were many different causes of indebtedness. Among the most obvious was that mentioned by the author of the 1913 Report, namely the abolition of slavery, and Government officials in Zanzibar were in-

---

the Colonies, 1932); C. F. Strickland, C.I.E., and Sir Alan Pim, K.C.I.E., C.S.I., *Zanzibar: The Land and Its Mortgage Debt* (London: Dunstable and Watford, 1932); C. A. Bartlett and J. S. Last, *Report on the Indebtedness of the Agricultural Classes, 1933* (Zanzibar: Government Printer, 1934); Zanzibar Protectorate, *Report of the Commission on Agricultural Indebtedness and Memorandum thereon by the Government of Zanzibar* (Zanzibar: Government Printer, 1935); B. H. Binder, F.C.A., *Report on the Zanzibar Clove Industry* (Zanzibar: Government Printer, 1936); and Sir Ernest M. Dowson, K.B.E., *A Note on Agricultural Indebtedness* (Zanzibar: Government Printer, 1936). Hereafter, whenever possible, these reports will be cited by author in the text.

[3] Quoted in Dowson, pp. 3-4.

clined to emphasize this factor more than any other. During its formative years and throughout the nineteenth century, the clove industry had been able to count on a supply of free labor, but when slavery was legally abolished many former slaves were reluctant to work in the clove areas, and wages soared rapidly. After World War I, Great Britain began to transport large numbers of migratory laborers from the mainland to work in the clove plantations. While this practice restored an abundant labor supply, it added somewhat to the costs of the industry, for the growers had to absorb the expenses of the migratory labor program.

Although abolition did lead to some increase in costs, its importance as a basic cause of indebtedness is limited. Not only had the problem of debt assumed considerable proportions long before abolition, but the importance of slave labor to the clove industry was small—slaves never constituted a very large proportion of the permanent work force. Once the initial labor of clearing the forests and planting the clove trees had been accomplished, the only remaining tasks were picking and drying during the harvest season. Most growers had always depended upon migratory paid labor recruited among the indigenous population, since it was unprofitable to maintain on a year-round basis a large group of slaves who could only be employed for a month or two. Thus, workers' wages had always been an important factor in the costs of the clove industry. Moreover, wages had begun to increase before the end of slavery and this was attributable to factors other than abolition, such as a rapidly expanding demand for labor as the industry grew. The real result of abolition was that it accelerated processes of change which had already begun to alter the cost-profit balance of the clove economy.

Probably the most important single cause of indebtedness was the irregularity of clove prices in world markets.[4] The problem of chronic economic instability is endemic in all nations dependent on a single crop with a highly variable return. In Zanzibar, periods of prosperity and high prices encouraged many clove growers to expand their landholdings. Competition for a diminishing supply of arable land forced up property values, leading to a highly inflated price structure, and most growers had to borrow heavily to finance their investments. Once the boom in world prices came to an end, they were left with debts far exceeding the deflated market value of their newly acquired acreage. This process occurred during the late 1870's and repeated itself with disastrous consequences between 1920 and 1925. A post-war clove boom ended abruptly about four years after the war and left many Arabs with debts amounting to two or three times the depressed value of their holdings.

Extremely high interest rates on loans charged by the Asian financiers aggravated the economic embarrassment of Arab farmers.[5] Many Asians at the time justified such rates on the ground that high risks were inevitably attached to agricultural loans. Their arguments were somewhat sardonic: the risk of not being fully repaid was great because, among other reasons, the rates of interest made it nearly impossible to repay. Often these rates were so high as to double the book value of the debt after only two or three years, and Asian lenders were legally able to assume possession of land and other property whose value was far in excess of the amount of the original loan.

Certain cultural practices and traditions of the Arab community also contributed towards an oppressive burden of debt. One was the Islamic religious precept about inheritance: property is to be divided between all legiti-

---

[4] See both Dowson, p. 14, and Bartlett and Last, p. 2.
[5] See Dowson, p. 11, Binder, p. 7, and Bartlett and Last, pp. 5-6.

mate heirs. This practice, together with polygamy and a tendency for wealthy Arab magnates to have many children, resulted in greater and greater fragmentation of Arab landholdings. Many once great estates were split up into smaller and smaller parcels which were scarcely sufficient to support even a small monogamous family. Many British civil servants analyzing the problem of debts have also commented on the prevalence of conspicuous consumption within the Arab community. Certainly Arabs have gained a universal reputation for cordial hospitality and even lavish entertainment of guests, and those in Zanzibar were no exception. It is possible that a culturally ingrained emphasis on gracious living made it difficult for Arabs to reduce personal expenditures during periods of economic difficulty. This was probably far less important in the whole debt problem, however, than the other contributing causes.

The extent of Arab indebtedness was the subject of several government surveys, but there was very little agreement among them. Numerous difficulties complicated the effort to achieve an accurate appraisal of the dimensions of indebtedness. The administration had never made a cadastral survey of Zanzibar, and thus did not possess authoritative and definite information about the distribution of land rights or ownership. Further, many of the persons involved (both Asians and Arabs) were reluctant to report their landholdings, and found ways to conceal ownership of property from government surveyors. Any estimate of land distribution, therefore, had to be based on incomplete knowledge and guesswork.

Political considerations, too, often interfered with realistic judgment of the problem. There was a division between those administrators favoring strong decisive steps to restore the Arab community to solvency, and those who felt that the government ought not to interfere in a strictly local matter. The former tended to adopt a very serious view of indebtedness, and in order to support their argument that without government intervention the economy would be ruined, their reports portrayed debt in the grossest possible terms. One official in this group claimed that "not less than half the agricultural property of these islands has passed to the hands of the money lending classes, and at least half the remainder is encumbered to them, most of it heavily."[6] Their opponents took strong exception to the notion that the Arabs were unable to extricate themselves from debt on their own initiative. The principal spokesman of this group of administrators argued that "the actual amount of debt does not appear extremely heavy . . . (and is not) a burden which a hard working man could not shake off by steady and intelligent effort."[7] Each side devised measurements best suited to its own position, and the result was a mélange of statistical information, from which an exploratory outline containing the basic historical and quantitative features of the problem of agricultural indebtedness may be derived.

Asians owned approximately 152,000 clove trees out of roughly three million in 1922, or slightly more than five per cent. After 1922, the government initiated an extensive planting program and the total number of clove trees in the country increased markedly, probably by about one-quarter of a million. A government tree census in 1933 established that within the preceding ten year period, Asians had radically increased their holdings; they now owned more than 500,000 trees and held

---

[6] Bartlett and Last, p. 14. The report goes on to say: "It is claimed, on behalf of the moneylenders, that they perform a useful, even essential function in financing agriculture. The majority have, in fact, used agriculture as a milch cow, which they have now almost milked dry."

[7] Strickland and Pim, p. 4.

virtually irredeemable mortgages on another 300,000.[8] Thus, at the very least, Asians either owned or controlled more than one-fourth of Zanzibar's clove output.

There is considerable basis for assuming that they controlled even more, for there were various forms of hidden ownership by which Asians concealed their actual holdings from government investigators. The most widely practiced method was known as the fictitious sale.[9] In a fictitious sale, the Arab farmer would be compelled under threat of complete foreclosure to agree to "sell" his land to his creditor in return for the discharge of a certain proportion of his debt. The Arab was then allowed to continue to reside on the land and to cultivate it, provided that his clove crop be handed over to the Asian creditor for a fixed price. This price was usually very low and the terms of the agreement often specified that the outstanding debt was to be accepted as payment. Since most Arab farmers lacked any alternative source of livelihood, even this cruel arrangement was preferable to eviction from the land. Fictitious sales of this sort added considerably to the total amount of land which passed from Arab to Asian control, but were rarely reported to government authorities.

An alternative method of measurement was devised to circumvent the problem raised by fictitious sales. Instead of attempting to calculate the amount of land or number of trees being transferred, officials attempted to compute the total value of outstanding debts on clove fields, as a proportion of the total aggregate value of all clove plantations in the Protectorate. Arabs and Asians were less reluctant to report exactly how much money they owed or were owed than such blatantly disreputable and embarrassing arrangements as fictitious sales.

---

[8] Binder, pp. 6-8, and Zanzibar Protectorate, *Report of the Commission on Agricultural Indebtedness*, pp. 2-4.

[9] Bartlett and Last, pp. 6-7.

This facilitated a comparatively easy calculation of total outstanding debt.

This method, however, was only slightly more successful than tabulating the transfer of trees. The principal difficulty was that the outstanding debt could be made to appear as either a large or a small proportion of the total value of all clove plantations, simply by varying the figure employed to represent the average value of a clove tree. According to the most reasonable and careful estimates, however, this alternative method indicated that Zanzibar's clove estates had a burden of debt amounting to well over one-half their aggregate value.[10] In slightly different terms, by 1933 Asians had become the potential legal owners of more than one-half of all clove property.

The large Arab clove estates bore a far heavier burden of the debt than small peasant farms owned by indigenous Africans. It was extremely difficult for peasant farmers to raise loans since they had little to offer as security. There was also a greater tendency for these small farmers to supplement their income from cloves by growing their own food or by harvesting other cash crops; they were hence more economically self-sufficient and less seriously affected by falling clove prices. Arab landowners, however, depended almost entirely upon the sale of cloves for their income. Though indebtedness affected all landowning communities to a degree, the disproportionate incidence of debt gave one special social meaning to this economic phenomenon. Agricultural indebtedness had assumed dimensions which threatened the economic survival of the Arab oligarchy.

Other less readily apparent consequences also flowed from the staggering burden of indebtedness. Debt had

[10] The Bartlett and Last report employed this standard of measurement, but Bartlett himself was widely known to be the strongest advocate of firm government intervention and the other official reports usually discounted his approach.

reduced the once dominant elements of the Arab community to a state of permanent insolvency, and transformed Zanzibar's political elite into a debtor class. Those Arabs living on estates already appropriated through fictitious sale had become virtual serfs, and the land, more and more held by absentee owners, suffered from poor agricultural practices and reduced productivity. This progressive demoralization of Zanzibar's most economically productive agriculturalists, together with the growing pattern of absentee ownership, posed a severe threat to the entire agricultural economy of the Protectorate.

Throughout the entire era of the indebtedness problem, the major administrative concern of British officials was to formulate and implement a remedy for Arab indebtedness. From 1923 to 1933 administrative efforts in this direction were mostly unsuccessful. Until 1928 agricultural policy was based upon a complex subsidy scheme designed primarily to provide Arabs with a means of acquiring ready cash to pay off their debts. Subsidies, in the form of bonus payments, were given to growers for planting additional clove trees. A correlative objective of the scheme was to increase the value of the plantations by replacing old and worn-out trees with new ones and by increasing the number of debt-free trees. In part the subsidy scheme failed because it required a degree of attention and supervision beyond the means of the small Department of Agriculture.[11] The main reason for its failure, however, was that the government had completely underestimated the magnitude of indebtedness. The subsidies were insufficient to pay even the recurrent annual interest obligation on the outstanding debt.

The scheme was finally abandoned in 1928 when its

[11] Troup, pp. 32-33. No other cause for the failure of the subsidy scheme was recognized at this time by the administration.

inadequacy had become apparent, and for several more years insufficient information about the size of the debt problem continued to hinder the formulation of an effective agricultural policy. Between 1927 and 1933 a small committee of officials of the Department of Agriculture had been assigned to handle the problem. The committee's objective was to unite the plantation owners in order to control the costs of production, especially labor rates, and to form a sort of growers' cooperative to market cloves, to provide cheap storage facilities, and to offer low-interest harvesting loans. The Clove Growers Association (CGA) was only partially effective. When it was founded in 1927 membership was made a prerequisite for receiving subsidies, and it had over nine thousand members, but after the subsidy scheme was dropped the CGA lost membership and became inactive. It was altogether unable to regulate the market price of cloves, largely because the indebted growers had made it a standard practice to mortgage their crops far in advance.[12]

The turning point in the administration's approach to the problem of indebtedness came in 1933, when a series of investigating commissions first began to make public their official knowledge of the economic jeopardy of the Arab community. This information elevated indebtedness in the eyes of the colonial authorities; from a mere matter of economics it now became a fundamental test case of Britain's political and constitutional relationship to Zanzibar's Arab rulers. One administrator commented that: "The real case for taking measures for the preservation of the Arab against himself rests on grounds which are not economic. . . . The State of Zanzibar is Arab in origin and constitution. The British Government destroyed the whole basis of their social organization . . . (and must now) take the necessary steps

12 Strickland, pp. 10-11.

to adapt them for meeting the new condition."[13] This concept of the Protectorate as a special political obligation to preserve Zanzibar's Arab elite was widely held in expatriate administrative cadres, and it became accepted as a sufficient motive in itself for undertaking a concerted effort to ease the Arabs' economic position.

The problem confronting British administrators was that any effective remedy for Arab indebtedness might offend the economic interests of the Asian community. Official determination to restore the Arab oligarchy to solvency would thus have profound political consequences. The most serious of these would be that restorative policies would inevitably provoke disagreement and strong opposition from Asian leaders. Under the official majority system there was no question that colonial authorities could pass any legislation they wished. But open debate in the Legislative Council also meant that they would be accused publicly of prejudice and partiality in their attitudes towards the local population. The administration's choice was between steadily worsening economic conditions—both for the Arab community and the Protectorate—and an immediate political struggle with the powerful and influential Asian community.

Between January and June of 1934 agricultural and economic experts in the Protectorate government developed a comprehensive legislative and administrative program designed to alleviate Arab indebtedness. The most controversial piece of legislation in the program was a law forbidding the alienation of land from the Arabs or Africans to Asians, except with the consent of the British Resident. At the same time, a temporary moratorium was declared on all debts. The purpose of these two measures was to put an immediate stop to the

---

[13] Strickland and Pim, p. 14.

flow of all types of property and funds from the Arab to the Asian community. Both were conceived initially as purely temporary measures; they would remain in effect only until the more fundamental long-range reforms contemplated in the program could begin to take effect.

The principal long-range reform was the resuscitation and reorganization of the Clove Growers Association. Previously the CGA had been a kind of voluntary cooperative society which government agricultural officers simply helped to organize. It assisted the growers on a strictly mutual self-help basis. The agricultural reform program of 1934 endowed the CGA with semi-official status. Its main function was still to help clove growers to harvest and market their crops economically; but, as a recognized agency of the government, it had a better financial position and was given important regulatory and supervisory powers over the entire clove industry. It was, for example, exempted from taxes and fees and given a share of all the revenue duty collected on cloves. Its supervisory powers, which constituted the fourth section of the government's program, enabled it to police the business practices of the Asian community and to impose quality controls on exports.[14]

During the Legislative Council debates on the agricultural reform programs, Government spokesmen gave full public expression to their belief that the interests of the Arab community held the position of highest legislative priority. The Attorney-General, for example, said: "This is an Arab state. It is the duty of the protecting government to assist the protected people. It is impossi-

---

[14] For a detailed summary of the 1934 Agricultural Reform legislation, see Binder, pp. 5-6. The debates on these laws are found in Zanzibar Protectorate, *Debates of the Legislative Council, Eighth Session, 1933-1934* (Zanzibar: Government Printer, n.d.), pp. 56-67 and 79-111.

ble for us to stand by and take the risk of the expropriation of His Highness' people."[15]

Other official speeches supporting the program expressed the opinion that the indebtedness crisis was as much a political issue as an economic one. The existing danger, as it had come to be viewed by the government, was nothing less than the complete impoverishment and expropriation of the Arab landowning class. Administrators felt very strongly that unless the reform measures were accepted, the utter ruin of Zanzibar's plantation economy would follow. They were wholly supported in this position by the unofficial members of the Arab community.

The legislative representatives of the Asian community offered two major criticisms of the agricultural reform program. First, they bitterly argued that the program was blatantly discriminatory against Asians, and that it was a violation of their basic property rights. One important Asian leader accused the government of harboring virulent anti-Asian prejudices: "Suspicion has been growing . . . that the administration is, for reasons best known to itself, antagonistic to the Indian community. . . . The policy of the government has been anti-Indian for the last three years, and that sedulous antagonism has now broken out into the open and active hostility. . . . Let me ask, Sir, whether such a piece of legislation [a moratorium on debt payments] would have been undertaken if the money and rights involved had been of the British instead of the Indian community."[16] The legislative representatives directed the brunt of their attack against the alienation law because it was worded in explicitly racial terms. Asian leaders argued

[15] Zanzibar Protectorate, *Legislative Council Debates,* 1933-1934, p. 60.
[16] *Ibid.,* pp. 88-90.

that economic categories, such as "agriculturalists" and "non-agriculturalists," ought to have been employed.

A more fundamental Asian criticism of the program was that the agricultural reforms being offered by the government would not be effective. The gist of their argument on this point was that in preventing the sale of property to the only community in a financial position to purchase, the government had lowered property values still further since there would be a scarcity of eligible buyers. Thus, the government had imprisoned the indebted classes even more tightly in their own debt. This criticism was beside the point, however, since the purpose of forbidding alienation was not so much to keep land values high as to prevent the spread of absentee ownership.

Asian representatives had remarkably little criticism of the sweeping reforms contemplated in the character and powers of the CGA. A token objection was raised to the establishment of an official government body possessing strong regulatory powers and also operating as a marketing agency in competition with private entrepreneurs. The reluctance of the Indian National Association to pursue a sustained and vigorous attack on the CGA is indicative of the political temperament of the Asian community. Asian leaders seemed almost eager for economic reforms to extricate their community from an economic position which had become a source of considerable embarrassment and which had incurred the racial emnity of other groups.

Partially for this reason and partially because further protest would have been gratuitous anyway, the Indian National Association limited its opposition to the reform program to criticism within the Legislative Council. Its objective was to expose the discriminatory nature of certain of the reform laws, not to prevent creation of a government agency which might help indebted farmers.

Once the laws had been passed, there were only minor forms of protest, such as editorial commentary and private expressions of protest to government officials.

The CGA itself increased tensions between the Asian community and the government after the inauguration of the agricultural reforms. The business restrictions imposed by the CGA, which Asians viewed as a competitor, became a source of particular resentment. Among the most strongly resented of these were the requirements that Asian merchants obtain export licenses from the CGA, that all their cloves for export be submitted to the Association for inspection, and that the CGA be kept periodically informed of their clove purchases and sales. The administration further antagonized the Asian community by renewing from time to time its moratorium on the repayment of debts, and by deciding to make its restrictions on land alienation a permanent part of Zanzibar's legal code. Both these latter policies prevented Asians from recovering outstanding financial investments. To most members of the Asian community, the most galling aspect of their relationship with the government was their knowledge that local British authorities were committed—by constitution and by prejudice—to offer their full legislative support to the Arabs. This created a growing sense that mere parliamentary protest was an insufficient and inadequate mode of political action.

Tensions between the Asian community and the British administration reached their peak in 1937, and developed into a major political crisis when colonial officials decided to introduce additional legislation to expand the power of the CGA. The new legislation granted the CGA an exclusive right to purchase cloves from local producers. Although the earlier agricultural reforms had, to a degree, alleviated Arab economic distress, colonial authorities had been persuaded by an influential report that only monopolistic control over the local supply of cloves would enable the CGA to influence world prices, to determine the local price structure, and to increase the growers' share of the clove profits—its over-riding objectives.[17] The object of the legislation was to force Asian merchants to purchase all cloves for export from the CGA at a price determined by the Association, and thereby to reduce radically their share of the clove profits since they could no longer negotiate over prices with an indebted community of growers. This legislation was adopted and put into effect in July, 1937.[18]

After the legislation was passed, Asian leaders decided to break their uneasy truce with the government and to expand the arena of conflict beyond the Legislative Council by adopting extra-parliamentary techniques of political action. The Indian National Association proclaimed a boycott of the clove industry, and during the latter half of 1937 Asian dealers refused to buy or to export cloves. The boycott was insufficient by itself, however, since the CGA could purchase and export cloves, and since the CGA also began to draw on its financial reserves to guarantee agriculturalists a fair price for the 1937 crop. Paradoxically, Arab and African clove farm-

[17] The report mentioned here was Binder's *Report on the Zanzibar Clove Industry*. In the final pages of his otherwise carefully balanced evaluation of the indebtedness situation, Binder cast his principal recommendation in the most unqualified terms: "In my opinion, . . . a complete and continuous monopoly of supplies is necessary to assure the Association full and effective control, with a minimum risk to the funds employed by it, and therefore its present operations should be continued, but on a wider basis and with more extended power . . . viz; that all local buying of cloves should be centered in the Association on the same lines and with the same effects as if the Association were a Cooperative Society." Binder, pp. 40-41.

[18] For the full debate on this new legislation, see: Zanzibar Protectorate, *Debates of the Legislative Council, Eleventh Session, 1936-1937* (Zanzibar: Government Printer, 1938), pp. 61-67.

ers experienced a temporary economic boom during the early stages of the Asian boycott, since the CGA offered higher prices for cloves than the merchants normally gave. The success of the boycott thus required that clove exports be reduced significantly, for only in this way would the financial reserves of the CGA become exhausted.

Except for the fact that India was a major importer of Zanzibar cloves and accounted for more than two-fifths of the total clove exports, the Indian National Association's boycott might have been easily defeated by the CGA. It would probably have been extremely difficult for the INA to mobilize international support for its boycott in any other country. In India, however, this was a comparatively simple matter. The Indian National Association sought and received the support of the Indian National Congress, the nationalist movement of the Indian people, and the Congress organized a nation-wide consumer boycott in India against the use of Zanzibar cloves. In this way, the political support of the Congress became crucial to the Indian National Association. There were thus created two different boycotts: the boycott of Asian exporters in Zanzibar who refused to sell cloves anywhere, and the consumers' boycott in India which frustrated the CGA's exporting activities by depriving it of an essential market.

The Asian consumer boycott struck deeply at the position of the Zanzibar Government. It exhausted the CGA's reserves, and by sharply reducing exports it also lowered government revenue and created a severe budget deficit. At a private meeting with Asian leaders, the British Resident issued a stern warning about the social consequences of the boycott tactics: "Let us remove one obvious fallacy, namely that in this matter you can strike at the Government of Zanzibar without injuring the people of this country . . . you cannot strike effectively at Government except by harming and impoverishing the Arabs, and the Africans and yourselves. . . . The results [of the boycott] can be stated shortly. . . . Heavily increased taxation, drastic economies in the sphere of education and other social services, depressed internal prices for cloves, *a revised debt settlement scheme with repayment to creditors necessarily spread over many years,* poverty, discontent, commercial and economic stagnation" (italics mine).[19] This warning, however, only had the effect of informing the Indian National Association that its joint boycott with the Indian National Congress had been effective. The Congress intensified its consumer boycott, holding numerous mass meetings across India to rally its membership against purchasing Zanzibar cloves. Between the two boycotts, Zanzibar's overseas sales of cloves were reduced by considerably more than half.

By the early months of 1938, the political atmosphere of Zanzibar bordered on hysteria and racial violence. Arabs began to organize a succession of counter-boycotts against the Asian community. They persuaded African laborers not to work as clove pickers on Asian-owned plantations and made intensive preparations to launch a joint Arab-African counter-boycott of Asian shops. A group of about forty wealthy Pemba Arabs subscribed funds to form a trading syndicate and cooperative society, the object of which was to eliminate any need for rural Arabs and Africans to depend upon Asian traders.[20] Armed bands of Arabs roamed the rural areas intimidating Asian shopkeepers, in the hope that this would lead to pressure within the Asian community to abandon the clove boycott.

---

[19] The speech was made on March 3, 1938, and appeared in the March 12, 1938, issue of *Al Falaq,* the newspaper of the Arab Association.

[20] *Al Falaq,* March 26, 1938.

Instead, however, these efforts at intimidation strengthened the unity of all classes of Asians. Asian bus and lorry owners refused to transport cloves purchased by the CGA.[21] Many of the other Asian traders left the rural areas and emigrated to the greater safety of the city. Asian leaders, on their part, interpreted Arab violence as a government-sponsored effort to induce them to surrender, and because of this suspicion they rejected the efforts of local authorities to intercede even in the racial side of the dispute. Conflict between Asian leaders and the administration reached a total impasse. Asian merchants were determined to reject any compromise that would enable the CGA to retain its monopoly of the local clove supply, while officials were convinced that any control short of monopoly would be insufficient to assist the growers.

The Zanzibar Government had two choices. It could negotiate to weaken the CGA's monopoly and permit Asians to buy a certain proportion of their cloves from local growers or it could seek means to break the two boycotts. Government officials in the CGA believed that there was a strong possibility of pursuing the latter policy successfully. Their intelligence reports indicated that the Indian National Congress' consumer boycott did not have the full support of the Indian people, and that two critical groups in India (the clove importers and merchants and the Muslim segments of the Indian population) were prepared to oppose Congress policy. The importers had an obvious economic interest in seeking to frustrate the Indian National Congress' consumer boycott. Muslim discontent with the Congress stemmed from the fact that it was Hindu-dominated. The leader of India's Muslim community, Mohammed Ali Jinnah, had taken the view that "the question is not

[21] Clove Growers Association, *Board of Management Minutes,* July 1937–July 1938 (typescript), Item No. 933.

between the British and Indian community, but is purely an economic one in which the bulk of the people concerned are Muslims."[22] Jinnah and his supporters felt that the unity of Islam ought to cross racial lines and that Arab and Indian Muslims ought to be able to negotiate peaceably. The manager of the CGA believed that with the assistance of these two groups his Association would be able to export cloves to India.

During the closing months of 1937, the CGA's position was further strengthened by a break in the unity of the Zanzibar Asian community. A large Asian exporting firm approached CGA officials and "proposed to the Association that for a suitable remuneration they would undertake to export cloves to India destinations notwithstanding the attitudes and activities of local Asian exporters and that boycott conditions were obtaining."[23] This was extremely important, for the CGA had been reluctant to export directly to India fearing that such action would strengthen the position of Congress supporters of the boycott.

There was also evidence that popular support for the boycott among Zanzibar Asians was waning. While the wealthy Asians were able to endure fairly easily a prolonged cessation in their business activities, the boycott and Arab counter-boycott were producing considerable economic hardship among the poorer class of Asian traders.[24] This group had not been badly affected by the revised powers of the CGA because the Association employed them as its commissioned buying agents in the rural areas. Since these rural Asian shopkeepers depended upon Arab and African clove farmers as customers, they were somewhat anxious for a settlement

[22] Quoted in Zanzibar Protectorate, *Legislative Council Debates, 1936-1937*, pp. 75-76.
[23] Clove Growers Association, *Minutes,* Item No. 1083 and appendix.
[24] *Ibid.,* Item No. 1116 and attached memorandum.

that would be favorable to the agriculturalists. This group, however, was completely unable to exercise any influence on the policies of the Indian National Association, which was dominated and controlled by the wealthy exporters.

The CGA was finally restrained from encouraging clove exports to India by the close working relationship between the Indian National Congress and Zanzibar's largest exporters, who held the highest positions of leadership in the Indian National Association.[25] This relationship endowed the Indian National Association with an extraordinary power of reprisal. The Indian National Congress had consistently displayed willingness to take any measures sought by its embattled brethren. By virtue of its position as the majority party in the Indian Legislative Council, it held full legal authority to pass a legislative prohibition against the import of Zanzibar cloves. This implied threat of legislation against clove imports became the critical factor in the Indian National Association's dispute with the CGA. The CGA was unwilling to take the risk of provoking a legal embargo largely because such legislation seemed to imply a kind of finality about the termination of Zanzibar's clove trade with India. Once the CGA had decided that it was economically unwise to attempt to circumvent the boycott either by direct action or by employing the services of a maverick exporter, the Zanzibar Government was left with no recourse but to seek a compromise with the Asian community.

The government's decision to negotiate was also the result of an accumulation of pressures from British sources. The Indian National Congress had been able, at the crucial final stages in the dispute, to persuade the Colonial Government of India and the Indian Office in London to intercede with the Zanzibar authorities on

[25] *Ibid.*, Item No. 1335.

behalf of the Asian community. As a result, British officials in Zanzibar found themselves under pressure from high officials in London to abandon their intransigent attitude. The symbol of an imminent change in British policy and of London's desire for a conciliatory approach to the Indian National Association was the appointment of a new British Resident, J. Hathorn Hall, to serve in Zanzibar. The former resident, Sir Richard Rankine, was personally identified by Asian leaders as the prime mover of the 1934 reform program and as the major source of anti-Asian prejudice in government policy. Hall's arrival reduced the tension between the Asian community and the government, and fostered the atmosphere necessary for negotiation and reconciliation.

Though the Indian National Association had, with the aid of the Indian National Congress, forced the British government to come to terms, it did not exact a one-sided agreement. The terms of the compromise treaty—known as the "Heads of Agreement"—gave the CGA considerably more power than it received under the original 1934 reform program.[26] The key provisions of the Heads of Agreement were that the CGA would not exercise its authority to export cloves, and in return Asian exporters agreed to purchase a fixed proportion of all cloves for export from the CGA. That proportion was set at one-half. The remaining provisions of the Heads of Agreement were a sort of charter of business practices according to which both the CGA and the Asian firms agreed to conduct their affairs. With the funds obtained from the sale of cloves, the CGA was allowed to set a base price at which it would purchase all cloves offered to it, a practice similar to the American

[26] The "Heads of Agreement" has been reprinted in: Zanzibar Protectorate, *Debates of the Legislative Council, Twelfth Session, 1937-1938* (Zanzibar: Government Printer, 1939), pp. 129-131.

price-support program. This enabled the CGA and the Indian National Association to guarantee the Arab Association that growers would receive reasonable prices. The Heads of Agreement was signed on May 5, 1938, by all parties concerned, and for all practical purposes brought to a close the political portion of the agricultural indebtedness problem.

It might be added as a contemporary postscript that after 1961, when the Arab leaders gained full political power as the spearhead of a mass political movement, one of their earliest acts was to abrogate the Heads of Agreement. Their justification for doing so was that under a fully democratic and representative constitution, an agreement between a colonial government and a racial association could no longer be considered to have binding effect. Arab leaders did not, however, have an opportunity to implement any actual changes in the operation of the CGA before the African revolution.

CHAPTER V

The Emergence of Arab Nationalism

Anti-colonial protest was the most striking and profoundly important political innovation of the post-war period. This revolutionary phenomenon brought about a series of major changes in the character and pattern of conflict relations and in the assumptions people held about the nature of their political environment. Pre-war politics had been dominated by social and economic disputes among the local communities, especially among Arabs and Asians. With the one exception of the agricultural indebtedness crisis, the British colonial administration was not a party to these disputes, but had kept aloof as the supreme impartial arbiter. Its presence was taken for granted and its position could be likened to that of a judge whom the contending parties sought, by various means, to sway. After the war, political and constitutional issues became paramount, and the colonial authorities could no longer stand aside. They were drawn into active and direct conflict with those who considered their very presence illegitimate.[1]

An essential feature of this revolution in politics was the decrease in conflict between Arabs and Asians. Certain traces of their old animosity remained, but the Asian community, whose interests were commercial and economic, were by and large indifferent to constitutional considerations. Asian leaders did not seek a prominent role in constitutional discussions, and for this reason the Asian community receded as a major political

[1] This chapter and those which follow depend heavily for their information upon interviews conducted in Zanzibar during a year and a half of field research in the country. This field research began in June, 1962, and continued until November, 1963, and was made possible by a fellowship from the Foreign Area Fellowship Program (formerly administered by the Ford Foundation).

force. Its retreat from politics had considerable consequence: since Asians were not for some time replaced by
assertive African leadership, Arabs were left in sole possession of the political arena. This may help to explain
why Zanzibar nationalism was initiated by Arabs. Long
after nationalism had appeared in other countries on
the African continent—Egypt, Ghana and Kenya, for
example—Arabs were the only active political partici-
pants in Zanzibar.

That Arabs should have become nationalistic at a
time when there were no other nationalists in Zanzibar
seems, at the very least, puzzling. British colonialism
had in no essential way impaired the privileged political
and social status of the Arab community, and under a
system of racial representation in the legislative Council, the Arab Association would have enjoyed a greatly
disproportionate influence on government policy for a
considerable period of time. Further, Arab leaders were
fully aware that if Zanzibar should become a democratically self-governing state, the overwhelming African
majority (comprising approximately 80 per cent of the
population) could effectively swamp the Arab minority. No single factor is sufficient to explain the early ma-
turity of nationalism among the Arab minority. The motivation of the early nationalists was a complex blending
of simple patriotism, a rather naïve, religiously inspired
idealism, and a Machiavellian sense of enlightened self-
interest. All of these forces stimulated among a small
number of Arab intellectuals a determined impulse to
end colonial rule and to establish Zanzibar as a sovereign and independent state.

Arab anti-colonialism in Zanzibar undoubtedly had
certain historic as well as contemporary origins. When
Zanzibar was made a Protectorate at the end of the nineteenth century, the agreement was signed with an Arab
Sultan at the head of an Arab government. Zanzibar was

far more an Arab than an African state and the British practice of giving Arabs the highest constitutional and legislative priority only reinforced their belief that Zanzibar was an Arab country. For this reason, the sense of political loss engendered by the British intrusion was felt especially heavily by the descendants of the early Arab immigrants. An important part of their nationalistic ideology was the belief that the British Protectorate had subordinated a once sovereign and independent Arab nation under an Arab Sultan.

Islamic religious beliefs were also an important stimulant to the early Arab nationalists. In broad terms, the Koran postulates an essential and inevitable conflict between Muslim and non-Muslim (particularly Christian) communities, and it enjoins all faithful Muslims to wage an eternal struggle—*Jihad*—against non-believers.[2] The nationalistic implications of this creed against the political background of a British colonial state are obvious. Nationalism was endowed with an almost holy status as a sacred obligation, and became nothing less than a religious crusade against alien infidels.

Ibadhi Islam, the religious persuasion of the Omani Arabs, is notable for its heavy admixture of egalitarian and democratic tenets. The Omani Arabs believed, for example, that "the judgment of God could be expressed only through the free choice of the whole community."[3] Autocratic colonial rule was an obvious negation of this belief, and as such came to be viewed by many Omani Arabs as a profane obstacle to the realization of the will of their Creator.

The political implication of Islam's avowedly multiracial theology was also relevant to the intellectual formation of a nationalist mentality. Islam's religious

[2] H. A. R. Gibb, *Mohammedanism: An Historical Survey* (New York: Mentor Books, 1955), pp. 57-58.

[3] Alfred Guillaume, *Islam* (Edinburgh: Penguin Books, 1956), p. 113.

injunction that "all Muslims are brothers" has long had its political reflection in the belief that Zanzibaris must sublimate racial differences in a greater sense of Zanzibari citizenship and nationhood. Under the influence of this belief, some of the high ranking members of the Arab Association came to hold a profound conviction that their leadership could unite all the people of Zanzibar in a common struggle against colonialism.

Of all the motivations for nationalism, one stands out with particular clarity—the almost ominously uncertain political fate of an alien aristocracy within a gradually democratizing constitutional framework. The essence of the dilemma facing all Arab leaders was that, by the early 1950's, Great Britain was already clearly committed to a policy of introducing democratic political institutions and eventual independence in those colonies where there was no substantial resident white population. This meant that the elite status of their community could only be preserved either through an indefinite postponement of independence or through the creation of a policy which was other than egalitarian. The more forward-looking leaders of the Arab Association could not possibly have avoided the conclusion that if an immigrant aristocracy was to survive as such within a framework of parliamentary democracy, it would have to win the support and acceptance of a substantial portion of the African majority. This realization would suggest as a political strategy that it was necessary to wrest political power from the British before the growing African nationalism on the continent should spread to Zanzibar.

The emergence and growth of Arab nationalism in Zanzibar may be divided into three phases. *The proto-nationalist phase* consisted of a brief excursion into anti-colonial protest, and occurred between 1949 and 1953. Not yet wholly nationalistic, Arabs began at that time to formulate their ideology and to develop extra-constitutional agitational techniques. *The associational phase,* occurring between 1954 and early 1956, was the beginning of full nationalism. Arab nationalists fought to win over the Arab Association, and having done so, used it for a short time as the vehicle of their anti-colonial protest. *The multi-racial phase* began in 1956 and lasted until the African revolution. Having recognized the limitations of an associational-communal approach, Arabs assumed the leadership of a multi-racial nationalist movement, the *Zanzibar Nationalist Party* (ZNP), and employed it as the vehicle by which they sought to seize power from the British.

This sequence of phases represented a development of Arab nationalism along two separate dimensions of political behavior—organization and ideology. In organizational terms, Arab nationalism progressed from a tiny, exclusive caucus of forward-looking intellectuals to an extensive, purposeful political party with a highly elaborate structure and a broad membership base. In ideological terms, this progression involved a development from a limited, highly specific and issue-oriented attack on colonial policy to a universalistic assault on the concept and practice of colonial government.

The first post-war British proposals for constitutional advance have an extremely important place in the development of Zanzibar nationalism as an Arab creation. In line with the long established policy of working toward the ultimate democratization of the Legislative Council, the local authorities proposed in late 1948 that popular election replace governmental nomination as the method of electing Arab and Asian unofficial members.[4] The election was scheduled to be conducted on a communal basis; each community would elect only its

---

[4] Zanzibar Protectorate, *Debates of the Legislative Council, 23rd Session, 1948-1949* (Zanzibar: Government Printer, 1950), p. 6.

own representatives. In order that the Asian voters' list be as representative as possible, the government intended to make eligible for the franchise all resident aliens whose status was "British Protected Persons," as well as Zanzibar nationals. Inasmuch as the existing Zanzibar citizenship law made no provision for dual nationality, the vast majority of Zanzibar's Asian community was in the former category.[5] For Asians were reluctant to become naturalized Zanzibaris if this meant severing all their legal ties to India, Pakistan, and Great Britain.

Arab leaders objected strongly to including British Protected Persons on the voters' rolls. They wanted the franchise restricted to Zanzibar nationals in order to ensure that only persons permanently resident in the Protectorate would be able to participate. Arab Association representatives and governmental officials conducted confidential negotiations over this question for more than three years (1949-1951). Colonial authorities were unable to agree to the Arab demand for a restricted franchise since it would exclude from eligibility all but a minute fraction of the Asian community. The Arab negotiators were equally adamant in their refusal to cooperate with any election conducted on the basis of dual nationalities.

The relevance of these negotiations to the gradual formulation of a nationalistic ethic by Arab intellectuals is considerable. After a time the subject matter of the discussions developed into a broad concern with the political importance of Zanzibar nationality and with the real meaning of Zanzibar's constitutional status as a Protectorate. The logic of this wide frame of reference compelled Arab spokesmen to frame their arguments

[5] Zanzibar Protectorate, "The Nationality and Nationalization Decree," *Laws of Zanzibar, 1934*, Vol. III: *Decrees* (Chapters 83-135) (Zanzibar: Government Printer, n.d.), pp. 1700-1701.

for a restricted franchise in the broadest possible terms. Arab theoreticians slowly expanded the simple notion that aliens were potentially disloyal into a more universal and persuasive political theory of the state. For the first time, Arab leaders began to articulate the view that Zanzibar possessed a separate and constitutionally autonomous national identity, and that within this national community, as within any other, national allegiance must assume an importance greater than any other loyalty. In this way, Arab arguments for the restricted franchise developed into a patriotic defense of the Sultanate.

The principal leader of the Arab opposition to the proposal was the Vice-President of the Arab Association, Seif Hamoud. Born in Oman, Hamoud had emigrated to Zanzibar at the age of nineteen, and had become a Zanzibar national through naturalization. Though a member of the Royal Family and a respected figure in Arab circles, his views were more extreme than those of most of his colleagues in the Executive Committee. The major difference of opinion between them concerned political strategy.

Hamoud wanted to make a public issue of the franchise dispute and to mobilize popular opinion against the government. Most committee members were unwilling to go this far and would not allow the Arab Association's newspaper, *Al Falaq* (The Dawn), to editorialize about their quarrel with the administration. Hamoud founded his own newspaper, *Al Nahadha,* in early 1951 and began to publish articles condemning the government's position. His objective, to shame the Association into taking a public stand on the franchise issue, succeeded within a few months, and the Arab Association was forced to declare itself publicly as irrevocably opposed to extending voting or candidacy rights to alien residents. This statement transformed the once private disagreement between the Arab leaders and British officials into a major public controversy.

Once Hamoud had consolidated Arab Association opinion behind his position, he initiated an editorial policy of attacking the government in the strongest possible terms. He was several times arrested and fined for his columns. It was symbolic and indicative of subsequent developments that the first Zanzibari to suffer for public expression of anti-colonial sentiments was an Arab of alien birth and a member of the Sultan's family. Hamoud's editorials in *Al Nahadha* stressed two recurrent themes: first, that Zanzibar's status as a British Protectorate had not given Great Britain any constitutional or political right to confer fundamental civil privileges on alien residents. In Hamoud's own words: "It will be read by every generation that the British, Zanzibar's protector, has (sic) bestowed Zanzibar rights to other people having nothing to do with the ruling of this Sultanate. . . . Sir, this Sultanate is not a Crown Colony, nor is it a territory whose lands can be given away at one's will to anybody one likes. This Sultanate is only given to His Majesty's Government on trust; and out of her own will she kept herself under His Majesty's protection. Thus, your freedom of action in giving away our rights is not in keeping with the national laws."[6]

Hamoud's other favorite theme was a virulent racial attack on the Asian community, which he openly despised as a "political Trojan horse." In his view, enfranchisement of the Asian community would be equivalent to the "establishment of an alien force inside our legislature, a force which because of its nature and the location of its sympathy and allegiance, can paralyze progress and engender unrest."[7] The essence of his position was that only those Asians who had been natural-

[6] *Al Nahadha,* March 8, 1951.
[7] *Ibid.,* April 26, 1951.

ized, and who had therefore identified themselves permanently with the political and economic destinies of Zanzibar, had earned the privilege of political participation.

Hamoud and his sympathizers urged the Arab community to employ every tactic at its disposal to prevent suffrage for non-Zanzibaris. Among those specifically listed in *Al Nahadha* were: "We should not accept the system of Government. . . . We should proclaim that we are not responsible or bound to execute any form of constitution in this Sultanate. . . . We shall wash our hands from all Government committees and boards."[8] The agitational technique of total non-cooperation was not employed during this dispute, but it later became a primary weapon of Zanzibar nationalism.

The Arab Association's cause was greatly strengthened in late May (1951) by the decision of the Shirazi Association to support the demand for a limited franchise. This completely altered the Arabs' moral position vis-à-vis the colonial authorities and made it unnecessary for them to employ tactics of civil disobedience. With Shirazi support, Arabs were no longer a minority interest group but the spearhead of a united patriotic movement composed of both indigenous Africans and Arab immigrants. This clothed the Arab Association's position with unassailable political and moral virtue, and in September the government decided to abandon its election proposal and to look for a compromise agreeable to all communities.

The Arab Association's agitation over the franchise question was in many ways reminiscent of fully developed nationalism. In its patriotic fervor, its militantly critical attitudes towards colonial rule, and in the willingness to employ tactics of civil disobedience it exhibited several of the features of nationalism most visible everywhere in Colonial Africa. One crucial difference,

[8] *Ibid.,* May 10, 1951.

however, distinguished the franchise agitation from mature nationalism, namely a willingness to compromise on a goal short of independence. The entire franchise controversy was fomented by discontent over that one issue. Once the government had removed its election proposal, dissatisfaction subsided. By accepting a solution offered to it within the overall framework of colonial rule, the Arab Association stopped short of being a wholly nationalistic political movement.

The francise controversy had two lasting consequences. It gave rise to certain basic ideological principles of nationalism: the idea of the constitutional autonomy of the Sultanate as a national state, and the notion that it was the patriotic duty of all loyal Zanzibaris to defend their country by extra-constitutional means if necessary. Second, it led to a fundamental division within the Arab Association between those to whom these ideas were critically important, and those to whom they were not. Until mid-1953 the former group had only one effective member on the Executive (Seif Hamoud), and was not in a position to challenge the basic Association policy of close cooperation with the colonial authorities.

This weakness of the militant group first exposed itself when the Arab Association Executive and the British authorities compromised on the franchise dispute. The basis of the compromise was a new law allowing dual nationality,[9] thus enabling members of the resident Asian community to become naturalized Zanzibaris without completely forfeiting their previous nationality status. Although this arrangement clearly implied that in any future election the franchise would be limited to Zanzibar nationals, it was not acceptable to Hamoud.

[9] Zanzibar Protectorate, "A Decree to Make Provision for Zanzibar Nationality and for Purposes Connected Therewith," *The Laws of Zanzibar Revised* (Zanzibar: Government Printer, 1962), Chapter 39.

He argued that dual nationality was inconsistent with a sense of paramount national loyalty to Zanzibar, and insisted that the Executive Committee hold out for a single nationality system. In the absence of a critical public issue, Hamoud was unable to arouse any widespread popular support and could not prevent the law being passed in late December of 1952.

During late 1952 and 1953, the British authorities sought the cooperation of the Arab Association in a joint effort to achieve a new plan of constitutional advance which would meet with wide Arab approval. In order to placate the militant elements and avoid another constitutional crisis, some moderate members of the Executive Committee agreed to work closely with the British Resident, Sir John Rankine. Partly because Hamoud and the militant group had not yet begun to express a systematically nationalistic philosophy but were still seeking specific issues on which to agitate, and partly because the moderates failed anyway to understand their true intentions, there was a lack of communication between the two wings of the Executive Committee. Moderate members tended to view Hamoud's opposition to the dual nationality law as simply an extension of his old franchise agitation, and they wrongly interpreted his constitutional position as nothing more than a refusal to agree to an election unless there were a single nationality only. Both the moderates and the British Government failed to realize that the constitutional corollary of Hamoud's highly patriotic ethos was some form of national non-communal representation.

This failure may help to explain why Rankine's constitutional plan, submitted to the various associations in early 1954, recommended as its most central doctrine an indefinite continuation of appointed communal representation in the Legislative Council.[10] No constitu-

10 For an extended official discussion of the substance of the

tional recommendation possibly devised could have been less acceptable to nationalistically-inclined Arabs. For Hamoud and several other nationalists believed fervently that the ultimate position of the Arab in Zanzibar depended upon his ability to foster cordial political relations with the African community. A year earlier Hamoud had called for a multi-racial organization based on nationality: "A United Political Body (sic) has become an urgent need. . . . All Zanzibar subjects can join in such a United Political Body . . . it is obvious that only through such a United Body can common questions affecting the welfare of all the people and races residing in this Sultanate be effectively advanced. We therefore appeal to the leaders to rise to the occasion and work as Zanzibaris for the good of Zanzibar, and strive for all round progress leading to the attainment of the now cherished aim of self-government within the Commonwealth."[11]

Racial representation would at best have offered Arabs only temporary security by offering them a guaranteed place in the Councils of Government. In the long run it would have been disastrous, for it would have fostered a pattern of political loyalties based exclusively on racial identity. Total rejection of the Rankine Constitution was the only course of action consistent with the nationalists' intention of commanding the political allegiance of large numbers of Africans. From this point on, the brunt of the Arab nationalists' attack on British institutions in Zanzibar was directed against the practice of communal representation.

Not only did communal representation appear to the

Rankine proposals, see Zanzibar, *Papers Laid Before the Legislative Council, 1955*, Sessional Paper No. 9, "Constitutional Development, Zanzibar: Exchange of Despatches between the British Resident, Zanzibar and the Secretary of State for the Colonies" (Zanzibar: Government Printer, 1956), pp. 75-80.

[11] *Al Nahadha,* March 26, 1953.

nationalists to stand in the way of their working for African support, but sweeping democratic reforms suggested by Rankine in all other constitutional areas dramatized the urgent need for such action. Until this time, for example, it had been standard constitutional practice in Zanzibar to award numerically graded representation to the various racial communities. Under that system, Arabs received the largest number of seats, Asians the second largest and Africans the smallest. Under the new arrangements, Africans were for the first time to be given equal representation.[12] This made it very clear that the British Government intended to move rapidly towards a more fully representative Legislative Council with radically greater representation for the African population. Other suggested measures, such as the implementation of a constitutional form of monarchy, also held ominous meaning for Zanzibar's future. Arab nationalists knew that any further continuation of this type of constitutional policy would end Arab political hegemony and transform Zanzibar into an African state. The only possible solution for Arabs—short of complete abdication of their political preeminence—was to capture the leadership of a democratically self-governing country.

Their immediate problem was to win over the Executive Committee of the Association, and to persuade a majority of its members to refuse the constitution. At this time, however, Arab nationalism was still a highly elite phenomenon confined to a few prominent mem-

[12] The controversial passage in the Rankine plan was the following: "The Legislative Council should consist of the British Resident as President, four ex-officio members (being the four ex-officio members of the Executive Council) and nine official members and twelve unofficial members nominated by the Sultan on the advice of the British Resident. The present unofficial membership is eight only. *It is the intention that the twelve unofficial members should be four Arabs, four Africans and three Indians and probably one European*" (italics mine). *Zanzibar Voice,* October 9, 1955.

bers of the Association. The Executive Committee was deeply divided between the nationalist elements and those who were inclined to continue the more or less cordial relationship that existed between the Arab Association and the administration, but it was firmly in the control of the moderates. After July, 1953, nationalists had begun to assume an increasing number of positions on the Executive Committee, but when the proposed constitution came to a vote in March, 1954, they were still unable to muster a majority of members to oppose it, although by a very slight margin.

Two nationalists of special importance, Ali Muhsin and Ahmed Lemke, had become members of the Arab Association Executive Committee in the months just before the vote on the Rankine Constitution. The former, an independently wealthy journalist and former government agricultural officer, was principal editor of a tri-lingual (English-Swahili-Arabic) newspaper, *Mwongozi* (The Leader). During the franchise dispute he had actively supported Hamoud's views, and later he became perhaps the most famous of all Zanzibar nationalists as leader of the *Zanzibar Nationalist Party* (ZNP).

At this time, however, Lemke was by far the more colorful and influential figure. Born in Zanzibar in 1929 of an extremely wealthy Arab family, he had gone to Egypt for education at the age of ten and resided there continuously between 1939 and 1951. During the Arab-Israeli war he joined a communist movement opposed to King Farouk, and became deeply involved in its organization and propaganda activities. For this and other political offenses, he spent his last two years in Egypt in prison.

Lemke's direct personal contribution to the growth of Zanzibar nationalism is considerable and merits some comment. After being released from prison in Egypt he went to England, where he organized Zanzibar workers and students into a politically oriented multi-racial club called the Zanzibari Association. The principal purpose of the Zanzibari Association was to protest Great Britain's reliance upon racial institutions and racial organizations in its administration of Zanzibar. Lemke blamed England for having fostered a society in which the citizens were divided against one another along racial lines, and he hoped that the members of the Association would return to Zanzibar to work for the elimination of racial practices. Lemke's tendency to equate communal differentiation and the presence of British rule gave the Zanzibari Association its nationalistic overtones. In a letter to *Al Nahadha,* Lemke wrote of the Zanzibari Association and its multi-racial ideology as a necessary precursor of any political progress in the Protectorate: "We have realized the urgent need for unity and cooperation among all sections and elements of the Zanzibaris, and we intend to eradicate communal discrimination in our country, a disease that has stood as a stumbling bloc in the way of progress. . . . We are Zanzibaris in and out and detest any method used to inculcate racial discrimination, and widen the gulf between different sections of our people."[13] The Zanzibari Association included several men who later became prominent in the movement for independence. One, Jamal Ramadhan (a seaman and journalist), became a major impetus to the formation of an African nationalist party in Zanzibar.

Lemke's political ideas were a great influence on Hamoud, and in fact precipitated Hamoud's own cry for a "United Political Body." Lemke returned to Zanzibar in early 1953 and in April began to form a more overtly anti-colonial multi-racial organization, the *Zanzibar National Union* (ZNU). In its ideological emphasis on the concept of "Zanzibari" as a basis of loyalty transcending racial allegiances, and in the effort to employ this con-

[13] *Al Nahadha,* November 6, 1952.

cept to attract the political support of all racial communities, the ZNU was the prototype of the ZNP. Later
Arab nationalists added to the concept of "Zanzibar" the
notion that the Muslim faith was also a bond of identity
which transcended racial divisions, but the initial quest
for a trans-racial bond of solidarity and the first attempt
to test the idea of multi-racial political unity were
Lemke's. The ZNU floundered because it was unable to
maintain its African support. The best educated and
most politically conscious Africans at this time were civil
servants, and when the British Government circulated a
regulation forbidding their participation in politics, they
were forced to withdraw.[14]

This was a death-blow to the ZNU. Without African
support it could not hope to become a genuinely multi-
racial body, nor could it legitimately claim to speak for
all races within the Protectorate. For this reason and because of his own failing health, Lemke dissolved the
ZNU in late summer of 1953. His imprisonment in Egypt
had left him with a damaged heart and a severe nervous
condition, which prevented him from playing an important role in later nationalist organizations. He was,
however, the central figure in the nationalists' effort to
make the Arab Association adopt a nationalistic position. And, as the new editor of *Al Falaq*, Lemke continued to be a force in the anti-colonial movement.

Lemke and Muhsin were bitterly disappointed in the
Arab Association's acceptance of Rankine's plan. Failing
to alter the Committee's accommodationist position by
capturing a majority of the membership, they used another method to bring about concerted Arab opposition
to communal representation. With Lemke as editor of
Al Falaq, the most easily executed and immediately

[14] The African community's relationship to the ZNU and the effect
of this circular on the development of a nationalistic political awareness within the African community are fully discussed in the following chapter.

operative tactic was to mount a scathing editorial campaign against colonial rule. Since even the most moderate members would not publicly disassociate themselves from *Al Falaq*'s call for national freedom and non-racial institutions, they would be compelled to change their position on the constitutional question. A similar technique had been employed by Seif Hamoud when he wanted to force a recalcitrant Arab Association Executive to support his views on the franchise issue, and the history of the franchise agitation was well known to the nationalists.

This explains the suddenness and the militancy with which Arab nationalism emerged in the spring of 1954. Almost immediately after the acceptance of the constitution, Lemke began to publish a series of nationalistic articles condemning colonialism as oppressive and unjust. While his articles contained no specific reference to Zanzibar, their revolutionary meaning was clear and precise:

Wisdom of the Week:

> Oh my brother
> The Oppressors have exceeded the bounds
> It is right that we should wage *Jihad*
> It is right that we should redeem ourselves.[15]

The nationalists' strategy of embarrassing their moderate colleagues into opposing racial representation explains the apparently ambivalent character of the Arab Association's constitutional position during April and May. At the same time that the Association was formally committed to accept the Rankine Constitution, its official newspaper (*Al Falaq*) was calling for immediate constitutional reforms including common roll elections, universal suffrage, and the introduction of a ministerial

[15] *Al Falaq*, March 10, 1954.

system. This ambivalence was the public reflection of a fundamental disagreement within the Executive Committee over the merit of Arab-inspired nationalism.[16] An influential group of moderates were resisting the pressure to adopt a nationalistic position, not so much because they did not subscribe to a nationalistic ethic as because they questioned the wisdom of an Arab-led nationalist movement. They believed that Zanzibar Arabs ought to be prepared to abdicate their position of political preeminence as a means of averting political and racial antagonism.

The British Government's response to the nationalistic policies of *Al Falaq* probably had a great deal to do with healing this split in the Arab Executive and with unifying the entire leadership in favor of a policy of nationalism. For in June the administration arrested the entire Executive except for one member who had pre-

[16] This ambivalence encouraged the British colonial authorities to continue to pursue the Rankine plan in closed discussions with Arab Association leaders. There was a strong feeling on the part of the colonial administration in Zanzibar that so sudden a shift could not possibly reflect the opinion of the majority of Arabs or, for that matter, of Africans either. In a letter to the Secretary of State for the Colonies, the British Resident who succeeded Rankine and who was pursuing the negotiations over the Rankine Constitution wrote: "In March, 1954, Sir John Rankine had secured the agreement of all the unofficial members of the Legislative Council, representing all races of the Protectorate, to each of the measures now envisaged, and was hoping that the changes would be brought about before the end of the year. A few months later, however, the Arab Association of Zanzibar and two unofficial members of the Legislative Council who were members of the Association, decided to repudiate the agreement which had been reached. . . . The Africans, the Asians and the many, probably the majority, of the Arabs would have been happy to see the 1954 proposals put into effect before now, and I feel no longer justified in depriving the people of the Protectorate of the benefits of constitutional advances at the instance of a community or rather certain spokesmen of the community, who will agree to no advances except a rash leap to a position which may well be reached within no great span of years by a rational and orderly progression." Sessional Paper No. 9 of 1955, p. 77.

viously apologized to the British Resident. All those arrested were charged with sedition. Moderates and nationalists alike were held legally to blame for Lemke's
articles, tried, found guilty and heavily fined.[17] Not only
did this thoughtless action make the colonial regime an
object of intense enmity, but by assigning collective responsibility, the government forced the moderate committee members to stand publicly behind their nationalist colleagues.

The actions of the British administration during this
crucial period in 1953-1954 had a decisive impact on the
nature of emergent Zanzibar nationalism. Colonial officials not only prevented Arab-African collaboration by
barring the only Africans ready for political leadership
from all political activity, but also alienated the Arab
moderates by arresting and trying them in the company
of extremists. The primary objective of British policy
was to maintain strict control over emergent anti-
colonialism. The Mau Mau rebellion in Kenya, then at
its height, lent a special sense of urgency to the Zanzibar
officials' desire to ensure complete political stability and
may help account for the gratuitously repressive nature
of the administration's policy. In addition, some British
officials probably saw a possibility of forcing the Arab
Association to resume its traditional policy of close cooperation with the colonial government, both through
strong legal pressure and by isolating Arab intellectuals
from the African elite. In either case, colonial policy at
this time in effect drove a wedge between the Arab and
African communities and united the Arab political
leaders in favor of a militantly nationalistic position.

So united had the Association become during the
month of the trial that there was virtually complete
unanimity on a decision to repudiate the Rankine Consti-

[17] Zanzibar Protectorate, *The Crown, Prosecutor, versus Abdulla
Suleiman el Harthi et al.,* Criminal Case #1805 (1954).

tution and to adopt *Al Falaq's* constitutional program. As a means of dramatizing the militancy of their new constitutional demands, the Association also decided to institute a complete boycott of the Legislative Council and all other government bodies. Since it had been British practice to give Arabs key positions on its many statutory boards and commissions, the boycott depended upon the cooperation of a fairly large number of people. Perhaps the most dramatic evidence of the new-found solidarity of the Arab Association was the unanimous withdrawal of all these Arabs from their government positions. Furthermore, this unbroken solidarity enabled the boycott to be carried on with complete effectiveness for more than a year and a half.

Only one important Arab, Sultan Mugheiry (a retired police inspector), opposed his Association's policies. A member of the Executive Committee and one of the Arab Association's three nominated representatives in the Legislative Council, Mugheiry had publicly disavowed the *Al Falaq* editorials, and was the only member of the Executive Committee not tried for sedition. Mugheiry was the principal opponent of Arab participation in mass politics. When the boycott was declared he ceased to attend Legislative Council meetings, but unlike the other two Arab-nominated members, he refused to resign his seat. Widely vilified as a coward and a traitor, Mugheiry expressed his private views on the boycott in a personal letter to a close friend: "I do realize that some unthinking people and those who are bent to disrupt the harmony that the Protectorate enjoys would do a lot to cover their weakness, stupidity and evil intentions by focusing attention on me. But I know that I am right and from that thought I derive great strength. Let them say what they say."[18]

[18] Private letter of Sultan Mugheiry to H. M. Pelham Murphy, dated June 16, 1954.

In a desperate effort to break the boycott, Mugheiry began attending Legislative Council meetings in late November, 1955. His fate was grizzly evidence of the highly charged emotional atmosphere, for less than a week after he had appeared in the Legco he was brutally assassinated by a demented Arab fanatic.[19] At the very least, the significance of Mugheiry's murder was that it silenced the only remaining voice appealing to Arabs to remain outside politics. The tragic irony of his death was that at the end of 1955 the British Government had un-officially decided to suspend its proposals for racial representation, and to consider holding at least a modified common roll election.

The preeminence of the Arab Association at the earliest stage of Zanzibar nationalism and of Arab leadership throughout its development has led to a widespread misconception as to the origin of one of Zanzibar's major political parties, the *Zanzibar Nationalist Party* (ZNP). The most common misunderstanding of the ZNP has been to regard that party as the political projection of the Arab Association. The ZNP was not founded by the Arab Association, nor was it initially created by individual nationalistically-minded members acting independently. In that sense, while Zanzibar nationalism was the creation of Zanzibar's Arab minority, the Zanzibar Nationalist Party was not.

In mid-1955, at the height of the Arab Association boycott, a small group of peasants in the village of Kiembe Samaki (Fish Corner) formed a political party which they called *Hizbu l'Watan l'Riaia Sultan Zanzibar* . . . the *National Party of the Subjects of the Sultan of Zanzibar* (NPSS). Their party possessed a multi-racial ideology with an appeal for an end to communal repre-

---

[19] Zanzibar Protectorate, *The Crown, Prosecutor, versus Mohammed Hamoud*, Criminal Case #3585 (1955).

sentation in the Legislative Council and a demand for independence. During the first few months of its existence, the NPSS remained a tiny collection of semiliterate rustics, remote from the mainstream of Zanzibar political life, and altogether lacking in that articulate political leadership which would give public expression to its views. For this reason, very few people—either at that time or subsequently—heard of its existence. It was nonetheless the first nationalist political party in the Protectorate.

Certain very special features distinguish the NPSS from any number of other early nationalist parties in Africa. First, it was a party of the countryside and not of the city. Not only did its organizers and first elected officers reside in the plantation areas outside Zanzibar Town, but they were by occupation farmers and cattle herders rather than members of those elite professional groups (lawyers, teachers, trade-unionists, or government servants) customarily associated with the earliest stirrings of nationalism. Second, the NPSS did not spring from any already established social, economic, cultural or other potentially proto-nationalist organization. No trade union, social club, or communal group gave its originators previous experience in political action. The NPSS was wholly and completely the original creation of its founder members.

Since 1940, the Zanzibar Government had undertaken an extensive process of land acquisition for the construction of the Zanzibar airport. As the airport was gradually enlarged, more and more of the villagers' land had to be taken over. The policy of the government was to alienate as little land as possible at any given time in order to minimize dislocation of the villagers. The consequent piecemeal nature of the land alienation process led to bitter resentment of the government. The land crisis came to a head between 1949 and 1951 when the government sought to take over a parcel of land on which the village mosque was located. This property is permanently inalienable, in the eyes of Muslims, and the government's desire to acquire it added a feeling of religious persecution to already existing antipathies.

Just at this time, an anthrax epidemic broke out in the vicinity of Kiembe Samaki and the villagers refused to cooperate with the government in a cattle inoculation program. For their refusal, nineteen of the villagers were arrested and put on trial for a criminal offense. By 1951 Kiembe Samaki had already come to be widely known as a center of opposition to the government, and people of many other villages sympathized with the arrested herdsmen. The trial was marked by a major outburst of anti-governmental violence. During the morning of the trial (July 30, 1951), a crowd eventually numbering over five hundred persons gathered outside the courthouse, and grew increasingly restive as the trial went on. Word that the villagers had been found guilty and sentenced to imprisonment provoked an instantaneous reaction. Cries of *"Jihad"* rang out and transformed an angry crowd into a riotous mob.

Religiously-inflamed men armed with sticks and stones engaged in fierce hand-to-hand combat with police in an effort to prevent the convicted farmers from being taken to prison. The battle began at about one o'clock in the afternoon and went on until early evening. Several of the prisoners were, in fact, freed but they delivered themselves to the prison the following morning after order had been restored. For several days afterwards there were persistent rumors that the trade unions of the Protectorate were about to organize a general strike in sympathy with the imprisoned farmers. These rumors and the general atmosphere of unrest led government observers to conclude that the riots had been instigated by professional agitators, and the British administration feared that the cattle disturbances were to be used as a springboard for a more determined and systematic resistance to colonial authority.[20]

The July riots did have a certain close resemblance to a pattern of political violence often characteristic of incipient nationalism. The greatest similarity lay in their symptomatic character as an expression of widespread popular disaffection from colonial rule. In their religious inspiration also, and particularly in the passionate and volatile compulsion which drove the rioters to seek to fulfill the political obligation of the Islamic concept of *Jihad,* there was a close similarity to the motivation of later Arab nationalists.

The differences between the cattle riots and the many extra-parliamentary forms of protest employed by nationalists are perhaps more important and fundamental than the similarities. The riot was a purely momentary phenomenon, not part of a sustained assertive effort to achieve broad political and constitutional objectives. The grievance being given expression was a sense of injustice at the imprisonment of the herdsmen, and the mood of the crowd was one of resolved determination to prevent it, but the demonstrators offered no visible protest at the presence in Zanzibar of an alien colonial regime. For this reason it would be erroneous to assume that the desire to free Zanzibar of colonial authority and to establish an independent Zanzibar nation originated anywhere but in the Arab Association.

Only in Kiembe Samaki had there been fostered an abiding antipathy towards colonial rule, but even so the NPSS was not formed there until approximately four years later. In the light of the history of the previous

---

[20] For a full discussion of this riot and of the background events which led to it, see Zanzibar Protectorate, *Report on the Civil Disturbances in Zanzibar on July 30, 1951* (Zanzibar: Government Printer, 1952).

fourteen years, it is not surprising that the NPSS began where it did or that one of its founder-members was among the nineteen arrested herdsmen. The three principal founders considered themselves communally as "Swahili," a category of ethnic identification which had all but disappeared a generation earlier. This may have been a more important reason for their forming the party than was their residence in Kiembe Samaki, since communal loyalties and institutions held an extremely important place in Zanzibar life. The disappearance of the Swahili tribe had left those few individuals who preferred to remain Swahili in identity without any community to which to belong: Swahilis had become, in a sense, Zanzibar's detribalized Africans. More than any other group, they were alert and sensitized to new loyalties and patterns of identification. It is quite likely that the Arab Association's concept of "Zanzibari," and the corollary notion of a national community with the Sultan as paramount chief, were a functional re-creation of tribal membership and provided the Swahilis with a psychologically acceptable substitute for ethnic association. In this sense, the ideology of the Arab Association stimulated the formation of the NPSS.

The exact relationship between the founders of the NPSS and the Arab Association is obscure. They knew of the Association's boycott and of the political demands behind it. By December, 1955, they were in informal contact with Sheik Ali Muhsin, who had emerged as the foremost spokesman of the common roll policy and the principal leader of Arab nationalism. The unfamiliarity of the NPSS leaders with the exact meaning of the term "common roll" or "universal suffrage," their opposition to the more elaborate proposals for communal representation put forward by Rankine, and their informal contact with Muhsin all suggest that their constitutional demands were inspired by those of the Arab Association.

During January, 1956, the NPSS attracted public attention by voicing the Arab Association's constitutional views before a Constitutional Commissioner, Sir Walter Coutts, sent by Great Britain to inquire into the demand for a common roll election. Coutts found the NPSS members uninformed of the complex and technical constitutional questions involved: "The day before I left Zanzibar . . . I was asked to meet a group of people called "the Nationalist Party of His Highness' Subjects [an incorrect translation of the Arabic name of the party]. The main request was for universal adult franchise on a common roll . . . the majority of the people did not understand the real issues and the meeting was run by one Haji Husein. I was left with the impression that the theories were his."[21] Since the Arab Association was boycotting all relations with the government, the NPSS was the only group to express the demand for a common roll election before the Coutts Commission.

Coutts was reluctant to recommend that all unofficial representation be selected on a common roll basis because of the strong objections of the Asian and African communities. He adopted Rankine's suggestion that the unofficial side of the Legislative Council be expanded to twelve seats, but urged that only half of these be filled by racial nomination. The remaining six, he decided, could safely be filled in an experimental common roll election under a limited franchise.[22] This decision placed the Arab Association in an awkward and perplexing situation, for with an election imminent, it was more than ever essential to form a broadly based political party which had the support of Africans. Arab leaders realized, however, that if they openly founded a party them-

---

[21] Zanzibar Protectorate, *Methods of Choosing Unofficial Members of the Legislative Council,* by Sir Walter Coutts (Zanzibar: Government Printer, 1956), p. 25.

[22] *Ibid.,* pp. 4-8.

selves, the Arab Association would be accused of trying to dominate it.

It has been widely suggested that the NPSS was in fact a sort of political front organization surreptitiously formed by the Arab Association during its boycott, to create the appearance that Zanzibar nationalism was the product and intention of the African community. The NPSS beyond question fitted the Arab Association's need for a multi-racial party which Arab leaders could join, and from this point of view the timing of its appearance could not have been more propitious. But there is simply no evidence to suggest that the NPSS was artificially created. Arabs maintained confidential relations with the party before its existence was widely known and were among its first financial supporters, though they sought to keep this secret.[23] Their desire for secrecy, in fact, explains why they did not represent the party before the Coutts Commission, but it does not indicate that they had originated it. The most reasonable and likely hypothesis is that once the NPSS had been started, Arabs almost immediately saw its value and began to support it with funds and political advice.

Shortly after the NPSS had established its authenticity, Arabs began to join openly and soon became its real leaders. Ali Muhsin and Amour Zahor (another nationalistic member of the Arab Association Executive Committee) were its first Arab members; they began the laborious process of winning wide popular support from their own and other communities. They changed its name to the Zanzibar Nationalist Party (ZNP) and transformed it from a rural peasant league into an Arab-dominated urban nationalist movement. The NPSS had in any case been highly vulnerable to such an Arab

[23] One of the major financial supporters of the NPSS during its first few months of existence was Mohammed Hamoud, the assassin of Sultan Mugheiry.

takeover. It was altogether lacking in competent, politically experienced leadership, but of more importance was the fact that it suited the Arab need for a political organization which could legitimately claim African origin.[24]

The ZNP, ever since, has reserved the positions of Party President and Vice-President for its African founder-members, and this practice was widely advertised as evidence of its multi-racial character. It was purely a symbolic gesture, however, and had little to do with the ZNP's national executive. Here, inter-ethnic relations could more accurately be described in terms of the domination of the highly educated, politically sophisticated Arab intellectual over the simple peasant villager. This pattern was a permanent feature of the ZNP throughout its development as a nationalist movement.

The ZNP next proceeded to create a nationwide organization of local branches which would be able to recruit African supporters for the coming election campaign. As the sole nationalist organization in the country, it enjoyed the singular advantage of having no opposition as it appealed for members in rural African villages and settlements. From the very beginning it was able to preempt completely the symbols of nationalism, and at once became exclusively identified with the call of "freedom now." On the international level, as well, the ZNP was able to present itself as the only national-

[24] There is some evidence that Haji Husein, who led the NPSS in its appearance before the Coutts Commission and who held the position of vice-president in the party, did foresee what would happen if the Arabs were allowed to join and was strongly opposed to their membership. In any case, as the acknowledged leader of the Swahili group and certainly the most influential of the party's founders, he represented the greatest obstacle to an Arab takeover. Shortly after Muhsin and Zahor joined the party, Husein was dismissed from his post as vice-president for what party spokesmen referred to as "proud behavior," and thereafter he served as transportation officer in the ZNP.

istic party in Zanzibar and thereby to gain the financial and moral support of various world bodies committed to the cause of African nationalism.

The objective of the ZNP was to infuse Zanzibar society with a radically new political culture, and one conducive to wide popular support for a multi-racial nationalist movement. The key concepts of this culture—patriotism, anti-colonialism and the essential unity of all Zanzibaris—defined a normative frame of reference for legitimately nationalistic political expression. Any specification of the differences between Zanzibar's ethnic communities was considered unpatriotic and disloyal. Indeed, communal differentiation was explicitly identified by official ZNP party dogma as a colonial legacy. The ZNP's official history, for example, opens with the sentence: "For decades the imperialists segregated the Zanzibaris into tribal and traditional groups."[25] The terms of this mystique made any articulation of the glaring economic differences between the various racial groups a basic violation of nationalistic political norms.

Wholesale national acceptance of this ideology was the most critical prerequisite of Arab political survival and the precondition of ZNP electoral success. Unless it could foster a national climate of opinion hostile to open political expression of the economic and social grievances of the African community, it would be unable to prevent the eventual emergence of an assertive united African political movement.

The ZNP benefited considerably in this effort from the ethnic division within the African community between Shirazis and mainland Africans. Many Shirazis did not think of themselves as Africans, nor of Zanzibar as a part of Africa. These Shirazis thought of Zanzibar as a separate national and cultural entity, close to Africa only

[25] Zanzibar Nationalist Party, *Whither Zanzibar? The Growth and Policy of Zanzibar Nationalism* (Cairo: published by the authors, n.d.), p. 7.

in terms of geography. By portraying the Mainlander as an unwanted intruder in a land where Shirazis and Arabs had always lived together in peace, the ZNP was able to employ the Shirazis' sense of separateness as a means of gaining their political support. This appeal was especially effective among the Pemba and Tumbatu Shirazis.

In its drive to recruit members, the ZNP was also aided by the conservative attitude of some mainland African leaders. In their own deputations to the British authorities, the Mainlanders had argued that constitutional progress ought to be delayed until further educational advancement should enable all Africans to compete on equal terms with Arabs in a representative system of government.[26] Arabs in the ZNP publicly vilified this position as the worst sort of racism, an admission of racial inferiority, and appealed to Shirazis to repudiate it by joining their party. Inasmuch as Shirazis regarded themselves as the heirs of a rich cultural legacy, a sense of shame at the constitutional conservatism of their mainland brethren lent a powerful impetus to their joining with Arabs in the ZNP.

Perhaps the most important factor contributing to the ultimate success of the Arab drive towards a seizure of power was the absence of a politically active African elite. Within the ZNP this meant that Arabs would inevitably be the most effective and influential leaders, no matter how many Africans joined the party. Most Africans, however, were suspicious of the ZNP's Arab leadership, and began to look elsewhere for political expression. For this African majority, the absence of their own politically active elite meant that there was simply no prospect of a party endowed with organizational skill comparable to that possessed by the ZNP.

[26] Zanzibar, *Methods of Choosing Unofficial Members of the Legislative Council*, p. 4.

CHAPTER VI

The African Response

Nationalism in Africa has generally been viewed as a progressive, liberalizing, integrative force—an attempt to accelerate political and social change, to end alien colonial rule and to establish representative majoritarian government. This was not the case in Zanzibar. The essential characteristic of Zanzibar nationalism was its failure to unite Zanzibaris and to establish a genuinely democratic political environment. Arab nationalism, despite its liberal multi-racial ethos, was basically a conservative if not altogether reactionary phenomenon. It was an effort to return Zanzibar to a pre-colonial political condition, namely oligarchic rule by a small land-owning minority. While this would have been disguised in the form of a multi-racial party operating through formal parliamentary institutions, the political reality of autocratic rule by a small ethnic elite would, for all practical purposes, have been a return to the condition existing in the nineteenth century before the establishment of the Protectorate.

The nationalism of the African community in Zanzibar also had numerous conservative overtones. It was conducted almost wholly as a reaction to the Arabs' thrust towards a seizure of power. This basic character—a response to a threat—stamped African nationalism as a movement of fear rather than hope, and accounts for the African leaders' initial desire to retain colonial rule as long as possible. African conservatism was an effort to gain time until African organizations were sufficiently powerful to prevent Zanzibar's reconstitution as an independent Arab state. Because of chronic organizational weakness, this conservatism was not abandoned until two or three years before independence.

Origins of Political Conflict

The gestation and early development of African nationalism may, for conceptual purposes, be divided into two separate phases: the first, an *initial exploratory assault,* occurred during 1952 and 1953. African leaders adopted an agressive militant stance during this period; they actively specified and articulated the grievances of their community and sought to mobilize popular support behind a demand for political and social reform. The second phase, an extended *recession into conservatism,* may be dated from roughly 1954 until about 1959 or 1960. The initial African attack crumbled during this period, and African leaders withdrew from their original militant posture into a mildly pro-colonial position. This abrupt and dramatic retreat in the African community was a direct response to changes which were occurring in Arab nationalism. Arab nationalism had emerged into the public eye, moving from cloistered internal group politics towards an open, unconcealed effort to terminate colonial rule. Arab nationalism had become clearly evident only after the formation of the ZNU in 1953 and the heavily publicized *Al Falaq* trial in 1954.

The key hypothesis here is that an operative conflict relationship between Arabs and Africans was not fully established until this emergence occurred. Until then, African leaders perceived their political conflict relations as exclusively with the British colonial regime, and by the same token viewed anti-colonialism as a monopolistically African phenomenon. Their early aggressive, optimistic nationalism was appropriate to this political condition. But the public appearance of Arab nationalism challenged the Africans' monopoly and thereby gave rise among Africans to a very realistic fear that the result of successful nationalism would not be an African state in Zanzibar. This explains why the African anti-colonial movement, with its background of organizational weakness, receded from an open, aggressive nationalism to a defensive, conservative position.

An African nationalist movement of any sort was severely handicapped by the lack of a politically active intellectual elite. Non-African immigrant groups had traditionally monopolized secondary education and most of the elite positions in Zanzibar society. This prevented the growth of an African intellectual class, and as a result, the entire number of university-trained Africans in the Protectorate probably did not total half a dozen. Those few Africans who had managed to acquire higher education usually found it very difficult to participate freely in politics. Nearly all were employed full-time in professional occupations or as government civil servants, and at best could participate in African organizations only in their spare time; for unlike members of the Arab elite, the African intellectuals were not economically independent and could not afford to lose positions which were their sole source of income.[1]

As long as the British did not strictly enforce their policy of forbidding civil servants to participate in political organizations, it was still possible for a small number of African intellectuals to form a nucleus of political leadership. In 1953, however, the British administrators sternly enjoined participation by all civil servants in any but the most innocuous organizations. There is no doubt that this regulation operated with special severity against the African community, since practically the entire African elite came from the civil servant class. The loss of its sole area of leadership recruitment left the African political movement, handicapped by poor organization to begin with, no choice but to retreat be-

[1] The most important Arab nationalists—Hamoud, Lemke, and Muhsin—had well-to-do families and did not need remunerative employment. This comparative economic freedom enabled them to participate much more actively in politics than their African counterparts.

fore the prospering militant nationalism of the Arab community.

For a brief period just before the appearance of Arab nationalism, a small group of African civil servants had been covertly active in politics. Interpreting loosely the government's restrictions against political activity they attempted indirectly to foster an African political awakening. Most of those who were active in this endeavor belonged to a small social club called the *Young African Union* (YAU), founded in 1951. Their membership in the YAU caused it to become an organizational center for politically conscious Africans. The YAU had semi-official status as the youth league of the *African Association,* a far larger and more heterogenous body which was an all-purpose social, welfare and political organization for the mainland African community. Through this relationship a nucleus of YAU members sought to stimulate the African Association to adopt a militant assertive position towards the government. In particular, they wanted its leaders to demand government action to alleviate the hardships of Zanzibar's African population.

The YAU's efforts to stimulate its parent body produced the first bold, dramatic assertion of African discontent. Under the influence of this aggressive intellectual leadership, the African Association embarked upon a systematic enumeration and articulation of African grievances. Its newspaper, *Afrika Kwetu* (Our Africa), became the vital medium in a joint YAU-African Association drive to alert and inform African public opinion. Their objective was to mobilize the urbanized African community and to gain mass African support in their drive to secure a series of reforms.

Together the YAU and African Association leaders carried out a wholesale attack on the existing social and political structure of Zanzibar. Their criticism was not directed against any particular institution, but against the entire pattern of human and race relations in the Protectorate. For analytical and conceptual purposes, the African demand for radical and thoroughgoing reform may be considered under five separate complaints.

1). *The African community found itself politically dominated by alien immigrant races, and the British Government had no clear policy as to whether its constitutional policy included provision for more democratic arrangements.*

"Our interests have for too long been represented by the alien races and the result is . . . the alien races have become the masters and the real natives of the islands and we the Africans in these islands have become the alien races denied of all justice and all the rights that a native should have."[2]

"The Zanzibar Government has no definite policy and it is overdue that the Zanzibar Government should at least state their broad line of policy. There is no clear and uncompromising declaration of the aims to which the Zanzibar Government is committed with regard to its plural societies. It appears that the authorities concerned have been purposely evading this problem."[3]

2). *The Africans were being seriously underrepresented not only in the Legislative Council, but in all other statutory boards and government committees. The Africans' inability to give legitimate political expression to their grievances bred added resentment of the more privileged races.*

"We want more representation in the Legislative Council. We want more representation in all boards existing in Zanzibar. We want more facilities in all walks of life. . . . Let us hope that the prevailing anti-African policy will be changed by the administrators concerned. . . . It is no use preaching the doctrine of 'Plural Socie-

[2] *Afrika Kwetu,* September 25, 1952.
[3] *Ibid.,* August 21, 1952.

ties Living Together in Harmony' when everything done at the back door encourages racial prejudice and racial antagonism."[4]

3). *Educational discrimination against African children was a major factor in the African community's inability to move ahead economically and socially.*

"The educational system in Zanzibar has always been such as not to give the same facilities for higher education to Africans as given to Asians. What facilities are there for the African for Secondary School? Theoretically the facilities are there, but we are no longer interested in theories. . . . Let (those interested) see for themselves if the number of Africans in the Secondary School is comparable to the number of Asians who are statistically in the minority in Zanzibar."[5]

4). *The cumulative result of alien political domination and government neglect was that Africans lived in miserable conditions of poverty and ignorance.*

"We Africans still live in poverty and squalor; our minds are warped by hatred and suspicion as to the aims and policy of the Zanzibar Government. It is no good blaming us for we are an ignorant, backward uneducated lot; . . . the alien races have and are making us politically hopeless by denying us equal facilities."[6]

5). *The government's policy of treating Shirazis and mainland Africans as distinct groups for purposes of representation and administration prevented the African community from uniting in common cause. The concept of a united African community comprising all the various tribal groups was a much more essential and fundamental political reality than any other concept of identity.*

"Whenever we say 'Africans,' we mean all people who

---

4 *Ibid.,* September 11, 1952.
5 *Ibid.,* August 21, 1952.
6 *Ibid.,* August 28, 1952.

are officially called Africans; that is the Pemba, the Tumbatu and those Africans resident in Zanzibar who are His Highness' Subjects and who are supposed to have come from the mainland of Africa, as though the other above mentioned Africans originally came from the moon! !"[7]

The forcefulness of these complaints and the nature of the problems which they described made this attack the prototype for all subsequent African political expression. Between 1952 and 1964 only two other major concerns were added to the intellectual arsenal of African nationalism, and these were not fully developed until the period just preceding the African revolution.

As African leaders in later years began to build a nationwide political organization, they expanded their attention beyond the needs of the limited urban African community and began to seek appeals which would enlist the support of a rural agricultural population. Here, the issue of land alienation became a vital ingredient in their party program. In addressing themselves to this problem, the African leaders argued that a basic economic injustice existed so long as most of the country's best land was in the hands of minority elements. The constitutional orientation of African leaders also changed in later years. They ceased to petition for the redress of individual grievances within a colonial milieu, and began to call into question the very presence of British—and Arab—colonialism. The leaders insisted that the only real solution to the problem of the African community was that Zanzibar be constituted as an independent African state.

The initial exploratory thrust of African nationalism represented by the 1952 agitation came to an abrupt end the following year. High government officials, aware of the composition and role of the YAU, decided to en-

[7] *Ibid.,* August 28, 1952.

force the regulations which prohibited civil servants from engaging in politics. During the second half of 1953 they issued a special circular, warning government employees of the severe legal penalties for political activity. This severed the emergent link between African civil servants and the large African political organizations, and the African Association entered an extended period of political dormancy. By the time it began to recover from the government's restrictions, Arab nationalism had emerged publicly. This forced African leaders to respond to a set of political circumstances wholly different from those which existed in 1951 and 1952.

The government's circular had several profound and far-reaching consequences. It forced several of the African leaders to withdraw from Ahmed Lemke's newly organized ZNU as well as to curtail their activities in the YAU and African Association. Two of these men, Othman Sharif (an agricultural officer) and Aboud Jumbe (a secondary school teacher) were unable to rejoin the cause of African nationalism until after 1960. Their membership in the ZNU had created a close personal relationship at the level of top leadership between the Arab Association and the African community. If the ZNU had been able to survive, it might have been able to foster peaceful cooperation between the leaders of the two races, but when Sharif and Jumbe resigned from the ZNU and Lemke dissolved his party, the only political link between the two communities was broken. This made it practically inevitable that Zanzibar nationalism would emerge as a solely Arab creation, instead of a joint Arab-African enterprise. When that happened, leaders of the two communities pursued separate political paths.

The YAU underwent a succession of changes during 1954 and abandoned altogether its character as a political body. Its leadership renamed it the *Young African Social Union* (YASU), drew up a new constitution limiting it to purely social activities, and ceased to perform an agitational role with the African Association. The African Association itself was changed; the president, Herbert Barnabas, was forced to resign since he was a government doctor, and Abeid Karume, a former seaman, replaced him.

In sum, the government's decision to enforce more strictly the concept of a politically neutral bureaucracy had at least two major long-range consequences. It destroyed permanently an embryonic pattern of political communication between African and Arab leadership. By forcing African intellectuals to withdraw from political activity it ensured that the Arab community would for some time continue to possess the only politically active elite. And it meant that from 1953 onward, African political organizations would remain in the hands of men who had very limited administrative, political and organizational experience.

The wholesale exodus of African intellectuals from politics was immediately followed by a visible decline in the assertiveness and militancy of the African community. African parliamentary spokesmen and the African press began to display a lack of confidence in their relations with other ethnic communities, and became unable to express forcefully and systematically the needs of their own community. The new African leaders lacked the breadth of social and economic vision of the civil servant group and were motivated far less by concrete issues of injustice and underrepresentation than by fear of Arab domination. Instead of continuing the attack on the unfair distribution of political influence, wealth, and social services in Zanzibar, they lost the initiative and began to assume a purely defensive position. The new objective of African political organization was not to win needed reforms for the African population, but to protect Africans against Arab nationalism.

This change was most apparent in the area of constitutional policy. African leaders ceased to agitate for major democratic reforms and adopted a highly conservative position, supporting the administration against the militant demands of the Arab Association. They accepted the proposed Rankine Constitution as a fair and reasonable political advance, for example, although it gave Africans only one-third of the unofficial legislative seats. A year later, in April, 1955, representatives of the Arab Association asked Africans to join with them in rejecting the Rankine proposals and in seeking an immediate common roll election.[8] The African Association declined, and when its spokesmen appeared before the Coutts Commission in early 1956, their position was that nominated communal representation ought to continue for at least another five years.[9]

This constitutional conservatism reached its peak in late 1956. Coutts had recommended earlier in the year that the Zanzibar Government accept the Arab Association's demands and hold a common roll election. An announcement that this election would be held during

[8] *Ibid.*, May 5, 1955. The African Association's response to the idea of cooperating with the Arab Association in constitutional matters was negative in the extreme. This issue of *Afrika Kwetu* commented: "It is quite true that the African Association of Zanzibar and Pemba does not favor the proposed Round Table Conference. As we are the backward community in these islands, we shall ever beg *our* needs and claim *our* rights for the benefit of Africans in this Protectorate for it is the adopted policy of the African Association to achieve advancement and endeavour to win rights for ourselves so long as we are sons and daughters of the soil. So our immigrant friends should not forget that our aim is African self-government, . . . not Zanzibari self-government."

[9] Zanzibar Protectorate, *Methods of Choosing Unofficial Members of the Legislative Council,* by Sir Walter Coutts (Zanzibar: Government Printer, 1956), p. 4. See also *Afrika Kwetu,* February 9, 1956, and July 6, 1956.

1957 created among Africans an almost paralyzing sense of the unpreparedness of their community—first, because they knew that education and income requirements for the franchise would prevent large numbers of Africans from achieving suffrage and, second, because of their more diffuse fear that the political inexperience of the African community would be a major handicap in an election campaign. Mr. Shaaban Sudi Mponda, a retired school teacher and the first mainland African nominated to the Legislative Council, expressed his community's bitter opposition to the election: "I beg to state plainly before this Council that we the Africans do not welcome this election with open hearts. . . . This (type of election) is applicable only to that country where the citizens have the same opportunities in the management of the activities of their government. Here, . . . we the Africans are backward people due to our lack of educational facilities; we therefore do not have those said opportunities. . . . Owing to my people's ignorance of election (sic), I suggest that they should be given enough time to learn."[10] The *Afrika Kwetu* issue of January 3, 1957, went so far as to urge its readers to boycott the election.

One explanation of the conservatism of African leadership was their belief that the various constitutional reforms being sought by the Arabs would, if introduced prematurely, work against the deepest political interests of the African majority. Given the scarcity of qualified African administrators and politicians, the immediate establishment of a democratically self-governing state would necessitate the formation of a multi-racial government. Africans found this far less to be preferred than colonial rule because of the danger that Arab dom-

[10] Zanzibar Protectorate, *Debates of the Legislative Council, Thirty-first Session, 1956-1957* (Zanzibar: Government Printer, 1958), p. 55.

ination would become too entrenched ever to be routed. They were adamant in their insistence that the only acceptable course of constitutional evolution was from Protectorate to African nation. *Afrika Kwetu* had commented nearly two years earlier that: "We wish to assure all the so-called Zanzibaris . . . that anything short of an African state will never be accepted when self-government is achieved in this Protectorate. . . . We are also opposed to multi-racial government in these islands. It is against all this Association stands for. We want Zanzibar to become an African state like the Gold Coast."[11]

African fears about the coming election also stemmed from the historical inability of Shirazi and mainland African communities to cooperate in achieving common political aims. Throughout the contemporary political period Shirazis and mainland Africans have maintained separate communal associations. The African Association was formed in 1934 and immediately sought semi-official status as an affiliate of the Tanganyika African Association.[12] The Shirazi Association was not established until 1939, beginning first in Pemba and then in Zanzibar. The two associations contested bitterly over the allocation of the nominated seats in the Legislative Council reserved for representatives of the African community. The fact that until 1956 these places were in every case awarded to a leader of the Shirazi Association offended mainland African leadership and created a deep split between the two groups.

Disunity between Shirazis and Mainlanders was the principal obstacle to the formation of an all-African political party. Several times during 1956 Julius Nyerere, President of the Tanganyika African National Union (TANU), came to Zanzibar to try to persuade African

11 *Afrika Kwetu*, May 5, 1955.
12 *Ibid.*, January 26, 1956.

leaders of both communities to forget past differences. The mainland Africans were strongly in favor of a merger of the two associations, but Nyerere's proposal for an Afro-Shirazi Union had only limited success among the Shirazis.

The Nyerere visits provoked a crisis of unity and identification within the Shirazi Association. The Shirazi leaders of Zanzibar and Pemba were deeply divided over the issue of whether or not to join in the newly proposed *Afro-Shirazi Union* (ASU). The Hadimu Shirazi leaders Ameri Tajo (a Koranic School teacher) and Thabit Kombo (a former railroad engineer) were in favor. They felt that the need for a common African response to the threat of Arab domination posed by the ZNP made it essential for Shirazis and mainland Africans to become reconciled. They began to canvass the Hadimu community, seeking popular support for a decision on their part to link the two associations. For many Shirazis, however, the merger was unacceptable. There was considerable resistance to the formation of any political party which involved subordinating a separate Shirazi identity to a more all-encompassing concept of the integral unity of the African people. In Zanzibar there was strong local resistance among the Tumbatu people in the northern peninsula areas. The heaviest Shirazi resistance to joining with the African Association, however, came from Pemba.

The unwillingness of many Shirazis to cooperate with mainland Africans in a single political movement was partially the result of factors that had separated the two groups long before the emergence of Arab nationalism. Their differing occupational structures and residential patterns, for example, had probably created a sense of social distance between them. The major reason why Shirazis and mainland Africans could not cooperate, however, lay precisely in the fact that the sole motive for cooperation was resentment and fear of the Arab community. Since the emergence of the ZNP the place of the Arab in Zanzibar had become the sole issue around which all African politics revolved, and the menace of an Arab seizure of power obscured all the social and political problems which had united Africans in common political action in 1952. For a variety of historical reasons, the place of the Arab community was the one issue on which Shirazis and mainland Africans had completely different attitudes: on this subject they could not possibly unite.

Many Shirazis, particularly in Pemba, looked back upon a history of warm and friendly relations with the Arabs of Zanzibar. They recalled with pride that they served as local administrators in the Sultan's government or as seamen in the Indian Ocean trade. Shirazis were very rarely bought and sold as slaves, and to a very large extent their daily lives were unchanged by the establishment of an Arab Sultanate in Zanzibar. There were numerous Shirazis, especially in remote rural areas, who had grown to accept Arabs as the rightful and legitimate rulers of Zanzibar. For all these reasons, large numbers of Shirazis were profoundly reluctant to enter into any political party predicated on the idea that the purpose of African unity was to defeat and overthrow the immigrant Arab minority.

The most vivid historical memory of the mainland African community, on the other hand, was that Arabs were the instigators and perpetrators of the East African slave trade. Mainlanders were frequently aware that their own presence as a community in Zanzibar was largely attributable either to the Arab slave trade or to the need for immigrant agricultural labor in the Arab clove fields. They were strangers in Zanzibar, unable to regard it as home and yet often removed by several generations from their countries of origin. Furthermore, they occupied the lowest place in the social structure. For all this the Arab aristocracy seemed to be to blame, and there appeared to be little reason for entering politics other than to defeat the Arabs and create an African state. Thus, the first active efforts to form a united African political party were made in response to the threat of permanent racial subjugation by the ZNP. The motivation for African unity was only a continuation of earlier constitutional conservatism; its stimulus was far less an awareness of the revolutionary changes occurring elsewhere in Africa than a fear that Zanzibar might move ahead too rapidly.

In February of 1957, only a few months before the scheduled election to which the British had agreed in early 1956, leaders of the African and Shirazi Associations met together. They had hoped to form a joint political party, but very little unity was achieved. Although they agreed to form the Afro-Shirazi Union and to co-operate during the coming election campaign, there was to be no merger of the two associations. Even this modest agreement covered only the African and Shirazi Associations of Zanzibar and not those of Pemba.

The Pemba Shirazis refused as a group to join the ASU. In preliminary negotiations they indicated that they would be prepared to affiliate themselves with the new party only under two conditions: first, that the Shirazi Association of Pemba be allowed to name the party's candidates for both constituencies into which Pemba had been divided. They felt that as their association represented 85 per cent of Pemba's African population, it could legitimately claim to speak for the interests of indigenous and immigrant African groups. Their second condition was that the name of the party should not include any reference to the racial composition of its membership, hence that the designation "Afro-Shirazi" be avoided in favor of a term such as

"National Congress." They wanted a non-racial political organization which would be nationalistic rather than anti-Arab in character. Since neither of these two conditions was acceptable to the African Association, Pemba Shirazi leaders had not even attended the February meeting when the ASU was formed.

The mainland Africans' militantly anti-Arab political views repelled these Shirazis not only from the ASU but paradoxically from the ZNP as well. For the preeminence of Mainlanders as leaders of the ASU also accentuated the dominant role that the Arab immigrant minority had begun to assume in the ZNP. The disproportionate political influence of these immigrant minorities engendered among the Pemba Shirazis a sense that they were innocent bystanders in a species of cold war waged on their soil by alien elements.

Although the ZNP fulfilled at least the second of their two conditions, Shirazis were reluctant to join because they knew that they would be subordinate to its Arab leaders. They were seeking a political party which would not be excessively influenced either by the Arab or the mainland African minorities, and which would have Zanzibar's Shirazi majority as its constituent basis. The Shirazi leaders Mohammed Shamte (a retired school principal) and Ali Sharif (a landowner and brother of Othman Sharif) formed a political group which they called *Ittihad ul'Umma* (The People's Party)[13] in late 1956. It never became a fully organized political party: a proposed constitution was drawn up but never adopted, permanent leaders were never elected, and no official program was ever promulgated. Throughout a very brief existence it remained an informal gathering of influential Shirazi leaders from

[13] *Mwangaza* (The Searchlight), January 2, 1957. The editor of this newspaper, Abdulla Amour Suleiman, was a Hadimu Shirazi and played an important part in the formation of *Ittihad ul'Umma*.

Pemba who met from time to time with one or two sympathetically inclined intellectuals and communal leaders in Zanzibar. *Ittihad ul'Umma* never attained any serious public following, declined markedly in the early months of 1957, and was finally disbanded during the election campaign. The principal reason for its failure was that it could not gain the support of Zanzibar Shirazi leaders Tajo and Kombo. These men were seeking a somewhat more anti-Arab organization, and therefore preferred to remain in the ASU.

Despite its transitory existence, the brief appearance of *Ittihad ul'Umma* was of penetrating significance in the development of Zanzibar's political party system. The party's founders (Shamte and Ali Sharif) were extremely influential leaders in the Pemba branch of the Shirazi Association. They stood as independent candidates in the two Pemba constituencies and their widespread personal following among Pemba Shirazis enabled them to defeat not only their ZNP opponents, but also an Afro-Shirazi Union candidate. Their presence in *Ittihad ul'Umma* gave the party its special character as an attempt by Pemba Shirazis to avoid political involvement with the mainland African community of Zanzibar. The lasting importance of the party was that the impulse to use Shirazi solidarity as the basis for a separate political organization had, albeit momentarily, been given concrete expression. The same impulse later furnished the political inspiration for the formation of Zanzibar's third major political party, the *Zanzibar and Pemba People's Party* (ZPPP).

The decision to scuttle *Ittihad ul'Umma* left Zanzibar for the time being with a modified two-party system, but there were numerous unaffiliated ethnic groups seeking national political expression. This lent the two-party system an impermanent, unstable quality. During the brief period between the earliest stirrings of modern nationalism in 1954 and Zanzibar's first election in July, 1957, the nationalist impulse had become fused to highly separatist ethnic loyalties. Even before the election campaign began, political solidarities were defined in terms of ethnic fears. The nearly unanimous aspiration towards independence was all but obscured by the determination of communally based parties to prevent an independent Zanzibar from falling into the hands of their communal enemies.

In the course of the election campaign,[14] both the ZNP and the ASU made nationalist demands for independence within the British Commonwealth and for a more rapid recruitment of local people into the civil service. Both parties also expressed loyalty to the Sultan and declared themselves in favor of constitutional monarchy as the form of government most appropriate to an independent Zanzibar nation.[15] The parties differed, however, on the pace of constitutional advance. The ASU, in keeping with its self-identification as the party of the deprived and impoverished African masses, sought a policy of gradual constitutional development. In that way, they argued, the African majority might move closer to the other racial communities in educational and social achievements. The ZNP, setting itself up as the militant instrument of patriotic nationalism, favored immediate self-government and independence.

The essential differences between the parties lay not so much in their official programs as in the contrasting nature of their appeals to the electorate. The ASU, drawing its principal support from the mainland African and Shirazi communities, emphasized the unity of all Africans and appealed strongly to common fears of Arab

[14] The writer is indebted to Professor Carl G. Rosberg of the University of California, Berkeley, for having made available a private collection of materials on this election.
[15] *Tanganyika Standard*, July 18, 1957.

domination. ASU propaganda repeated continually the idea that: "Both the Arab Association and the National- ist Party as a whole are composed of a majority of aliens, most of whom are foreign Arabs from Oman. The Arab Association and the ZNP jointly represent the immigrant minority class . . . the ZNP was only organized as a bait to gain a majority [of African supporters] but it was and still is a vain attempt."[16]

The ZNP leaned heavily for its initial support upon Arabs and Asians. Seeking to broaden its membership, it emphasized multi-racial concepts such as Islam's relig- ious unity and the common cultural and historical past which linked all Zanzibar's ethnic groups. In a special effort to gain Shirazi supporters, it appealed to the national unity of all Zanzibaris and to indigenous fears of mainland influence in Zanzibar politics. *Al Falaq,* for example, made a clear distinction between Shirazis and mainland Africans, and claimed that "the majority of Africans in Zanzibar are aliens . . . the merger of Shi- razis with the Africans was not a sensible move and for- eign hands are really responsible for the great blunder which Shirazis were led to commit. And that, too, for the benefit of foreigners!"[17] In this view an ASU victory would place the government of Zanzibar in the hands of people with whom Shirazis shared neither nationality nor cul- tural ties. The purpose of this appeal was to win Shirazis away from the ASU by providing them with a patriotic sense of identity—a more attractive appeal than the simpler ASU notion of racial solidarity.

In the election (see Table 9) the ZNP was completely defeated.[18] It contested five out of the six constituencies

[16] *Afrika Kwetu,* May 9, 1957.

[17] *Al Falaq,* April 17, 1957.

[18] See: Zanzibar Protectorate, *The Report of the Supervisor of Elections on the Elections in Zanzibar, 1957* (Zanzibar: Government Printer, 1958), p. 39. This report, however, erroneously indicated that the two victorious candidates in Pemba, Mohammed Shamte

TABLE 9

1957 Election Results

Constituency	Candidate	Affil.	Support	Vote
Zanzibar South	Ameri Tajo	ASU	ASU	5,380
	Amour Zahor Said	ZNP	ZNP	1,679
Zanzibar North	Daud Mahmoud	ASU	ASU	3,687
	Haji Mohammed Juma	Indep.	ZNP	3,221
Pemba South	Mohammed Shamte Hamadi	Indep.	Shirazi Assoc.	5,851
	Rashid Ali el-Khaify	ZNP	ZNP	1,488
	Abdulla Seuleiman Ali Busaidy	Indep.	Indep.	1,075
Pemba North	Ali Sharif Mussa	Indep.	Shirazi Assoc.	3,386
	Rashid Hamadi Athumani	ZNP	ZNP	3,182
	Shaaban Sudi Mponda	ASU	African Assoc.	657
Stone Town	Sher Mohammed Chowdhary	Indep.	Muslim Assoc.	519
	Rutti A. Bulsara	ZNP	ZNP	494
	Anverali Hassan Virji	Indep.	ASU	392
	Abdul Qadir Mukri	Indep.	Indep.	49
Ngambo	Abeid Amani Karume	ASU	ASU	3,328
	Ali Muhsin Barwani	ZNP	ZNP	918
	Ibuni Saleh	Indep.	Comorian Assoc.	55
Total				35,361

into which the Protectorate was divided but did not gain a single seat. And in both constituencies where ZNP and ASU candidates opposed each other directly (Zanzibar South and Ngambo), the ZNP candidates were de-

---

and Ali Sharif, were members of the ASU. As Table 9 indicates, Ali Sharif was opposed in his constituency by a member of the African Association, Shaaban Sudi Mponda, who received the endorsement of the ASU. The ASU had intended to stand an African Association candidate to oppose Shamte as well, but reconsidered at the last minute and withdrew from Pemba South constituency. The reason for the error in the *Report* was that the election commissioner, Mr. J. C. Penney, identified the Shirazi Association of Pemba (which endorsed both Shamte and Sharif) with the ASU of Zanzibar.

feated by overwhelming majorities. Although it had campaigned as a multi-racial nationalist movement, it polled only about 32 per cent of the vote; it had failed almost completely to gain the confidence of the African population.

The decisive ZNP defeat was widely interpreted as an event which marked the end of Arab domination in Zanzibar. The notion that a major political revolution had been brought about by peaceful constitutional means was heavily publicized by international observers. The London Times, for example, had commented that: "If the Arabs (the ZNP) fail to secure the election, the issue will be for them exceedingly serious. For their great predominance . . . among the landholders, the professional class and the politicians . . . will have been undermined at a critical point. The knell of their hegemony which once extended to the whole of East Africa may well be sounding in their last stronghold upon the Coast."[19] The assumption here was that a tiny racial oligarchy like the Arabs could not survive the introduction of majoritarian institutions, and that as constitutional advance occurred, parliamentary democracy would transform Zanzibar into an African state. Subsequent events proved this interpretation erroneous. The ZNP recovered, and in later elections it was able to win parliamentary majorities and to install an Arab-led government.

On closer examination, the results of the 1957 election did not provide a sound basis for assuming the eventual victory of anti-Arab forces. The mistake made by observers at the time lay in identifying ZNP defeat with ASU victory. This was far from the case. Only in Zanzibar where it had gained more than 60 per cent of the popular vote did the ASU emerge as the dominant political force. As a national phenomenon, however, the

[19] *London Times,* July 22, 1957.

election results did not represent a victory for the party of anti-Arab opinion. The three ASU victories in Zanzibar were its only successes. They gave the party just one-half of the six elected seats in the Legislative Council and only one-fourth of the total unofficial representation. The ASU had sponsored or supported five candidates and all together these men polled less than two-fifths of the total vote throughout the Protectorate. The ASU did not even exist as such in Pemba, where the African and Shirazi Associations continued as completely separate bodies.

The poor national showing of the ASU suggests that some factor other than anti-Arab prejudice may have been a more universal and important determinant of voting behavior. Close inspection of Table 9 indicates that the common denominator of electoral success in every constituency was affiliation with or sponsorship by an established communal organization. The three victorious candidates who were not members of the ASU, for example, had all been publicly sponsored by ethnic organizations. The Stonetown seat was won by the candidate of the Muslim Association, a newly-formed political group whose membership was composed almost exclusively of Muslim Asians.[20] The two Pemba seats were also won by candidates with strong communal ties; Shamte and Ali Sharif, though formally designated as "independents," had been given the official public endorsement of the Pemba Shirazi Association. Ethnic loyalties also played a major part in the ASU's victories in Zanzibar, for the ASU had been able to present itself as the legitimate heir of the African and Shirazi Associations. Communal identity had been virtually institutional-

[20] Throughout most of Zanzibar's contemporary history, Asian Hindus and Muslims cooperated in the Indian National Association. But when India became independent in 1947 and was partitioned into two separate countries (one Hindu and the other Muslim), the Muslim Asians of Zanzibar withdrew from the Indian National Association and formed the Muslim Association.

ized as the sole basis of political and social organization
since long before the era of nationalism. The strength
of communal separatism was exemplified in broad and
long-standing acceptance of the practice of racial representation in the Legislative Council, in the presence of
innumerable racial and communal bodies, and in the
fact that even sports, social life, and the local press were
organized on communal lines. The election demonstrated the persistence of these communal loyalties and
revealed that they had entered the modern parliamentary arena as the most powerful basis of political affiliation.

That the election did not reveal an emergent pattern
of anti-Arab voting was of decisive significance in the
subsequent history of the ZNP. Top ZNP leaders realized
that as a matter of practical party strategy they need
campaign only for broad acceptance of multi-racialism,
and did not have to excuse their party for its Arab
leadership. They also knew that if they could discredit
communalism and bring the old pattern of ethnic loyalties into disrepute, they would weaken the real basis of
affiliation of many ASU supporters. This strategy had its
greatest prospect of success in Pemba, where local voting
patterns as well as the absence of the ASU confirmed that
an anti-Arab policy had virtually no appeal to the local
population. The ZNP had received almost 30 per cent of
the popular vote in Pemba, a figure nearly double its
Zanzibar total. In Pemba North constituency the African
Association candidate who had been given tacit ASU support ran far behind a ZNP rival, and in many rural areas
and villages of Pemba, ZNP candidates had received a
majority vote.

In the last analysis, the 1957 election revealed Pemba
as a critical weak spot in the Afro-Shirazi's organization
and thus in their prospects for popular support. Not
until several months after the election did the Pemba

Shirazi Association agree to a limited form of cooperation with the African Association. The two elected representatives from Pemba joined the ASU—now renamed the *Afro-Shirazi Party* (ASP)—and sat in the Legislative Council as its members. The Shirazi Association refused, however, to merge with the African Association as the two Zanzibar associations had agreed to do immediately after the election. The Pemba Shirazi Association insisted on the right to maintain separate organizational facilities and to continue as an autonomous political body separate from the ASP. This demand symbolized the continuing profound reluctance among Pemba Shirazis to become involved in a full political partnership with mainland Africans, and it also dramatized the deep disagreement between the two communities over the race issue. Within two years this disagreement led to a major split in the ASP. The Pemba Shirazis withdrew to form their own political party, and thereby made it impossible for the ASP ever to win sufficient electoral support in Pemba to gain a national parliamentary majority.

PART III

COMPETITIVE PARTY POLITICS
IN ZANZIBAR

✲ CHAPTER VII
Party Conflict in the Electoral System

Competitive party politics were a new phenomenon in Zanzibar. The political culture of the Protectorate lacked an accumulated tradition of established practices and precedents which defined the boundaries of partisan activity and set it clearly apart from other forms of behavior. There was no clear cultural differentiation between political conduct and conventional modes of social interaction. As a result, the political antipathies which had been stimulated by the 1957 election infected practically every aspect of life and infused the entire range of individual and group relations with partisan emotions.

Day-to-day activities became a battleground in which every individual act was invested with highly symbolic significance as a demonstration of party membership and solidarity. Performance of the most routine daily tasks—marketing, working and commuting, for example—was viewed as an integral facet of the national political struggle. Practically every individual construed his personal behavior as an opportunity for a direct contribution to the cause of ultimate party victory. Supporters of opposed parties boycotted their rivals' buses, refused to share their wells, and in numerous farming and fishing villages ceased to work collectively. Sports and social activities were organized and attended on strictly party lines. Even religious life was affected. Funerals, weddings and worship itself were subjected to an almost unanimously imposed segregation; each party's members refused to attend ceremonies initiated by or identified with supporters of the opposite party.[1] By early 1958 no

[1] Zanzibar Protectorate, *Annual Report of the Provincial Administration for the year 1958* (Zanzibar: Government Printer, 1959), p. 1.

dimension of social behavior remained politically neutral. Even private quarrels and disputes which had long preceded the formation of modern political parties were absorbed into the pattern of partisan conflict.

This intrusion of political strife into conventional realms of social behavior was accompanied by mounting racial antagonism. The election campaign of April to June, 1957, had aroused widespread and vocal expression of communal prejudices. The intensive electioneering of the two principal parties converted latent ethnic biases into publicly debated principles of party affiliation.

This was especially apparent in the rural plantation areas of Zanzibar, where there was close daily contact between Arab landlords and the African squatter-farmers who lived on their estates. These two groups had traditionally enjoyed good relations, for squatter-farming was an institution of mutual benefit. It had grown up after the abolition of slavery when freed slaves simply settled on plantations where they had formerly worked. Later, many mainland Africans began to practice squatter-farming because it held some significant economic advantages; they were allowed to live rent-free and to cultivate their own food crops, while performing only minimal services for the landowners. Squatter-farming also helped the landowner; it was a deterrent to thievery, the squatters furnished a ready supply of laborers for hire, and their cultivation of food crops kept the ground beneath the clove and coconut trees cleared.[2] Thus there had emerged an acknowledged body of reciprocal rights and obligations which served to protect the interests of both groups.

After the 1957 election, however, the landlord-squatter relationship became subject to extreme unrest;

[2] John Middleton, *Land Tenure in Zanzibar* (London: Her Majesty's Stationery Office, 1961), pp. 43-47.

there were sporadic outbreaks of violence and soon the landlords began to expel the squatters from their farms. These evictions caused considerable suffering and potentially threatened the lives of thousands of persons. Fear and resentment aroused by the evictions caused intense hatred between Arabs and Africans in the rural areas, and many Arabs moved into town in order to avoid reprisals. In the ensuing controversy over squatters' rights, the ASP began for the first time to call into question the very legitimacy of Arab landownership.[3] Both among the mainland African squatter-farmers of the fertile area and among the Shirazis of the remoter villages, the problem of Arab land alienation became a salient political issue.

An intensification and effusion of conflict also characterized the competition between the two political parties. The pressure of the election campaign had forced the ASP and the ZNP to channel their energies and to focus all their attention on the single specific objective of achieving a popular electoral majority. Once that pressure was removed, they began to explore other possible arenas of competition. Both parties were seeking

---

[3] The substance of the controversy was the ASP's claim that under the traditional system of land tenure which had existed in Zanzibar, land was community property and therefore legally inalienable. In a famous speech, ASP President Karume argued that the land of the country still belonged to the Africans and that the squatters therefore had an inalienable right to settle on and cultivate the plantations. He asserted that this right was not subject to any infringement by the Arab plantation owners and that they could claim legitimate ownership only of the trees and movable property, not the land itself. The Arabs viewed land relations through the perspective of an Islamic legal tradition which recognizes private ownership, and they asserted a right to freehold tenure. There had, in the past, been considerable litigation over this problem, but because Islamic law had official recognition, land issues were usually decided in favor of the Arab owners. See Sir John Gray, *Report on the Inquiry into Claims to Certain Land at or near Ngezi, Vitongozi, in the Mudiria of Chake Chake, in the District of Pemba* (Zanzibar: Government Printer, 1956).

means of gaining decisive popular and organizational superiority and of demoralizing the supporters of their opponent. Between 1957 and 1963 each party was anxious to find and employ every technique that might help toward victory.

The ZNP possessed an important advantage in the support of the wealthy and landowning classes. This group furnished the party with a steady supply of funds for organizational and recruiting activity and also provided it with large numbers of dedicated workers. In addition, their membership meant that the ZNP, although a minority party, indirectly controlled the major sectors of the economy such as the clove and coconut industries. ZNP members were the country's largest employers outside of the government, and this gave the party considerable leverage against the African population. With the high level of unemployment, the ability of ZNP members to confer or withhold work became a powerful instrument of patronage which the party used to expand its membership among the African and Shirazi communities.

Labor organizers employed by the ZNP immediately began to form agricultural trade unions. Their first substantial success was in the coconut industry, which employed large numbers of workers on a year-round basis. The informal cooperation of the owners of the large coconut plantations was critical. It enabled the organizers to make union and party membership the precondition of receiving employment, which compelled practically the entire labor force in the coconut industry to join the party. ZNP organizers also attempted to organize the workers in the clove industry, but were less successful because of the seasonal nature of employment and the extremely large numbers of workers needed at harvest time.

Since the large landowners were nearly all deeply

loyal and active members of the ZNP, the ASP made little counter-effort to organize trade union support in the rural areas and, from 1958 on, the agricultural workers' unions of the Protectorate were nearly always controlled by the ZNP. These unions were not only a major vehicle through which the party built up a mass popular following among Africans, but because of the direct affiliation between the Agricultural and Allied Workers' Union and the ZNP, it was also an important source of party funds.

The ZNP also attempted to recruit waterfront labor by forming a party-sponsored dockworkers' union in opposition to two such unions already in existence.[4] As most of the dock and transport workers in Zanzibar Town were mainland Africans, their sympathies and the sympathies of their unions were heavily on the side of the ASP. The employers' organization, known as the Schooner Captains and Owners Association, was predominantly Arab and loyal to the ZNP. A pattern of union organizer-employer relations emerged which was practically identical to that in agriculture; the Schooner Captains and Owners Association cooperated informally with ZNP labor leaders to freeze out the mainland African workers. The employers planned to replace them with workers committed to the ZNP, primarily Tumbatu Shirazis.

By sponsoring a Shirazi dockworkers' union the ZNP also managed to exploit latent economic tensions between mainland Africans and Shirazis. The party presented itself to Shirazis as the defender of their economic rights against cheap immigrant labor. Official party spokesmen and union organizers argued that Mainlanders were not Zanzibar citizens and that Shirazis, who were citizens, ought to have first preference for all em-

---

[4] Zanzibar Protectorate, *Report of the Arbitrator to Enquire into a Trade Dispute at the Wharf Area at Zanzibar* (Zanzibar: Government Printer, n.d.).

ployment. This argument enabled the ZNP to recruit numerous members among urbanized Shirazi workers.

The ASP organized its own economic warfare against ZNP supporters. Party leaders encouraged Africans to boycott all Arab-owned shops both in the towns and in the rural areas and, in order to implement the boycott, the party organized a chain of consumer cooperatives so that Africans would be able to buy from party-managed stores. The boycott and the consumer cooperative movement forced hundreds of Arab shopkeepers out of business. It is indicative of the dominantly racial pattern of party conflict that the Arabs who suffered under the ASP boycott were not members of the politically active elite stratum, but were Manga Arabs. These shopkeepers, as recent immigrants, were disinterested in party conflict and in sheer economic terms were much closer to Africans.

Political tensions rose to such a pitch that towards the end of 1958 persistent outbreaks of disorder threatened to engulf the society in chronic racial warfare. The British Government attempted to mediate between the parties in an attempt to prevent further violence. In October, local authorities summoned a Round Table Conference which was attended by representatives of the ASP, ZNP and various racial associations. The purpose of the Conference was to provide an informal meeting-ground where the party leaders themselves would face the responsibility of finding ways to reduce racial friction. For this reason, the government officials did not participate actively in the discussions and did not exert real pressure for a solution. The Round Table Conference yielded little in the way of enduring results.[5] Most of the meetings were taken up with discussion of the more obvious symptoms of racial enmity—bus and

[5] Zanzibar Government, *Minutes of the Round Table Conference Held in October, 1958* (Zanzibar: mimeograph, 1958).

shop boycotts and squatter evictions. In the presence of government officials, party leaders merely denied any complicity in these events on the part of their respective organizations. The parties' delegates did sign a modest agreement, however, and offered to try to alleviate the racial difficulties. Little attention was paid to the basic differences in political and constitutional outlook responsible for the racial crisis.

A more influential and effective effort to avert open clashes between party supporters was made by the *Pan African Freedom Movement of East, Central and Southern Africa* (PAFMECSA), an international organization of African nationalists. PAFMECSA's first meeting was held at Mwanza, Tanganyika, in mid-September, 1958, and was attended by leaders of both of Zanzibar's political parties. In the congenial and sympathetic environment furnished by a convention of African political leaders, the Zanzibar delegates freely voiced their constitutional differences.[6] The ZNP representatives presented their party as a militantly nationalistic, multi-racial body demanding immediate independence. ASP leaders portrayed their party as the voice of the African masses and argued that its conservative constitutional position was dictated by the dual nature of colonialism in Zanzibar. This disagreement appeared so fundamental that the Mwanza Conference postponed making any concrete recommendations and asked the Zanzibar leaders to wait until a special delegation could be sent to Zanzibar to investigate the situation for themselves.

The PAFMECSA delegation, which consisted of Mr.

[6] Pan African Freedom Movement of East and Central Africa, *The Minutes of the Mwanza Conference of PAFMECA* (mimeograph, n.p., n.d.). At the time, this international movement was called PAFMECA, and did not actually become PAFMECSA until after 1958 when nationalist leaders from South Africa began to attend. The official title is used here because that is now the accepted designation of the movement.

Francis Khamis of Kenya and Mr. Kinyame Chiume of
Nyasaland, arrived in Zanzibar in late November and
met with both political parties.[7] The ZNP argued that the
ASP was harming the cause of nationalism in Zanzibar by
its unwillingness to demand immediate independence,
and requested that the ASP be asked to abandon its conservatism and its anti-Arab views. The PAFMECSA representatives were critical of the ASP because they were inclined to accept the militant nationalism of the ZNP at
face value. They concluded that the ASP was allowing its
racial feelings to delay Zanzibar's independence, and
recommended that ASP and ZNP leaders form a united
front to work for racial harmony and immediate independence.

These recommendations were a triumph for the ZNP,
for they placed the ASP in an extremely difficult position.
If the ASP refused it would be cutting itself off from the
mainstream of East African nationalism. If it accepted,
the ASP faced the ignominious task of changing its constitutional and racial policies to bring them into line
with those of a party which it had far surpassed at the
polls. ASP leaders chose the latter course, and in late
1958 they joined with the ZNP in a "Freedom Committee." They urged their followers to forget old racial differences, and changed their target date for independence
from 1963 or later to 1960. Throughout the fifteen
months that the Freedom Committee lasted, the ASP presented the spectacle of a party which publicly repented
past mistakes and conceded the superior virtue of the
policies of its chief rival. As a result, the ZNP increased
its stature immeasurably in the eyes of Africans.

Throughout 1959 party leaders toured the country together, frequently appearing on the same platform, to
dramatize publicly the new-found spirit of unity. Party

[7] *Afrika Kwetu,* November 11, 1958.

spokesmen urged their followers to work together to restore good race relations, and gave wide publicity to a
joint ASP/ZNP declaration which said: "We jointly and
publicly condemn all acts which are directed at causing
hatred and disharmony among the people of Zanzibar.
We jointly agree to work for the eradication of all hatred
and to establish a joint nationalistic front for the liberation of Zanzibar from imperialism and colonialism . . .
we reiterate our determination to establish in Zanzibar a
joint national freedom movement and accordingly to
form a Territorial Freedom Committee of both our
parties as a step towards that end."[8] The result of the
formation of the Freedom Committee was a visible
lessening of political and racial tensions in the Protectorate. This was evidenced by the cessation of eviction in
the rural areas, the restoration of more or less cordial relations between squatters and landlords, and the aban-
donment of the shop and bus boycotts.[9]

Once the immediate racial crisis was resolved, the ASP
became reluctant to continue its participation in the
Freedom Committee. PAFMECSA's deep commitment to
inter-party unity, however, exerted considerable pressure toward continuing cooperation with the ZNP. In
mid-April, PAFMECSA held a conference in Zanzibar and
its leaders chided Zanzibaris for allowing past racial animosities to stand in the way of independence. Julius
Nyerere, for example, commented that "the atmosphere
of masters and slaves still exists in Zanzibar . . . politically the parties all agreed to one objective but they
opposed each other because of race."[10] Most ASP leaders
accepted PAFMECSA's criticisms as an implied mandate to

[8] *Afrika Kwetu,* December 4, 1958.
[9] Zanzibar Protectorate, *Annual Report of the Provincial Administration, 1959* (Zanzibar: Government Printer, 1960), pp. 1-3.
[10] Pan African Freedom Movement of East and Central Africa,
Minutes of the PAFMECA Conference at Zanzibar, 14-15 April, 1959
(mimeograph, n.p., n.d.).

work with the ZNP, at least until independence was achieved.

Some ASP leaders and influential supporters were bitterly opposed to the idea of multi-party unity and advocated withdrawal from the Freedom Committee—even at the expense of antagonizing PAFMECSA. Their disagreement later led to a major split in the ASP and the formation of Zanzibar's third political party, the *Zanzibar and Pemba People's Party* (ZPPP). The heaviest opposition stemmed from a small, highly militant, youth group called the *Zanzibar African Youth Movement* (ZAYM). ZAYM had originally been organized by Jamal Ramadhan, who had become an important member of the ASP Executive Committee, during the racial crisis of 1958. He had formed the group in order to help the party intensify and extend its boycott of Arab and Asian businesses and, as a consequence, ZAYM members were deeply committed to a policy of economic warfare against the ZNP. When the ASP changed its political approach (i.e. abandoned the boycotts and joined the ZNP in the Freedom Committee), Ramadhan and ZAYM were in complete disagreement with the new policy of inter-party unity.[11]

ZAYM conducted a series of public meetings at which Ramadhan and other influential ASP members criticized their party's leadership for the decision to cooperate with the ZNP. Ramadhan also kept up a running attack on the Freedom Committee in his own newspaper, *Agozi* (the African General Organization for Zanzibar Independence). He argued that Afro-Shirazi leaders were destroying the basis of the party's appeal by appearing on the same platform with leaders of the ZNP and by urging ASP followers to forget racial differences. In Ramadhan's view, the political and social differences be-

[11] *Mwangaza*, May 13, 1959.

tween African Zanzibaris and non-African Zanzibaris
were critical. "We are tired of being led by other people
every day. Now we will lead ourselves because we already know that other people want to sit on Africans'
heads forever. And rule them until doomsday. But they
are mistaken. It is not fair for anybody to push himself
forward and want to oppose African progress. We see
that every time we say something or do something, other
people come and sit in front of us. For example, if Africans want independence in 1963, there will emerge people who boast that they are civilized, educated and better than us and give their view that independence
should be in 1960."[12] Ramadhan felt that the sudden
shift in constitutional policy was confusing to the party's
supporters. He urged the party to sever its ties with the
ZNP and return to its former constitutional program.

Ramadhan gained firm support for his views from at
least three separate sources within the Afro-Shirazi movement: YASU, regional and branch leaders, and members of the ASP parliamentary group. YASU's overt political activities were restricted as it was still composed essentially of government servants, but it was widely
known to sympathize with Ramadhan and to support
ZAYM's political activities. Regional and branch leaders
also began to be disenchanted with top party leadership
because they felt that they had not been adequately consulted about the sudden change in party policy. The
disaffection of subordinate leadership, the growing
crowds attending ZAYM meetings, and the gradually increasing circulation of *Agozi* all indicated that Ramadhan's campaign to force the ASP to secede from the Freedom Committee had a considerable popular following.

Ramadhan's third principal source of support came
from members of the ASP's parliamentary group. Some
parliamentarians held moderate or gradualist constitu-

[12] *Agozi*, May 4, 1959.

tional views which led them to disapprove of the Freedom Committee because of its demand for immediate independence in 1960. Just before the Freedom Committee was organized, the ASP had committed itself to a gradualist constitutional policy in a resolution passed at its first annual conference held in early November, 1958.[13] This resolution requested the British Government to name a definite date for the achievement of internal self-government, and added that unless such a date were announced the ASP would seek internal self-government in 1963. Ameri Tajo had emerged at the time as the foremost advocate of this stand, and after the Freedom Committee began he was widely identified with the view that the party ought not to have changed its constitutional policy without first convening another conference. This placed him squarely on the side of Ramadhan.

Tajo's views on the constitutional issue raised by the Freedom Committee were directly opposed to those of ASP President Abeid Karume. Karume was the leading proponent of the Committee and of the militant constitutional policy of independence in 1960 which it espoused. The confrontation of these two men gave the entire issue the complexion of a dispute between Shirazis and Mainlanders. Since there were already tensions between the two groups, arising principally from the difficulties experienced in forming the party, there was an almost natural tendency for them to take opposite sides on any issue. During the Freedom Committee period this tendency was accentuated by several factors. The President of YASU at this time was Othman Sharif who, like other YASU leaders, was strongly opposed personally to ASP cooperation with the ZNP. He was widely suspected of trying to influence his brother, ASP parliamentarian Ali Sharif, to support Tajo. Since all these

13 *Mwangaza*, November 12, 1958.

men were Shirazis, a kind of concerted Shirazi opposition to the Freedom Committee could be said to exist.

The specific incident which brought the crisis of party unity to a head occurred towards the middle of 1959. Tajo accepted a substantial donation from a wealthy Zanzibar philanthropist for the purpose of constructing a new YASU building.[14] Though the donation was purely charitable and Tajo acted only as intermediary, he was criticized by the top party leaders, who felt that his sponsorship of YASU implied public approval of ZAYM, which YASU was supporting. At a large public meeting, Tajo was openly vilified as a traitor and expelled from the ASP. This harsh and humiliating treatment offended the two Shirazi members from Pemba, Mohammed Shamte and Ali Sharif, who resigned from the party in protest. In late 1959 these three men founded the Zanzibar and Pemba People's Party (ZPPP).

Like *Ittihad ul'Umma,* the ZPPP was open to members of all races but specifically designed for those Shirazis who wished to avoid involvement in a heavily Arab-influenced ZNP or a mainland-African ASP. The ZPPP was immediately given the full support of the Pemba Shirazi Association, which had continued to maintain its separate organization throughout the Freedom Committee period. This support was critical to the survival and success of the ZPPP, for the Shirazi Association in effect merged with the ZPPP and became the organizational structure of the party. Thus the ZPPP was born with a full-fledged network of regional and local committees in Pemba.

Though the Freedom Committee dispute, the ensuing quarrel over YASU and finally the expulsion of Tajo were the final causes of the rupture, the formation of the ZPPP really represented the basic inability of Pemba Shirazis and mainland Africans to cooperate in a com-

14 *Mwangaza,* October 14 and 21, 1959.

mon political party. The Pemba leaders wanted to be free of the restrictive anti-Arabism of the ASP, and wanted to pursue their own policies towards the Arabs. In this respect, their personal attitudes towards ASP participation in the Freedom Committee were quite complex. They approved it as an attempt by the party to move toward a multi-racial nationalistic position, but they also realized the extreme reluctance with which most ASP leaders had joined the Committee. They viewed this as a fairly definite indication that the party would imminently resume its old position.

By the time the ZPPP was formed, the honeymoon of the Freedom Committee had practically ended. The Committee had effectively muted any open expression of inter-party conflict. But the basic political and social differences between the parties and the ubiquitous racial and communal fears had been in no way resolved by public protestations of harmony. An announcement that Zanzibar's second general election would be held in July, 1960, led both the ASP and the ZNP to begin disengaging themselves from the Committee. The imminent introduction of a ministerial system now offered control over important departments of the government, and because of such high stakes, the election campaign had to be conducted along vigorous party lines.

The ASP withdrew from the Freedom Committee in early 1960 and attempted to rebuild its weakened organization and faltering membership. The ZPPP split had left the ASP with only two of its five parliamentarians remaining in the party, but of more importance was the loss of the fragile unity between mainland Africans and Shirazis which had been achieved in 1957. The ASP was to enter Zanzibar's second general election in desperate condition—bereft of leadership, divided over policy and torn by internal ethnic conflicts.

The date of the election was postponed from July, 1960, to January, 1961, largely because of administrative difficulties. The 1960 report of Zanzibar's second Constitutional Commissioner, Sir Hilary Blood, had proposed wide constitutional changes which would bring Zanzibar to the stage of "responsible government." Sir Hilary had recommended that Zanzibar's Legislative Council be reconstituted to include a majority of elected members, that the Protectorate be divided into twenty-one single member constituencies, and that a ministerial system be created so that local leaders could exercise the highest executive responsibility.[15] This report was not submitted to the Zanzibar Government until late May. There was not sufficient time to organize all these changes before July, and since Zanzibar's clove harvesting season (entailing widespread migration of voters) normally begins early in August and lasts until early December, it was impractical to conduct the election before early 1961. As a result of the delay, the parties were given an extra six months in which to campaign.

Both major parties campaigned along lines quite similar to those they had adopted in the 1957 election. The ZNP represented itself as a militantly nationalistic and patriotic body. Its election manifesto began with the words: "The Zanzibar Nationalist Party is contesting the election not as a mere party among parties but rather as a MASS LIBERATION MOVEMENT OF THE PEOPLE dedicated to wrest power from the colonial regime. . . . The Zanzibar Nationalist Party is a spontaneous expression of the people who have through painful experience learnt that their only salvation from misery, squalor, poverty and disease lay in NATIONAL INDEPENDENCE."[16] Party leaders gave heaviest em-

[15] Sir Hilary Blood, *Report of the Constitutional Commissioner, Zanzibar, 1960* (Zanzibar: Government Printer, 1960), pp. 1-20.
[16] Zanzibar Nationalist Party, *Election Manifesto* (Zanzibar: Zanzibar Nationalist Party, January, 1961).

phasis to non-racial political doctrines and attempted to discredit racial political thinking. They argued that the economic and social differences between the various communities were the product of seventy years of British colonial government and accused the ASP of assisting colonialism by making a racial appeal. The ethic of multi-racialism also infused the party's domestic program, which was prefaced by a commitment to conduct social and economic programs in a non-discriminatory fashion.

The objective of ZNP campaign doctrine was to foster a non-African sense of national identity. This would help the party to undermine the more communally and class-oriented appeal of the ASP and provide a more receptive environment for its multi-racial views. ZNP propaganda minimized the African content of Zanzibar nationalism by employing a heavy religious and cultural symbolism. Thus, although the party officially endorsed the concepts of "African unity" and "pan-Africanism," its election campaign made greater use of the idea of Zanzibar as a culturally autonomous Islamic state. Party speakers continually implied that the Muslim faith distinguished ZNP nationalism from that of continental Africa and that common religious devotion united Zanzibaris of all communities. Repeated demonstrations of loyalty to the Sultan also played a critical role in the campaign. The ZNP employed these demonstrations to buttress the concept of multi-racial religious solidarity with the added symbolism of a commonly shared institution.

The ASP's campaign was characterized by an intense effort to create a sense of common political identity among Zanzibar's African majority. The party displayed prominently a variety of symbols which dramatized the essential commonality between Zanzibar nationalism and African nationalism, and which identified it exclusively with the Pan African Freedom Movement. The ASP's flag and anthem were copied from those of Tanganyika, pictures of Julius Nyerere and Jomo Kenyatta were placed alongside those of Karume and Kombo, and well-known African leaders from nearby countries were invited to speak at ASP meetings. Since 1957 the party had also brought its constitutional policies into line with those of African nationalist movements and was now seeking immediate evolution towards self-government.

Officially, ASP doctrine declared multi-racialism and loyalty to the Sultan as basic principles, but the party's views on both these questions were much more conditional than those of the ZNP. ASP leaders reemphasized that their party was the political instrument of the deprived African majority, and they stressed heavily the need for a domestic policy which would balance the economic and social privileges of all the racial groups. In a thinly veiled allusion to the Sultanate, ASP leaders also declared that they would not accept either British or Arab colonial institutions as permanent features of Zanzibar society.

The ZPPP made its basic appeal to Shirazi voters. It emphasized the special interests and needs of the Shirazi majority and asserted that these could not be fully represented by either of the major parties. The ZPPP was closer to the ZNP than to the ASP on constitutional, domestic and racial questions; its declared objectives were constitutional monarchy, rapid evolution towards independence, and non-racial government policies. On nearly all these questions, however, the party had difficulty distinguishing itself clearly from its two larger rivals.

The election results revealed concretely that the Freedom Committee and its attendant consequences had done considerable damage to the ASP. Out of twenty-two constituencies (thirteen in Zanzibar, nine in Pemba), the ASP won only ten.[17] Its weakness lay in Pemba, where it received less than one-fourth of the popular vote and won only two seats. The ZNP radically improved its parliamentary position. Though it remained fairly weak in Zanzibar where it gained only five of the thirteen con-

TABLE 10

January, 1961 Election Results

Constituency	ASP	ZNP	ZPPP	Total
Zanzibar Island				
Stone Town North	62	1,109	23	1,194
Stone Town South	52	860	16	928
Darajani	1,400	1,765	27	3,192
Raha Leo	3,100	846	76	4,022
Jangombe	3,028	406	44	3,478
Northern	1,648	2,614	24	4,286
Mkokotoni	3,723	1,209	—	4,932
Mangapwani	1,831	2,049	5	3,885
Chaani	4,052	931	32	5,015
Koani	1,197	748	—	1,945
Chwaka	3,023	1,091	287	4,401
Fuoni	2,064	1,539	24	3,627
Makunduchi	2,315	388	1,388	4,091
Pemba Island				
Konde	255	2,388	1,779	4,422
Wete	932	1,826	683	3,441
Pandani	78	1,786	2,473	4,337
Piki	171	1,445	2,484	4,100
Ziwani	625	2,913	1,684	5,222
Chake Chake	1,538	1,537	819	3,894
Chonga	815	1,094	1,554	3,463
Kengeja	2,190	2,676	1,061	5,927
Mkoani	2,599	1,504	1,058	5,161
Total	36,698	32,724	15,541	84,963

stituencies, it won four seats in Pemba, making a total of nine. The ZNP thus emerged from the election with only one seat less than the ASP (see Table 10).

The most important feature of the election was that the newly formed ZPPP, which won the remaining three

[17] Zanzibar Protectorate, *Reports of the Supervisors of Elections on the Registration of Voters and the Elections held in January, 1961* (Zanzibar: Government Printer, 1961), pp. 60-63.

Pemba seats, held the balance of power and was in a position to decide which of the major parties would form a government. The leaders of each courted the three ZPPP representatives with the objective of forming a coalition. But this raised once more an issue which had so often and so deeply divided Shirazis in the past—whether to join with the ASP or the ZNP.

The three ZPPP members split. The party president, Mohammed Shamte, still smarted from the humiliating and insulting treatment of Tajo by the ASP, and was adamant against cooperating with a party that was led even partially by mainland Africans. He felt that the ZPPP ought to form a coalition government with the ZNP and persuaded a ZPPP representative, Bakari Mohammed (President of the Pemba Shirazi Association), to join him. Ali Sharif, however, refused to accept Shamte's decision and resigned from the ZPPP rather than support a ZNP/ZPPP coalition. He decided to rejoin the ASP. The twenty-two elected representatives were thereby split into two equal camps, neither of which was able to muster a parliamentary majority. An interim caretaker government was formed, and another general election was called for in June. In order to avoid any possibility of another parliamentary deadlock, the government created a twenty-third constituency in southern Pemba.

The only major change in the conduct of this campaign was the formation of an electoral coalition between the ZNP and the ZPPP so that their candidates would not oppose each other within the same constituency. Therefore, there were no three-cornered fights in the June election; in each constituency an ASP candidate was opposed by a candidate from either the ZNP or the ZPPP, but never by both. The parties continued to employ the same appeals which they had used in January, and there were no significant changes of party

TABLE 11

June, 1961 Election Results

Constituency	ASP	ZNP	ZPPP	Total
Zanzibar Island				
Stone Town North	52	1,046		1,098
Stone Town South	62	862		924
Darajani	1,493	1,569		3,062
Raha Leo	3,301	363		3,664
Jangombe	3,162	278		3,440
Northern	1,841	2,792		4,633
Mkokotoni	3,915	1,261		5,176
Mangapwani	1,922	2,174		4,096
Chaani	4,318	965		5,283
Koani	1,325	740		2,065
Chwaka	3,219	1,368		4,587
Fuoni	2,373	1,592		3,965
Makunduchi	2,448		1,852	4,300
Pemba Island				
Konde	1,074	3,576		4,650
Wete	1,384	2,257		3,641
Pandani	2,355		2,278	4,633
Piki	1,548		2,995	4,543
Ziwani	1,100	4,336		5,436
Chake Chake	1,761	2,374		4,135
Chonga	886		2,884	3,770
Mtambile	1,552		2,402	3,954
Kengeja	1,479	2,590		4,069
Mkoani	2,602	1,538		4,140
Total	45,172	31,681	12,411	89,264

strength between the two elections. Even the formation of an electoral alliance between the ZNP and the ZPPP changed the result in only one constituency (see Table 11).[18]

Table 12 indicates the distribution of Legislative Council seats according to party in the January and June elections. What in effect determined the outcome of the June election was a pre-election agreement between the ZNP and the ZPPP that if they gained a majority of the seats they

[18] Zanzibar Protectorate, *Report of the Supervisor of Elections, June, 1961* (Zanzibar: Government Printer, 1961), pp. 27-29.

TABLE 12

Distribution of Seats in the Legislative Council
January and June 1961

PARTY	January			June		
	Zan.	*Pemba*	*Total*	*Zan.*	*Pemba*	*Total*
ASP	8	2	10	8	2	10
ZNP	5	4	9	5	5	10
ZPPP	0	3	3	0	3	3
Total	13	9	22	13	10	23

would form a coalition government. Having won thirteen out of the twenty-three constituencies, they possessed a clear legislative majority and formed a government. The ASP thus became an opposition party.

The election precipitated several days of uncontrol-
lable rioting on Zanzibar Island. There were two separate patterns of violence. Disturbances broke out in
Zanzibar Town early on election day, June 1, and continued until armed reinforcements flown from the mainland helped the Zanzibar police to restore order.[19] These
disturbances consisted principally of street-fighting between ASP and ZNP supporters. Being confined to the urban area and of not very great intensity, they were put
down fairly easily.

On June 2, violence increased radically in intensity
and spread to the rural areas. News of the ZNP victory
and wildly distorted versions of the election-day fighting
had spread to the remoter villages where there were
strong ASP majorities. For several days numerous bands
of Africans roamed the plantation area of Zanzibar Island and looted, pillaged and murdered. Many clove
plantations were devastated. The official death toll was

[19] See Great Britain, *Report of a Commission of Inquiry into Disturbances in Zanzibar during June, 1961* (London: Her Majesty's
Stationery Office, 1961), Colonial No. 353.

placed at sixty-eight, of whom sixty-four were Arabs. Practically all of those killed were Manga Arabs, petty traders and small shopkeepers who lived either on the plantations or in villages in the plantation area. The number of people injured and beaten approached four hundred.

The roots of the trouble lay in the very nature of Zanzibar politics. The entire procession of political events between 1957 and 1961—especially the squatter evictions, labor disputes and economic boycotts of 1958—had engendered hatreds and animosities that persisted long afterwards as an ineradicable feature of competitive party politics.[20] Four particular features of this pattern of development may be singled out as especially relevant causes of the June, 1961, violence.

1). *Since the election of 1957, party and racial conflict had become practically synonymous, for party membership was based essentially on racial divisions. Indeed, members of all communities viewed their party affiliation as a projection of the ethnic hostilities between their own community and others in the society.* The fundamental division was between Arabs and Africans. This pattern was so prevalent that the Swahili terms for Arabs and Africans were used everywhere in the Protectorate as euphemisms to describe the ZNP and ASP respectively. The Arab-African racial dichotomy between the parties was particularly acute in the plantation belt and immediately surrounding areas where violence occurred.

---

[20] The proceedings of the Commission of Inquiry are an invaluable source of information on the development of Zanzibar politics between 1957 and 1961. See, *Commission of Inquiry into Civil Disturbances on 1st June, 1961 and Succeeding Days* (mimeograph, n.p., n.d.). This document, approximately 1,500 pages in length, is a verbatim transcript of the testimony given before the three man investigating committee both by administrative officials and leaders of the three political parties. The author is indebted to Mr. A. L. Pennington of the Office of the Civil Secretary, Zanzibar, for having made this document available.

For although the ZNP had a large African membership, it was concentrated in Pemba and in northern Zanzibar Island. Since the racial differences between the parties were more apparent in and around the fertile area, the economic discrepancies between party supporters were also especially visible. More than anywhere else in the entire Protectorate the clove and coconut plantations contained wealthy, landed Arabs who supported the ZNP and poor, landless Africans who supported the ASP.

2). *A tradition of political violence had long been established in Zanzibar. Violence had become a recurrent method of resolving conflict before the era of nationalism.* Riots involving loss of life had occurred in 1928, 1936 and again in 1951 during the cattle innoculation trials.[21] The assassination of Sultan Mugheiry and forcible squatter evictions were also a part of this violent tradition. Competitive party politics led to a marked increase in the frequency of political violence. This manifested itself in a variety of ways. It became a common practice for youthful extremists in both major parties to participate in heavily armed para-military youth wings which would bait and assault members and leaders of the opposite party.[22] Attempts to gain votes through in-

[21] There is no published report on the riots of 1928. These involved a sort of private blood feud between Omani and Manga Arabs. Long-standing tensions between these two groups were touched off when a prominent Omani family failed to invite some influential Manga Arabs to a wedding. The 1936 riots were indirectly related to the indebtedness problem. The colonial administration attempted to impose quality controls on the export of cloves and copra (dried coconut meat) in an effort to gain the highest available prices on world markets. Manga Arabs felt that this was an attempt to force them out of the coconut drying industry and attacked the offices of the Department of Agriculture and the CGA. See: Zanzibar Protectorate, *Report of the Commission of Enquiry Concerning the Riot in Zanzibar on the 7th of February, 1936.* (Zanzibar: Government Printer, 1936).

[22] There is an extensive account of the activities of these youth groups in Zanzibar Protectorate, *Papers Laid Before the Legislative Council, 1959,* Sessional Paper No. 7, "Report of the Select Com-

timidation and coercion were also frequent and several candidates were badly beaten during both the January and June, 1961, election campaigns. Violence was a natural corollary of the diffusion of political conflict into all realms of social life. By 1961 it had become so commonplace that under the atmosphere of hysteria engendered by two successive election campaigns, conventional restraints against violent behavior broke down.

3). *The Manga Arabs had figured prominently in the entire pattern of violence in Zanzibar, and thus their community was singled out to bear the brunt of the June riots.* Manga Arabs had instigated the earlier riots of 1928 and 1936, and had acquired a universal reputation as a violently inclined community. Because of this reputation, the Manga Arabs became widely (and erroneously) known as the secret military wing of the znp. During the racial crisis of 1958 it appeared to Africans that Manga Arabs were to blame for the squatter evictions, for in numerous cases landowners justified the expulsions on the grounds that the squatters were boycotting Manga shops. In a few instances, members of the Manga community fell heir to the land from which Africans had been removed. Their reputation as a znp militia, their implied role as accomplices in the squatter evictions, plus the normal frictions inherent in the relationship between farmer and shopkeeper classes made the Manga community an object of intense resentment to many Africans. This resentment together with the Manga Arabs' exposed and isolated position as rural shopkeepers probably accounts for the large number of Manga deaths.

4). *Although the parties differed on a variety of policy questions, their appeals to the electorate were based on*

---

mittee Appointed to Enquire into the Public Order Bill" (Zanzibar: Government Printer, 1960), pp. 33-44.

symbolic rather than programmatic differences. Much of the election campaigning was of a singularly intemperate sort, exploiting both racial and religious fears. The Commission of Inquiry appointed to investigate the riots regarded this factor as the basic reason for the outbreak of violence. Its report commented that ". . . the major cause was the bombardment of words, both written and spoken, which the people of Zanzibar were subjected to more or less continuously after the first General Election of July, 1957."[23]

The ZNP/ZPPP coalition had sought to portray the ASP as an agency of pernicious alien forces. The principal feature of this campaign was an attempt to stigmatize the ASP by identifying it with a penetration of mainland African religious influence into Zanzibar, and it portrayed the ASP as a party covertly supported and dominated by foreign Christian interests. In speech after speech, spokesmen of the ZNP/ZPPP asserted that if the ASP were elected, it would convert Zanzibar to Christianity and hand it over to Tanganyika. The following quotations have been excerpted from some ZNP campaign speeches made just before the riots: "The ASP is fighting for Tanganyika. (Name of important Tanganyikan leader) wants to introduce Christianity into our country and abolish Islam."[24] "It is ASP policy to bring mainlanders into Zanzibar to dominate, spread Christianity, and to suppress the Muslim faith."[25] "The ASP aim is to sell this country to Tanganyika, bring Christianity

[23] *Report of a Commission of Inquiry,* Colonial No. 353, p. 24.

[24] As a normal measure of security and intelligence, police officials in Zanzibar attended party meetings and recorded speeches in shorthand and on tape. These recordings and transcriptions were made available to the Commission of Inquiry during its visit in Zanzibar. They form a large portion of the documents submitted in evidence before the Commission and a part of the record of its proceedings. The speeches will be referred to by place and date. This speech was given at Mkoani, Pemba on April 13, 1961.

[25] Dunga, Zanzibar, April 27, 1961.

into Zanzibar and to destroy the Islamic religion."[26]
"The ASP is built on hatred. They want to bring in im-
migrants and create unemployment and starvation.
(ASP leaders) visited Tanganyika and returned with
Christian books. The ASP does not want the Sultan."[27]

These same themes were reiterated in the ZNP press. In
an article on the problem of unemployment, *Mwongozi*
commented: "There is work for thousands of citizens,
but we have been overpowered by foreigners. . . . This
has happened because there is not a good system of immigration in this country—the door is open to a certain
race from our neighboring countries. Confusion reigns;
the rights of citizens are enjoyed by aliens; and the
indigenes have no work."[28] And on the issue of domination by Tanganyika, *Mwongozi* commented: "We have
given publicity to a statement by (ZPPP leader) . . .
about a conversation with (Tanganyikan leader). (Latter) stressed the ease with which he could dispose of the
existing dynastic and administrative setup and rule the
Protectorate from Dar es Salaam with the assistance of
one D.C. It will be recalled further that it was the dis-
covery of these plans which brought (ZPPP leader) onto
the side of the ZNP, because he knew that the ASP (his
former party) was ready to sell Zanzibar to her enemies."[29]

The ASP's campaign was based largely upon establishing an identity between the ZNP and the Arab oligarchy.
This idea appeared in one form or another in the great
majority of ASP speeches, and there were very few ASP meetings at which the term ZNP was not used as a synonym for
Arab political domination. The real emotional force of
this issue lay not so much in the mere possibility that a ra-

---

[26] Uzini, Zanzibar, May 21, 1961.
[27] Chake, Pemba, April 13, 1961.
[28] *Mwongozi,* November 18, 1960.
[29] *Mwongozi,* April 21, 1961.

cial oligarchy would preserve itself as in the historical association between Arab rule and slavery. The character of
any prospective Arab-led government was envisioned by
ASP leaders and supporters in terms of the brutalities and
horrors of slavery.

Imagery about the cruelty of slavery was so widespread and well known among ASP supporters that party
speakers did not often refer to it directly in their
speeches. The ASP press played an important role in
keeping this imagery alive. A stylized version of the history of slavery became a prominent editorial topic in the
final weeks before the June election. One African newspaper, *Sauti ya Afro-Shirazi* (The Voice of the Afro-
Shirazis), carried the following item as a commentary on
an ASP public meeting. "Today we would like to . . . re-
mind our African brethren who are insisting on helping
the Arabs . . . (of) the actions done by the Arabs during
their time alone. The Arabs made the people sweep
with their breasts; the Arabs pierced the wombs of the
women who were pregnant so that their wives could see
how a baby was placed. The Arabs shaved the peoples'
hair and then used their heads as places for knocking
their toothbrushes. The Arabs made the people cas-
trated like cows so that they might converse with their
wives without wanting them. The Arabs made the African old men chew palm nuts without breaking them in
order that they may laugh."[30] These stories and many
others like them pervaded the African villages and the
rural areas. African old-timers presented them to
younger fellow-villagers as personally verified experiences of extreme physical suffering under Arab overlordship. Direct person-to-person repetition of such
stories endowed them with a legendary authenticity,
and created an atmosphere of apprehension and terror
far greater than could ever have been aroused in the

[30] *Sauti ya Afro-Shirazi,* May 5, 1961.

209

more ebullient environment of an open public meeting.

This type of campaigning was significant as much for its duration and intensity as for its content. Since it had originally been anticipated that an election would be held in mid-1960, the parties began to campaign early that year. The postponement of the election from July, 1960, to January, 1961, and the need to hold a second election in June, 1961, added a full year of heavy campaigning. The final result was that competitive propaganda activities were carried out on a daily basis for nearly a year and a half. Throughout this period, the parties went to further and further extremes to find ways of stimulating flagging interest. With each successive delay desperation increased and the parties became more and more acrimonious in their attacks on one another.

The extraordinary dimensions of propaganda activity are best indicated by the sheer size of Zanzibar's partisan press. At the time of the riots, Zanzibar possessed twenty-three daily or weekly newspapers, sixteen of which were associated with or directly sponsored by the various political parties and their affiliated organizations. Table 13 lists the partisan newspapers and their approximate circulation. Though absolute circulation figures may seem low, these newspapers were almost invariably passed from hand to hand many times before being disposed of. And, since so many Zanzibaris were illiterate, the newspapers were frequently read aloud before substantial groups of people. Thus, the audience reached by their circulation was far greater than the number of copies printed would appear to indicate.

Few of these newspapers were actual news media in the usual sense of that term. Very little of their contents pertained to the transmission and dissemination of information about the day-to-day events of a current political process. Zanzibar's newspapers could be compared to partisan pamphleteering more than to anything else.

TABLE 13

Partisan Newspapers at Time of Riots

NEWSPAPER	Political Affiliation	Frequency of Publication	Approx. Circulation	Language
Afrika Kwetu	ASP	Weekly-Thurs.	1,039	English & Kiswahili
Mkombozi	ASP	Sat. & Wed.	1,100	Kiswahili
Kipanga	ASP	Daily	300	Kiswahili
Z. News Agency	ZNP	Daily	1,000	English & Kiswahili
Kibarua	ZNP	Daily	400	Kiswahili
Worker	ZNP	Daily	400	English
Jasho Letu	ASP	Irregular	400	Kiswahili
Sauti Ya Jogoo	ZNP (Pemba)	Irregular	400	Kiswahili
Al Falaq	ZNP	Fortnightly	500	Arabic & English
Mwongozi	ZNP	Weekly (Fri.)	1,000	Kiswahili, English & Arabic
Adal Insaf	ZNP	Weekly-Sat.	500	Gujerati, English & Kiswahili
Mwangaza	ASP	Weekly (Wednes.)	350	English & Kiswahili
Agozi	ASP	Weekly-Mon.	300	Kiswahili
Sauti ya Afro-Shirazi	ASP	Weekly-Mon.	300	Kiswahili
Umma	ZNP	Daily	1,000	Kiswahili
Sauti ya Wananchi	ZNP	Daily	500	Kiswahili

They were purchased and read on almost exclusively party lines, and performed a symbolic rather than a communication function. Their content was strictly editorial and consisted basically of a constant repetition of party symbols, myths and stereotypes. Their basic purpose was to reaffirm the convictions and the loyalty of party supporters and thereby to strengthen an already existing commitment.

The immediate aftermath of the June riots was a national state of emergency. Colonial authorities feared a repetition of the violence and decided to assume special powers to deal with any crisis that might arise. British troops were stationed on Zanzibar Island and for the next twenty months made daily patrols to maintain order in the rural areas. A series of emergency decrees was enacted which gave the British Resident personal authority to forbid any partisan activity and to suspend any publication which he felt might ignite violence or reinflame racial feelings. These decrees muted overt political conflict; there were almost no mass meetings or other activities of campaign type, and the tone of the local press subsided sharply. Because of a constitutional disagreement between the ZNP/ZPPP Government and the Opposition ASP, it was widely expected that there would not be another election for at least three years. The parties themselves were not anxious to resume their competitive campaigning at once.

The Government and Opposition disagreed profoundly over the priorities and timing for the next stage of constitutional advance. The two coalition parties argued that their clear parliamentary majority of thirteen to ten was equivalent to a popular mandate, and that they should therefore be entrusted to carry Zanzibar through the remaining stages of constitutional change. They argued that internal self-government and independence ought to occur immediately and should therefore precede the holding of Zanzibar's next election, which was not scheduled to be held until mid-1964.[31]

Opposition leaders insisted that an election was necessary to determine which political party would lead the country into internal self-government and independ-

[31] See: Colonial Office, *Report of the Zanzibar Constitutional Conference, 1962* (London: Her Majesty's Stationery Office, 1962), Cmnd. 1699.

ence. They argued that since the ASP had received slightly more votes than the two coalition parties combined, the Government's parliamentary majority did not constitute a popular mandate. The Opposition also asserted that there was no constitutional justification for proceeding immediately to internal self-government. Sir Hilary Blood's 1960 Constitutional Report had declared explicitly that the governmental and legislative changes it suggested were not intended to furnish Zanzibar with the institutional foundation for any advance beyond responsible government. It had said: "My recommendations are such as to allow a ministerial system to be introduced, not to create an internally self-governing state."[32] The ASP interpreted this to mean that further executive and legislative changes were necessary, and its declared position was that these would be meaningless unless a new government were chosen to implement them.

This disagreement sprang from more deeply rooted fears on both sides. The ASP was afraid that if the ZNP ever came to preside over an independent Zanzibar, it would employ all the resources of the state—finances, propaganda, police control and patronage—to consolidate its position. Further, unless the British Government were present to supervise the next election, there could be no adequate guarantee that it would be conducted along fair and impartial lines. The ZNP was concerned that it might not be able to win another election. Its percentage of the popular vote had dropped noticeably between the January and June, 1961 elections, and the ASP was exploiting the ZNP's popular weakness in an intense effort to win over the ZPPP representatives.

These fears pervaded a major constitutional conference held in London in late March and early April of 1962. Both Government and Opposition parties clung to

[32] Blood, *Report of the Constitutional Commissioner,* p. 6.

their original positions and were unwilling to compromise. The British Government urged a coalition government of all three parties, but negotiations over this proposal also broke down. The ZNP/ZPPP offered the ASP three out of nine ministerial positions and a veto over all cabinet decisions; the ASP wanted parity membership in the cabinet and continued to insist that an election must be held before independence.[33] The efforts of the Secretary of State for the Colonies, Mr. Duncan Sandys, failed to resolve this dispute.

In early spring of 1963, Sandys visited Zanzibar in a further effort to end the constitutional deadlock. He wanted Zanzibar's independence to be accelerated so that it could be timed to coincide closely with that of Kenya. After consultations with leaders of all the parties had again failed to produce any agreement, he decided to impose a compromise plan whereby constitutional progress might be resumed. According to the terms of this compromise, internal self-government would be introduced in late June and followed just two weeks later by a general election in early July. The granting of full independence, however, would await the outcome of the election.

There was very little to distinguish the parties' formal campaigns in 1963 from those of 1957 or 1961. Both employed the same clusters of opposing symbols that had initially been developed just prior to Zanzibar's first election. The ZNP contrasted its idea of Zanzibar as an Islamic multi-racial society to the ASP's concept of Zanzibar as an emerging African state. The ZNP/ZPPP coalition had hardened into a virtual merger of the two parties, and there was now no visible difference between their appeals to the electorate.

Leaders and supporters of all the parties realized that

[33] Great Britain, "ASP Letter to Mr. Daniels," *Proceedings of the March, 1962, Constitutional Conference* (Mimeograph, n.p., n.d.).

since this was the last election before independence, victory would give the winning party a powerful advantage in the competition for permanent control over the government. Popular feeling therefore ran very high, and as in 1961, there was widespread apprehension and fear about the consequences of defeat. Policy differences between the parties again reflected racial stratification and not degrees of liberalism or conservatism within the society. Despite this, parties' campaigns were far more subdued in intensity than those of 1961.

The comparatively temperate election campaign stemmed partly from the government's severe restriction of all public meetings and its close surveillance of the local newspapers. In larger measure it stemmed from the fact that by 1963 the basic ideological position of each party had become well known and the popular following of each had become highly stabilized; there was very little that any form of propaganda activity could do to change the voting patterns of significant segments of the population. The parties therefore concentrated their energies on more organizational activities. They sought to secure the registration of as many of their supporters as possible, and tried to form a local organizational structure which could actually get out the vote on election day.

The quiet, indeed almost silent quality of the campaign concealed the fact that, with independence approaching, the parties had become deeply divided over a number of basic issues of public policy (see Table 14). Of these, land reform and Zanzibarization of the civil service stood out as having special importance. The ASP had indicated its basic position on these questions at the March, 1962, Constitutional Conference. Othman Sharif said: "Economically, socially and politically the distribution is rather in the inverse proportion to the population [gave population figures]. . . . Suffice it to say that some 80% of the fertile land and the bulk of the

TABLE 14

Basic Political Issues

ISSUES	ASP	ZNP/ZPPP
The Sultanate	Official declaration of loyalty; emotional commitment was highly conditional; some leaders were openly opposed to monarchical government.	Official declaration of loyalty; strong emotional commitment.
Pan-Africanism	Consistent official support; high emotional commitment. Strong organizational ties to Pan-African movements.	Official support. Conditional emotional commitment by ZNP; ZPPP was indifferent. ZNP had organizational ties but its leaders resented implied African support for ASP.
East African Federation	Very strongly in favor, on both economic and political grounds.	Officially in favor; emotional commitment was negative. Both coalition parties offered strong economic and political reasons for loose form of association and maximum local autonomy.
Coastal Strip	Cede to Kenya.	Cede to Kenya; sought guarantee of religious protection for Muslim population.
Immigration and Naturalization.	Favored open immigration from mainland; easy citizenship for mainland Africans.	Favored restrictive immigration policies. Instituted expensive and difficult naturalization process.
Land Reform	Redistribution of some fertile land to Africans.	Emphasis on nonracial policies.
Zanzibarization of Civil Service	Sought policy of recruiting more Africans into higher levels of administration.	Emphasis on nonracial policies.

trade and industry are in the hands of the minority, and that practically all the administrative positions of importance are occupied by them. This state of affairs calls for

adjustment and change."[34] ASP leaders wanted a concerted land redistribution program which would adjust
the radical imbalance of ownership between Arab and
African landowners.

ASP views on civil service recruitment were borrowed
in part from an egalitarian social ethic that had first
been developed in Tanganyika.[35] The ASP stressed that
under existing social and economic conditions Africans
would never be able to compete equally for administrative posts, for the educational advantages of Arabs and
Asians placed the children of these groups in a superior
competitive position. This, in the ASP's view, led to a
vicious cycle: the Arab and Asian communities maintained their middle and upper class position by monop-
olizing all the top occupational positions available; this,
in turn, led to disproportionate educational advantages
and the cycle repeated itself. ASP spokesmen asserted that
this cycle had to be broken artificially, if necessary. They
argued that in order to create a genuinely egalitarian
social system Africans must, for a time, be given special
preference for top posts. This would begin to create an
African middle class whose children would enjoy equal
access to higher education. Once this new African middle
class had taken on a self-perpetuating quality, special
preferences to Africans could be abandoned.

The ZNP disagreed completely with the ASP's views
on both these questions. The ZNP leaders asserted that
both a land redistribution program and artifical recruitment of Africans into the civil service would involve the
government in conducting policy along basically racial

[34] Great Britain, *Proceedings of the March, 1962, Constitutional
Conference*. Mr. Sharif's speech was made on the opening day.

[35] The author wishes to thank ASP leaders Othman Sharif and
Aboud Jumbe for their clear expression of their party's views on
these matters.

lines. They insisted that any policy which was based on an official recognition of racial differences was against

TABLE 15

1963 Election Results

CONSTITUENCY	*ASP*	*ZNP*	*ZPPP*	*Total*
Zanzibar Island				
Forodhani	175	2,403		2,578
Shangani	396	2,391		2,787
Mlandege	2,736	3,135		5,871
Kikwajuni	4,062	1,203		5,265
Mwembeladu	5,066	809		5,875
Kwahani	5,701		216	5,917
Nungwi	2,615	3,198		5,813
Tumbatu	2,310	3,667		5,977
Donge	4,564	545		5,109
Chaani	3,908	1,147		5,055
Mangapwani	1,898	3,290		5,188
Kiboje	2,958	618		3,576
Dole	2,965	1,518		4,483
Chwaka	3,785	720		4,505
Fuoini	3,534	1,928		5,462
Jozani	3,818		1,631	5,449
Makunduchi	2,741		2,725	5,466
Pemba Island				
Konde	1,585	3,565		5,150
Tumbe	1,810		2,971	4,781
Wingwi	4,390		1,705	6,095
Wete	2,719	3,140		5,859
Piki	2,563		2,756	5,319
Shengejuu	2,042		3,581	5,623
Ziwani	1,793	3,038		4,831
Ole	1,634	3,897		5,531
Chake Chake	2,347	2,627		4,974
Pujini	2,746		2,983	5,729
Chambani	1,569		3,469	5,038
Kengeja	2,573	3,506		6,079
Mtambile	1,913		3,572	5,485
Mkoani	4,169	1,605		5,774
Total	87,085	47,950	25,609	160,644[a]

[a] Represents the total *valid* vote cast. Over 165,000 people voted, but about 5,000 ballots were invalidated for insufficient marking, double marking, no marking, tearing, etc.

the basic multi-racial philosophy of their party. Indeed, their foremost campaign promise in all elections was that the ZNP would initiate no government policy that discriminated between Zanzibar's various racial communities. Beneath the surface of an almost silent election campaign, differing party viewpoints on these two issues represented an irreducible residue of hostility and antagonism between the ASP and the ZNP/ZPPP.

In preparation for Zanzibar's independence election, the country was divided into thirty-one constituencies, seventeen in Zanzibar and fourteen in Pemba. The election was conducted on the basis of universal adult suffrage and approximately 165,000 people, more than half of the total population of the Protectorate, registered and voted (see Table 15).[36]

A poll of over 99 per cent was concrete evidence of ubiquitous concern over the outcome. It also reflected the widely held belief that this election would determine the future rulers of Zanzibar, since the victorious party would be likely to consolidate and entrench its position after independence.

TABLE 16

Distribution of Seats in the Legislative Council—July, 1963

PARTY	*Zanzibar*	*Pemba*	*Protectorate*
ASP	11	2	13
ZNP	6	6	12
ZPPP	0	6	6
Total	17	14	31

The coalition of the ZNP and ZPPP gained a total of eighteen seats, the ZNP winning six in Zanzibar and six in Pemba, the ZPPP gaining six seats, all in Pemba (see Table 16). The death blow to the ASP was that it won only two of the fourteen Pemba constituencies. The

[36] Zanzibar Information Office, *Press Release on the Results of the July, 1963, Election* (Zanzibar: mimeograph, 1963).

significant feature of the election was that although the ZNP/ZPPP alliance gained a majority of five in the National Assembly, the ASP won more than 54 per cent of the popular vote.

The ASP's massive popular following led to considerable speculation that a three-party "national" government would be formed. In the despair of defeat many top ASP leaders viewed this as a more fruitful course of action than simply to form a parliamentary opposition. An ASP delegation began to negotiate with the ZNP/ZPPP over a possible three-way distribution of ministerial portfolios. The ZNP/ZPPP leaders, however, proved extremely reluctant to allow the ASP to help form a Government. They argued that they had offered the ASP an opportunity to form an all-party coalition at the 1962 London Constitutional Conference, but had been turned down.

Prime Minister Shamte offered the ASP only one possibility of joining the Government; he demanded that the ASP be dissolved completely and that its parliamentary representatives apply for membership in the ZPPP on an individual basis. The ASP interpreted Shamte's statement as the equivalent of a flat refusal to form a "national" government; at any rate the condition was so harsh and extreme that it was automatically rejected. This ended all the negotiations between the parties and created an even deeper bitterness among ASP leaders and supporters.

CHAPTER VIII

Voting Behavior and Party Organization

The ZNP/ZPPP Government had many characteristics indicative of enduring political stability. The parliamentary coalition of the two parties had proven to be extremely viable during the two years of its operation, and there was no indication at all that the ZPPP leaders were tempted to break with the ZNP and rejoin their former party. ZNP and ZPPP leaders were united not only by their mutual hostility towards the ASP, but by common attitudes on a whole series of symbolic and programmatic policy issues. Despite the ASP's popular majority, the ZNP/ZPPP coalition had won two successive general elections, gained a sizeable parliamentary majority, and would moreover be in control of the state upon the attainment of independence.

The decisive electoral victories of the ZNP/ZPPP coalition were the result of several intimately related factors. The nature and geographical distribution of voting support for the three parties was such that although the ASP was a majority party, the ZNP/ZPPP had every prospect of a continued parliamentary majority. There were vast differences both in the parties' organizational effectiveness and in their ability to appeal successfully to an economically and ethnically diverse population. And on these latter grounds, too, the ZNP/ZPPP possessed marked advantages.

The portentous feature of the two 1961 elections was the emergence of the ZNP as a major national political power. Since its utter defeat in 1957 the ZNP had nearly doubled its share of the popular vote and was now able to command electoral majorities in nearly half of the constituencies. This development reflected the success of more than three years spent in intense organizational activity, as a result of which the party had entered the 1961 elections as a highly disciplined, well financed and organizationally integrated body. Its swelling popularity was evidence as well of the party's growing ability to capture the mood of Zanzibaris with multiple political and religious appeals. Moreover, an almost unanimous confidence among ZNP supporters in the virtues and policies of the party leadership endowed the ZNP with a unique spirit of optimism and solidarity.

The ASP had emerged from the 1961 elections in undisputed possession of the largest single popular following. An increase of nearly seven per cent of the valid vote cast between January and June gave the ASP a slight majority of the electorate. It received over 54 per cent of the votes cast in the July, 1963, election and gained 13,000 more votes than the coalition parties combined. Its failure to translate this vast electoral support into a proportionate number of seats in the National Assembly is due to a variety of factors. The delimitation of constituencies favored the ZNP, which in 1961 won three seats with votes of less than 2,000 as opposed to one such seat won by the ASP. In both 1961 and 1963 elections, the ZNP was able to win easily in the two Stonetown constituencies which have a very small number of voters. The ASP was also hurt by the success of the ZNP/ZPPP electoral alliance which gave coalition candidates of either party additional non-ASP voters to draw upon in close constituencies. Finally, the ASP had been continually unable to command the financial and technological resources necessary to the conduct of a modern, nationwide campaign.

Structurally there were no major differences between the ASP and the ZNP. Each was composed of an ascending hierarchy of branches, branch committees and regional councils, at the apex of which stood the party executive.[1]

[1] Virtually all the descriptive materials on party organization in

Each party had organized a youth league and a women's section which functioned under the loose supervision of the national executive, and both had established official relations with trade unions. Both parties also operated a form of double national executive committee—a pure party executive and an expanded executive which included representatives of its youth movement and affiliated trade unions. After the formation of an electoral alliance and coalition government between the ZNP and ZPPP, the ZNP's expanded executive also came to include the parliamentary leaders and general secretary of its political partner. Both parties also instituted vigorously democratic procedures for the selection of all party officers at local, regional and national levels. All these similarities notwithstanding, vast differences in organizational strength and effectiveness separated the two parties.

The ZNP possessed an enormous political advantage in the power and refinement of its party structure. Though it was never more than a minority party, its better organization enabled it to make maximum use of a limited popular following. This organizational superiority did not stem from any simple difference in its formal constitution, but from the fact that its membership and leadership alike were infused with a spirit of militancy and dedication. This spirit was accompanied by a zealous and relentless devotion to the day-to-day tasks of fund raising, political propaganda, and membership recruitment. Unremitting attention to the smallest details of organizational solidarity transformed the ZNP from an electoral caucus of like-minded notables into a crusading instrument of anti-colonial nationalism. In the ZNP's progression from total defeat to national prominence, no other single factor was of such decisive importance as the excellence of its organization.

this chapter have been obtained through personal interviews with the leaders of the political parties.

The 1957 election had been a major catalyst to the development of this organization. The totality of the ZNP's defeat dispelled any lingering illusions about the ease of recruiting a multi-racial party and focused the attentions of party leaders directly on the task of creating a more effective electoral apparatus. From that very early moment in its history, the party was spurred to recruit new leaders and organizers among Zanzibar's educated elite. As a result, from 1957 onwards the ZNP benefited from a steady influx of young journalists, teachers and government servants, and soon became a party richly endowed with organizational skill—a resource not duplicated by any of the other parties.

Throughout its period of gestation and subsequently, the ZNP has enjoyed the nearly unanimous support of Zanzibar's plantation-owning class. This group, mainly Arab, has been of crucial assistance to party development in the rural areas. More financially independent than either the squatter-farmer or small-farmer communities and therefore free of the necessity of daily labor, this leisure class has been able to devote considerable time to political activities. As liaison between city and country and in the execution of their party's organizational policies, they furnished the ZNP with the equivalent of a full-time professional staff.

The organization was built from the center outwards; its local branches and committees were set up in an organizing campaign which emanated from the party's urban nucleus. Even the ZNP's trade union affiliate at this time, the *Federation of Progressive Trade Unions* (FPTU), owed its origin to the party's program of building a nationwide network of branches and affiliated bodies. This pattern of development enabled the top leadership to allow complete procedural democracy at the local levels while at the same time reserving for itself the greatest possible degree of autonomy. For the party's organizers were, from the start, in a position to specify the range of activities of local branches, restricting the discretion of local leaders to matters of organization-building and recruitment. They thereby retained for the central executive an unfettered flexibility of decision-making on matters of policy and tactics.

Certain distinctive structural features of the ZNP helped the party maintain the tightest unity within its now massive network of branches and among its far flung and disparate membership. One such feature was the party's practice of convening all branch secretaries in a weekly meeting attended by a representative of the national executive. This arrangement facilitated rapid two-way communication between branches and top leaders, keeping the party executive continuously informed of the state of affairs in the local areas and serving as a primary instrument for the dissemination of party policies throughout the organization. A result of still more importance was that the weekly meeting of branch secretaries engendered among local party leaders a strong sense of the party as a nationwide organization with national objectives. This all-pervasive sense of national purpose discouraged wasteful jealousies and rivalries between regional interests within the party.

The party also convened a weekly meeting of all the branch committees of Zanzibar Town. At first glance this practice might appear superfluous in the light of the branch secretaries' meeting. However, its function was altogether different: while the party's youth movement, *Youths Own Union* (YOU), and the FPTU had numerous members in the rural areas, it was in the city that these two bodies were most actively involved in party affairs. The frequent meetings of urban branch committees served to integrate youth leaders and trade unionists into the overall party structure.

The most impressive structural feature of the ZNP was

its administration of numerous philanthropic and benevolent operations. Through an elaborate system of
interlocking party subcommittees and voluntary groups
the party engaged in a ceaseless round of these para-
political activities. Its programs of charity and welfare
work, medical care and adult education were so extensive as to place the ZNP in competition with the government itself as a dispenser of social services. These activities furnished the party with a superb medium for the
recruitment of new members. They had an even greater
significance for the internal functioning of the party
organization, for administration of philanthropic and
benevolent services absorbed the energies and attention
of innumerable minor leaders and officials. This had
exactly the same consequences for the operation of the
party structure as did the restriction of local leadership
in matters of organization: namely, to endow the top
leadership of the executive committee with virtually
unchallenged authority over matters of party policy and
tactics.

The origin of the ZNP as a rural protest movement
was dramatized by its custom of reserving the highest
party offices—the presidency and vice-presidency—for
the founder members of *Hizbu l'Watan l'Riaia Sultan
Zanzibar*. As a result, these posts were solely honorary
and their holders had little actual influence on decision
making. The ZNP President, Vuai Kiteweo (a Shirazi),
continued to reside in his home village of Jambiani,
traveled to party meetings in the city only infrequently,
and took little part in party affairs. The acknowledged
and certainly most influential leader, Ali Muhsin, held
no official party position other than member of the
Executive Committee. This complete separation of formal office from effective influence gave decision-making
within the ZNP its distinctive quality as a collegial and
consensual process; since there was no role within the

executive which afforded its occupant any special authority over party policy there was no struggle for power over the purely ceremonial posts. Effective influence was purely a matter of ability to persuade one's colleagues.

Collegial decision-making led to a highly valued consensus on the collective responsibility of Executive Committee members for the party's policies. The most serious offense against the party was to violate that consensus by public criticism of party principles or leaders. As a result any conflict over issues was contained within the Executive Committee, policies had the unanimous public endorsement of leadership, and party followers were inspired with the solidarity of their cause. The ethic of collective responsibility enabled the ZNP Executive Committee to maintain effective party unity despite a severe ideological split which divided the top party leaders into two warring factions. The larger faction was led by Ali Muhsin, the minority faction by the General Secretary, Abdul Rahman Mohammed (Babu). These men disagreed bitterly over the proper philosophical foundation for the party's organizational and propaganda activity.

Muhsin's personal outlook was a combination of liberal Islamic reformism and a patriotically inspired nationalism. As a deeply religious person, he continually sought to base the party's social doctrines and its anti-colonialism on Koranic principles and to infuse the outlook of other party leaders with his own religiosity. Babu's social and political views were Marxist in inspiration. He was personally attracted to the revolutionary anti-colonial ethos of Communist China and sought continually to move the party away from its religious foundation towards a strict socialist viewpoint on domestic and international issues.

Muhsin and Babu performed very different roles in the party and this to some extent accounted for their different bases of support within the party structure. Muhsin's principal intra-party function was to mediate between the various ethnic communities from which the party drew its electoral support, and this enabled him to gain the confidence of those sectors of the party structure directly concerned with securing and maintaining its mass popular base. He was supported by practically the entire parliamentary group and virtually all the regional and branch leadership, so that he and his followers possessed a clear majority of the party's executive committee.

Babu's function was to build the party into an effective electoral apparatus. His principal activities were therefore devoted to expanding the ZNP's structural strength; he organized the regional and branch committees on a systematic basis, he presided over the formation of most of the affiliated organizations and personally recruited their personnel, and he enlisted international support and stimulated the party to establish legations in Egypt, Cuba and China. As General Secretary, he was the ZNP's principal strategist in its dual war against the British colonial government and the ASP. Though Babu was perhaps the chief architect of the ZNP's successive electoral victories, his support among the parliamentary group and from rank and file membership was small. Few of the party's influential leaders accepted his militant views. His principal support came from the leaders of the ZNP's ancillary bodies, particularly its trade unionist movement, the FPTU, and its youth league, the YOU. These groups had little strength on the Executive Committee, however, and Babu and his supporters were consistently unable to win the party over from its dominantly religious viewpoint to a more socialist appeal to the electorate.

The ZNP's appeal to Zanzibaris was dictated by the context of bitterly divided nationalisms, in which Islamic religion provided the only potential bond between members of all racial communities. It sought to present party affiliation as the sole allegiance consistent with the principles of the Faith and as the inevitable accompaniment to religious piety. Multi-racialism, loyalty to the Sultanate, and patriotism have all been expressed in the religious idiom, particularly in the rural areas where religious sentiments are strong.

The most constant theme of the ZNP press and of its public speakers was that Zanzibaris of every race must unite in common struggle. Party spokesmen stressed the spiritual meaning of this policy by quoting the Koranic precepts on the divine purpose of racial multiplicity. Deep spiritual meaning was also given to its role as "guardian of the Sultanate," which the party portrayed as a religious obligation due to established authority. Commonly regarded as the preferred party of the Royal Family, the ZNP benefited both from the high esteem in which the Sultan was held by the public and from the belief that political loyalty is the sacred duty of devout believers. Party ideology frequently identified the ZNP as the defender of Islam in a Muslim country threatened by powerful Christian enemies, and envisioned the consequence of its electoral defeat as the destruction of the Islamic faith in Zanzibar. Where these appeals were successful, the ZNP enjoyed a commitment which was highly religious in character and which was the product of a conviction that the political philosophy of the party embodied the social and moral teachings of Islam.

The appeal of the ZNP had a more political connotation in Zanzibar Township. In three key municipal constituencies the party was dependent upon majorities of Asian and Comorian descent, voters whose advantageous positions in government and commerce and whose status as minority aliens made them deeply apprehensive about the future. Here, the multi-racial composition of the party based solely on Zanzibar citizenship was stressed, and special emphasis was given to the fact that its policies did not interpret Zanzibar's social structure in racial terms. The plain implication that social change must not occur at the expense of deliberate discrimination against immigrant ethnic minorities was clearly suited to ease Asian, Arab and Comorian fears of government policies which might give special economic priority to socially underprivileged racial groups.

The ZNP assertion that Zanzibar citizenship was the chief political virtue attracted many Shirazis to its cause. Insistence on this point of ideology served to permeate its nationalistic ethic with a spirit of patriotic loyalty to country that provided Shirazis with political outlets for expressing their cultural pride in being the first Zanzibaris. By dramatizing the alien and potentially disloyal character of its main rival, the ASP, it furnished those Shirazis in competition with mainland Africans for employment and social services a political rationale for their claim to first preference. The overall effect of this appeal was to integrate within the party a multi-racial and socio-economically diverse body of supporters. Shirazi farmers and fishermen, plantation owners and urban commercial and middle-class elements were all united in a sort of league of patriots who served the Sultan, his subjects, and the Faith.

Probably the most important reason for the ASP's defeat in the 1961 and 1963 elections was the erratic and uncoordinated nature of its party organization. During practically the entire period between the elections of 1957 and 1961 the party did very little to recruit supporters or to establish local branches in areas where the ZNP was strong. Perhaps of greatest importance was the fact that the party had failed to recognize the consequences of the 1959 split and the emergence of the ZPPP.

That split stripped the party of its Pemba leadership and left it practically bereft of organizational strength there. The final product was a fatal structural imbalance —a powerful organization in Zanzibar which produced needlessly overwhelming majorities, and an organization in Pemba so weak as to be almost wholly dependent on the personal magnetism of the party's candidates.

The organizational failure of the ASP was the result of a chronic inability to transform the loose electoral coalition of 1957 into an integrated and disciplined political movement.[2] The origin of the party as an attempt to associate two autonomous associations affected every aspect of its development. It gave the party organization its distinctive quality as a purely electoral apparatus limited almost solely to the function of selecting candidates and assisting their campaigns. ASP local organization virtually disappeared between elections, and all those assorted political tasks which demand a permanent rural staff (fund raising, propaganda, intelligence work and recruitment) were left undone. Throughout the period following the first general election, ASP leadership remained virtually uninformed of the extent of the ZNP's growth, and in both 1961 and 1963 was forced to plan election campaigns on the basis of unrealistic and often exaggerated appraisals of its own regional strength.

The view of the ASP as strictly an electoral machine, widely held among its leadership, produced prolonged conflicts within the Executive Committee. It developed a habitual resistance to any attempt by the Executive to expand its authority to include the right of making policy decisions binding on members. The debate over participation in the Freedom Committee, for example,

---

[2] The concept of organization as the product of a federation of pre-existing units has been treated fully by Seymour Martin Lipset, Martin Trow and James Coleman in their book, *Union Democracy* (Glencoe: The Free Press, 1956).

was largely fought out within the party, on the issue of whether all Executive Committee members could be compelled to abide by the party's decision to cooperate with the ZNP. And the secession of Pemba Shirazi leaders which preceded the formation of the ZPPP was, in effect, provoked by what Pemba regarded as an unwarranted exercise of party discipline. In the absence of a sense that all leaders must ultimately come to share collective responsibility over policy, issue conflicts within the ASP seemed unsusceptible to any final resolution and factional squabbles were protracted over long periods of time. These conflicts drained off energies and talents that could more profitably have been devoted to improving organization, and also demoralized the party's supporters.

Failure to adopt a formal party constitution was partially responsible for the ASP's chronic inability to resolve internal conflict. Without a constitution, the ASP never possessed a clear set of binding rules for the conduct of its internal affairs. There was no decisive allocation of essential party functions between various members of the party executive or different sectors of the party structure, and as a result party leaders were in continual disagreement over the division of responsibility for various phases of party activity.

The ASP was wracked by regional, ethnic and ideological conflicts. Regional tensions over the distribution of party equipment and funds continually crippled the Executive Committee's ability to plan the most efficient utilization of slim resources. Pemba officials especially felt that they had been slighted in the allocation of finances and argued bitterly that, if sacrifices must be made, they should be made in Zanzibar where party support would remain constant. Conflicting regional interests, however, often forced the party to plan the logistics of its campaigns on the basis of placating dissident local leaders rather than on the basis of securing the largest possible number of seats.

Superimposed over a complex pattern of regional jealousies was an endemic power struggle between mainland African and Shirazi leaders, which split the ASP into two large factions engaged in interminable conflict over control of the party organization. This conflict had numerous dimensions, including that of private and personal animosities, but its fundamental component was a mutual distrust of the virtue and motivations of the two communities. The Shirazis believed that the ASP could never attract the vast majority of Shirazis as long as it was dominated by Mainlanders. At the same time, the Mainlanders were determined to prevent control over the party from falling into the hands of men whose loyalty to the cause of African nationalism they found suspect. The slight and uncertain unity between these two groups was preserved only by their maintaining an even and constant balance of members on the party executive.

The ideological disunity of the ASP expressed itself most graphically in a conflict of generations—between its parliamentary group and the young members of the party's trade union affiliate, the *Zanzibar and Pemba Federation of Labor* (ZPFL). The trade union leaders, some of whom had had higher education in Eastern bloc countries, wanted the party to abandon its gradualist approach to constitutional development and to take a more militant and socialist stand on both domestic and international political issues. Their demand for a larger representation on the party's branch, regional and executive committees, and their ability to coerce the party into adopting intransigent and extremist positions by threatening to withdraw their support antagonized the more conservative parliamentary leadership. These various patterns of conflict shattered the ASP into isolated

233

power blocs, each bent on altering the party to suit its own political aspirations. In the planning of campaigns, in the election of top leadership, and in the formulation of its policy, the party was nearly paralyzed by its own internal opposition.

The ASP was continually unable to recruit leadership that would enable it to compete on even terms with the more efficiently organized ZNP. The quality of its local leadership was especially poor. In the rural areas it was a party of fishermen, small farmers and squatters; in the city, of houseboys and manual laborers. As a result the ASP had to staff its local branches with leaders who lacked administrative ability, and who were unskilled in the strategies of agitational politics. ASP elite leadership at the level of the Central Executive was recruited late in the party's history, in fact the party's most effective spokesmen and organizers did not join until immediately prior to the first 1961 election. Thus they had very little opportunity, free from the pressure of campaigning, to recruit members in areas where the party was weak, or to accomplish the fundamental structural reforms necessary to improve communications between constituency organs and the center.

Frequently accused of being a purely racial party, the ASP has in fact tried to combine the idea of African unity with the view that in Zanzibar the Africans constitute an economically deprived community. ASP leaders sought to evoke an image of the ZNP as dominated by the well-to-do Arab minority, a party which acted in the interests of non-African upper-class elements whose affluence depended upon the economic misery of the African majority. In effect more a protest movement of the impoverished urban and rural masses than a revolutionary party, the ASP denounced the religiosity and patriotism of the ZNP as attempts to disguise the fact that Zanzibar society was stratified along racial lines. Because of their memories of slavery and of the privileged political position historically enjoyed by the Arab minority, ASP leaders singled out this group as the real enemies of African social progress. The ideology of the ASP asserted that Zanzibar suffered from two colonialisms, Arab and British, and that it was meaningless to achieve freedom only from the latter since the political condition of Africans would remain unchanged.

This appeal lacked universality, however, and alienated from the party most of the ethnic minorities of Zanzibar. The party had virtually no Arab supporters and only token support from the Comorians. Within the Asian community, the party basically gained support only from Parsees and Hindus who, as religious minorities, approved the ASP's desire to separate religion and politics. Numerous Shirazis, particularly in Pemba, were also alienated from the party because their racial discontent with the Arab minority was slight. The party's effort to create a spirit of commonality between Zanzibar African nationalism and continental African nationalism had limited success among the many Shirazis who had little sense of affinity with the African mainland. Their sense of a distinct Shirazi identity led them to prefer the ZPPP.

The ZPPP was a party in trouble long before the January, 1964, revolution occurred. The parliamentary negotiations of January, 1961, and the decision of the party president, Mohammed Shamte, to form a ZNP/ZPPP coalition government split the party, and led some of its most effective leaders to join the ASP. Among them were four of its parliamentary candidates and its general secretary. Their departure weakened the party, which had in any case achieved only the bare beginnings of an organization, and destroyed its hopes of ever becoming an independent third force in Zanzibar politics. The ZPPP was an effective electoral force only in Pemba, where more than four-fifths of its voting support was concentrated, and where its ability to command the allegiance of between one-fourth and one-third of the electorate created an almost evenly balanced three-party system. The party had virtually no popular support on Zanzibar Island and maintained only token organization or no organization at all in most areas. The only ZPPP stronghold on Zanzibar was the village of Makunduchi in the southern part of the island—the birthplace and home of the party's vice-president, Ameri Tajo. Here, however, its strength was largely the result of the personal popularity of Tajo, and the party was unable to extend its support sufficiently to pose an electoral threat in Makunduchi constituency.

The party lacked the support of any major ancillary organizations such as trade unions or youth movements, and consequently had great difficulty in replenishing its faltering organization with a fresh flow of vigorous new leadership. The decision to expand its relationship with the ZNP from government coalition to full electoral partnership revealed that by June the ZPPP had become almost wholly dependent upon the ZNP for organizational strength. In the period following that election, its own organization had become so inextricably merged with that of the ZNP that, in terms of party structure, it almost ceased to possess a separate identity.

Furthermore, the party was unable to formulate a basis of appeal which would distinguish it from its partner. In the past its recruitment of members was limited to those Shirazis who were dissatisfied with the ASP and ZNP, and who were attracted by the notion of a party of indigenous Zanzibar Africans opposed to both Arab and mainland African minorities. Since the party had now become completely identified with the ZNP it could no longer appeal on that basis and thus lost its chief source of popular support. Defectors from the ZPPP probably accounted for a sizeable portion of the gain registered by the ASP in Pemba during the 1963 election.

The ZPPP then faced a perplexing political dilemma. Its candidates had become dependent on the support of ZNP voters. Moreover, ZNP candidates stood to represent the coalition in a larger number of constituencies than did ZPPP candidates, and in all these constituencies ZPPP members were asked to vote for the ZNP on the grounds that the objectives and principles of the two parties were identical. The danger existed that in the absence of any clear policy differences between the two, ZPPP members would be drawn away by the more powerfully organized and actively proselytizing ZNP. Similarly many ZPPP supporters, when confronted with a clear choice between the ZNP and the ASP, seemed to prefer the ASP. If the ZPPP had left the coalition to maintain a more autonomous identity, it might have invited disaster at the polls. Since it remained in the coalition, it faced the danger of a gradual—but no less fatal—attrition of its popular following.

Because choice of party was basically a response to ethnic feelings and because all the parties came to symbolize clearly differentiated racial attitudes, personal preference had far less influence on the voting behavior of Zanzibaris than did party loyalty. In practically every polling area and regional voting division, the fortunes of the various parties were scarcely affected, as time went on, by shifts in their candidates. Each party had been able to count its safe and weak constituencies almost irrespective of the candidates it ran.

This pervasive commitment to party was particularly important to the ZNP/ZPPP electoral success in the June, 1961 election. It enabled these two parties in effect to pool their votes since most of the supporters of each party could be depended upon not to bolt, even when asked to vote for candidates of a different party. Thus at this time the ASP was unable to make significant inroads, even among ZPPP voters, when a ZNP candidate stood to represent the coalition. There was only one major exception to this pattern: Pandani constituency in northern Pemba, where Ali Sharif, victorious as a ZPPP candidate in January and again as an ASP candidate in June, had a substantial number of the same supporters on both occasions.

The key element in the ZNP/ZPPP coalition's electoral success had been the vast difference between the voting patterns of Zanzibar and Pemba. Put most briefly, *Zanzibar's Islamic multi-racial political culture produced considerable Shirazi voting support for Arab leadership only in Pemba. In Zanzibar there has always been an acute awareness of a separate African political identity, generated primarily by the ethnic pattern of stratification which exists in Zanzibar's society.* The result has been a completely different pattern of voting behavior on the two islands (see maps 3-5). The following tables (17, 18, and 19) show the strength of the political parties in the four general elections in Zanzibar, Pemba and the country as a whole.[3] (Figures are given as percentages of the total valid vote cast.)

Voting behavior in Zanzibar has been stable throughout, with the electorate roughly divided 60-40 between the ASP and its opponents in every election, despite a more than fourfold increase of the electorate between

[3] These tables have been compiled from figures in the official government reports on the four general elections. These are Zanzibar Protectorate, *The Report of the Supervisor of Elections on the Elections in Zanzibar, 1957* (Zanzibar: Government Printer, 1958); Zanzibar Protectorate, *Reports of the Supervisors of Elections on the Registration of Voters and the Elections held in January, 1961* (Zanzibar: Government Printer, 1961); Zanzibar Protectorate, *Report of the Supervisor of Elections, June, 1961* (Zanzibar: Government Printer, 1961); Zanzibar Information Office, *Press Release on the Results of the July, 1963 Election* (Zanzibar: mimeograph, 1963).

TABLE 17

Strength of Political Parties—Zanzibar Island

Party	1957	Jan. 1961	June 1961	1963
ASP	62.8	61.1	63.6	63.09
ZNP	15.7	34.6	34.2	31.49
ZPPP	—	4.3	4.0	5.42
Other	21.5	—	—	—

TABLE 18

Strength of Political Parties—Pemba Island

Party	1957	Jan. 1961	June 1961	1963
ASP	—[a]	23.3	36.6	44.39
ZNP	29.9	43.0	38.8	28.03
ZPPP	—	34.0	24.6	27.58
Other	70.2	—	—	—

[a] The ASP was not functioning in Pemba at the time of the 1957 election.

TABLE 19

Strength of Political Parties—Protectorate

Party	1957	Jan. 1961	June 1961	1963
ASP	35.1	43.2	50.6	54.21
ZNP	21.9	38.5	35.5	29.85
ZPPP	—	18.3	13.9	15.94
Other	43.0	—	—	—

1957 and 1963.[4] Here the ASP had its electoral support

[4] The total electorate in 1957 was about 36,000; in 1961 it was about 90,000 and in 1963 about 165,000. The small size of the electorate during the first election was a result of property and literacy qualifications for vote. The size of the voters' rolls was rapidly expanded through the enfranchisement of women and the reduction of property and literacy qualifications. See Zanzibar Protectorate, *Report of the Committee on the Extension of the Franchise to Women* (Zanzibar: Government Printer, 1959). Property and education requirements were completely eliminated for the 1963 election, and the voters' rolls were open to any Zanzibar citizen over the age of 21.

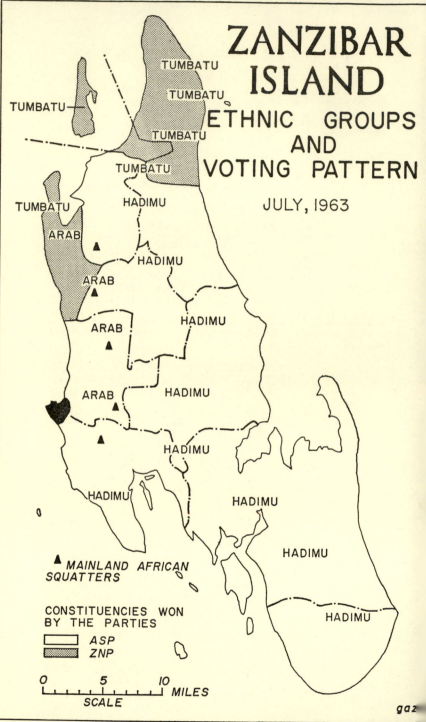

ZANZIBAR
ISLAND

ETHNIC GROUPS
AND
VOTING PATTERN

JULY, 1963

TUMBATU

TUMBATU

TUMBATU

TUMBATU

TUMBATU

TUMBATU

ARAB

HADIMU

HADIMU

ARAB

ARAB

HADIMU

ARAB

HADIMU

HADIMU

HADIMU

HADIMU

HADIMU

HADIMU

HADIMU

▲ MAINLAND AFRICAN
SQUATTERS

CONSTITUENCIES WON
BY THE PARTIES
☐ ASP
▨ ZNP

0   5   10
|_|_|_|_|_|_|_|_|_|_| MILES
       SCALE

gaz

MAP 3

ZANZIBAR TOWN

ETHNIC GROUPS AND VOTING PATTERN   JULY, 1963

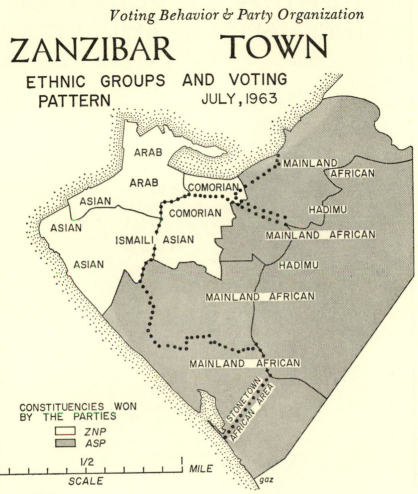

CONSTITUENCIES WON
BY THE PARTIES

☐ ZNP
▨ ASP

1/2 MILE
SCALE

MAP 4

almost exclusively among the mainland Africans and the vast majority of Hadimu Shirazis. In the two 1961 elections and in 1963 the ASP swept the north-central, central, eastern and southern areas of the island where the population is almost entirely Hadimu. In Zanzibar Township, the ASP has scored consistent victories in the con-

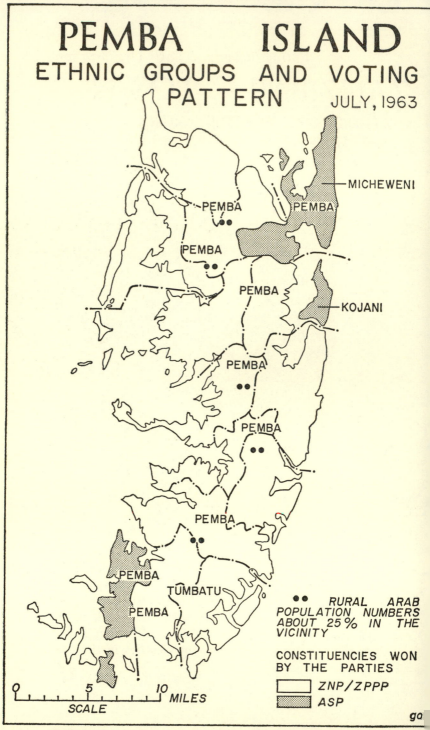

PEMBA ISLAND
ETHNIC GROUPS AND VOTING
PATTERN
JULY, 1963

MICHEWENI

PEMBA

PEMBA

PEMBA

PEMBA

KOJANI

PEMBA

PEMBA

PEMBA

PEMBA

TUMBATU

PEMBA

•• RURAL ARAB POPULATION NUMBERS ABOUT 25% IN THE VICINITY

CONSTITUENCIES WON BY THE PARTIES

ZNP/ZPPP

ASP

0   5   10 MILES
SCALE

MAP 5

stituencies where the population is overwhelmingly mainland African. This Hadimu and mainland African support on Zanzibar gave the ASP eight out of the ten constituencies it won in June, 1961, and eleven out of the thirteen constituencies it won in July, 1963.

The ZNP's principal success on Zanzibar was among ethnic minorities and the Tumbatu Shirazis. It consistently won the predominantly non-African seats in Zanzibar Township; two in the Stonetown area represent the domicile of many wealthy Arab landowners and of the Asian commercial and middle-class elements, and in a third constituency there is a preponderance of Comorians and Ismaili Asians. All of the rural constituencies in Zanzibar won by the ZNP are located in the north and northwestern area of the island, where there is a majority of Tumbatu Shirazis. The support of ethnic minority elements and of Tumbatu Shirazis gave the ZNP five out of ten of its constituencies in June, 1961, and six out of twelve of its constituencies in July, 1963.

Neither the ZNP nor the ZPPP ever won a constituency in which the majority of the inhabitants were Hadimu Shirazis or mainland Africans. The ZNP had some popular strength in the fertile area where Arab plantation owners sympathetic to the party had strong local influence, and where the agricultural workers' unions organized by ZNP leaders had much of their membership. But its support here was insufficient for it to gain any of the constituencies in the plantation belt. The ZPPP never won any of its constituencies on Zanzibar Island and had only a scattered popular following there.

Voting behavior and party affiliation in Pemba were nearly antithetical to that in Zanzibar. In the two 1961 elections the ZNP and the ZPPP gained almost two-thirds of the popular vote in Pemba, and in both 1961 and 1963 the coalition parties won all but two Pemba seats. Despite the recent ASP gains among the Pemba electorate, a clear majority of Pemba Shirazis showed a consistent preference for the other political parties. This preference was the basis of the ZNP/ZPPP coalition's continual electoral successes.

A partial explanation of the vast differences in the voting behavior of Pemba and Hadimu Shirazis lies in their very different historical experiences with Omani colonialism. With the transferral of the Omani Sultanate from Arabia to Zanzibar and the establishment of Zanzibar Town as its administrative center, Arab control over Zanzibar at once became highly effective. The Busaidi regime almost immediately established decisive political and administrative paramountcy over the Hadimu people and began to impose tax payments and demands for forced labor. In this way, the Shirazi of Zanzibar came to know the Omani Arab as an intruder and as a colonial administrator.

The Pemba Shirazis' early contact with the Busaidis was far more of a meeting between political equals. Pemba was under the strict control of the Mazrui dynasty of Mombasa until early in the nineteenth century, and a local chronicle records that several indigenous African rulers of Pemba sought and received the assistance of the Busaidis in their effort to evict the Mombasa Arabs. Furthermore, Omani Arabs did not settle in Pemba until after they had signed a treaty with the Pemba chiefs. These events have passed into the mythology of Pemba, and many Pemba Shirazis now view the Arabs not as intruding colonial administrators but as willingly received settlers. Since Pemba was some distance from the capitol at Zanzibar Town, Busaidi administration was never as effective nor as obtrusive as it was in the Hadimu areas. This reinforced the Pemba Shirazis' conviction that their historical relationship with Omani Arabs had been a voluntary one, and not one of enforced subordination. These historical beliefs predisposed most

Pemba Shirazis to resist an anti-Arab political appeal.

A second explanation of the differing voting patterns of Zanzibar and Pemba is that Arab land alienation has been much more extensive and apparent on the former island. Within a brief period after the establishment of the Sultanate on Zanzibar, Arab immigrants had displaced the few indigenous Africans from the fertile land area surrounding the town. These immigrants soon came to enjoy nearly exclusive occupation of the best land (see map 6).[5]

It is likely that Zanzibar's fertile area was, in fact, very sparsely settled before the arrival of the Omani settlers, since it was the Arab colonists who first introduced the clove tree to Zanzibar and since that land had previously consisted only of dense forest which was little used and heavily infected with malaria. Whether the concentration of Zanzibar's Arab community on the best cultivable soil was by historical accident, by legitimate acquisition or by force, the fact is that Zanzibar Shirazis have come to reside in a sort of native reserve on soils unsuitable for the intensive cultivation of cloves or coconuts. This has introduced an additional element of strain into Shirazi-Arab relations in Zanzibar and today has fostered a political myth of major importance. The Zanzibar Shirazi believes, rightly or wrongly, that he was forcibly and illegitimately deprived of his land by the Arab intruder. The present relative poverty of the rural coastal fishing villages as opposed to the moderate prosperity of the clove and coconut area, the hardship of country life as opposed to the comparative luxury of an urban existence (the Arab population of Zanzibar is 52 per cent urbanized), combined with the Shirazis'

---

[5] Map 6 has been drawn from information found in John Middleton, *Land Tenure in Zanzibar* (London: Her Majesty's Stationery Office, 1961), pp. 82-83 and Zanzibar Protectorate, *Review of the Systems of Land Tenure in the Islands of Zanzibar and Pemba* (Zanzibar: Government Printer, 1945), pp. 14-15.

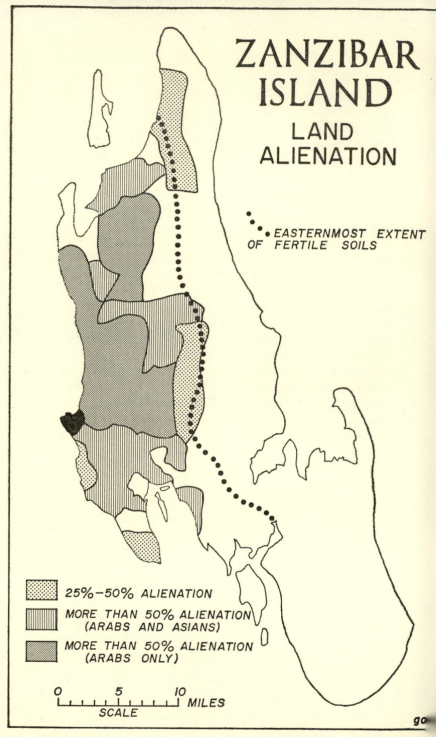

ZANZIBAR ISLAND

LAND ALIENATION

EASTERNMOST EXTENT
OF FERTILE SOILS

25%–50% ALIENATION

MORE THAN 50% ALIENATION
(ARABS AND ASIANS)

MORE THAN 50% ALIENATION
(ARABS ONLY)

O   5   IO
|_|_|_|_|_|_|_|_|_|_|_| MILES
        SCALE

go

MAP 6

belief that they were forcibly evicted from the best land —all these factors have generated among many Shirazis of Zanzibar Island the conviction that because of Arab colonialism they enjoyed at best the status of poor relations in their own land.

Land alienation in Pemba has not been so extensive or so readily apparent that it seriously harmed race relations between Shirazis and Arabs there. Good quality clove and coconut soils are common throughout Pemba; both Arabs and Shirazis occupied land of roughly similar arability, and as a result Pemba Shirazis did not develop any sense that the immigrant Arab minority had come to enjoy exclusive occupation of the best land. This perception was reinforced by the overwhelmingly rural character of the Pemba Arab population. Less than one-fourth of the Pemba Arab population lived in the three large towns on the island. Arabs lived side by side with Shirazis in the rural areas, so there did not develop that strong sense of social estrangement based on variant patterns of residence which figured so prominently in Zanzibar. The following three tables on land ownership (20, 21 and 22) reveal clearly the great difference between Zanzibar and Pemba with respect to the problem of land alienation.[6] They thereby help to explain the differing voting patterns of the Zanzibar and Pemba electorates. Arabs owned, as of 1923, about three-fourths of the trees in Zanzibar as opposed to less than half of the trees in Pemba. Furthermore, Arab landowners in Zanzibar averaged approximately twelve times as many trees per plantation and trees per owner as did the Zan-

[6] Table 20 has been based on figures quoted in R. S. Troup, *Report on Clove Cultivation in the Zanzibar Protectorate* (Zanzibar: Government Printer, 1932), p. 8. Tables 21 and 22 are based on figures taken from Edward Batson, *Land Ownership*, Vol. xv; *The Social Survey of Zanzibar*, Department of Social Studies, University of Capetown (Capetown, by the direction of the Zanzibar Government, n.d.).

zibar Africans, whereas in Pemba the ratio was only two or three times as many trees per plantation and trees per owner. Tables 21 and 22 differentiate among the three indigenous tribes with respect to land ownership.

TABLE 20

Clove Plantations in the Protectorate, 1923

ISLAND	Owners	Plantations	Trees	Trees/ Plant	Trees/ Owner
Zanzibar					
Arabs	1,218	1,869	735,554	394	604
Africans	4,840	7,070	236,758	33	49
Pemba					
Arabs	2,973	6,819	888,750	130	298
Africans	8,717	15,117	896,439	59	103

TABLE 21

Land Ownership by Size of Clove Plantation, 1948

PLANTATIONS	Hadimu	Tumbatu	Pemba	Arab
Very Large 3,000	—	—	—	165
Large 1,000—2,999	10	5	100	320
Medium 250—999	120	300	810	1,885
Small 50—249	730	700	3,715	1,990
Very Small 0—50	2,330	2,100	2,400	1,640
Total Population	41,425	43,965	57,585	44,605

TABLE 22

Land Ownership by Type of Plantation, 1948

PLANTATIONS	Hadimu	Tumbatu	Pemba	Arab
Clove	940	2,005	5,725	4,375
Coconut	2,760	2,500	5,015	4,035
No. of owners of all types[a]	3,190	3,105	7,025	6,040

[a] Some owners possessed more than one type of plantation.

The Pemba are closest of the three Shirazi tribes to the Arabs in terms of number and size of property holdings. Furthermore, there is considerable difference between Pemba holdings and those of the other two tribes. In the medium and small landowner categories there are well over four times as many Pemba landowners as Hadimu or Tumbatu landowners. The social structure of the Pemba tribe is quite similar to that of the Arab community, in that roughly eight to ten per cent of the population of each group is composed of small farmers and petty landholders. There are more than twice as many Pemba landowners of all types as Hadimu and Tumbatu landowners. For all these reasons, the problem of land alienation has been of negligible influence in arousing anti-Arab feeling among the Pemba population.

Regional ecological variations within Pemba furnish strong confirmation of the close relationship between land problems and voting behavior. Two separate areas of Pemba do possess poor, rocky soil comparable to that in the infertile areas of Zanzibar. Here, as in eastern Zanzibar, land conditions unsuitable for the intensive cultivation of cloves and coconuts have prevented Arab settlement—but both areas are adjacent to more fertile land where Arabs have settled and prospered. These areas are Micheweni-Kojani in northeastern Pemba and Panza-Mkoani in the southwest. It is in these two areas that the ASP gained its only Pemba constituencies.

A third cause of the vast differences in the voting behavior and party affiliation of Pemba and Hadimu Shirazis is their very uneven contact with the mainland African community. (Table 23 shows the Shirazi, African and Arab populations of Zanzibar and Pemba.[7])

[7] This table has been compiled from figures in Zanzibar Protectorate, *Notes on the Census of the Zanzibar Protectorate, 1948* (Zanzibar: Government Printer, 1953).

TABLE 23

Population of Ethnic Communities in 1948

COMMUNITY	Zanzibar		Pemba		Protectorate	
	No.	*Per Cent*	*No.*	*Per Cent*	*No.*	*Per Cent*
Shirazi	81,150	61.2	67,330	60.2	148,480	60.8
African	37,502	28.3	13,878	12.4	51,380	21.0
Arab	13,977	10.5	30,583	27.4	44,560	18.2
Total	132,629	100.0	111,791	100.0	244,420	100.0

In Zanzibar there are more than twice as many mainland Africans as in Pemba and there has been intense social contact between them and Hadimu Shirazis. The Hadimu Shirazis frequently migrate to Zanzibar Town where they become socially and politically assimilated into the mainland African community and pick up its racial views. Many migrants return to their villages and strengthen existing anti-Arab sentiments. This system of cyclical reinforcement has created an almost impenetrable ASP stronghold in the Hadimu areas of Zanzibar Island.

In Pemba there is no urban concentration of Mainlanders which functions as a center for the dissemination of the ASP style of nationalism. Here the mainland African, not the Arab, is more commonly regarded as an alien and an "unknown stranger," and his racial views and political attitudes have gained little currency with the indigenous population.

The antipathies of many Pemba Shirazis towards mainland Africans in that crucial period between 1957 and 1963 were rooted in a kind of social prejudice. Though practically the entire mainland community was of the Muslim faith, there was a tendency for Shirazis to view the mainland in terms of a strongly Christianized Tanganyika and hence to disapprove of the mainland immigrant as a potential Christian influence. Shirazis frequently felt that the mainland African's national loyalties, especially those of the more recent immigrants, did not ultimately reside in Zanzibar. Proud that they had lived in peace with the Arab minority, many Pemba Shirazis strongly disapproved of the mainland Africans' antipathies towards the Arabs. In recent years, Pemba Shirazis perceived the Mainlanders playing a prominent role in incidents of political violence, and added to their former biases an image of the mainland African as a troublemaker. Economic issues aggravated these feelings: there was a general conviction that the mainland African was a cheapener of labor and that Shirazis, as indigenes, should have had special priority for government and other jobs.

All of these factors produced a separatist attitude which was first expressed dramatically in the refusal of the Pemba Shirazi leaders to join in the Afro-Shirazi Union. Later, this attitude was the real force behind the formation of the ZPPP. The fact that it was so entrenched among the majority of the Pemba Shirazis meant that the ASP was never able to gain more than limited support among the Pemba electorate.

The different geographical patterns of historical-political contact with Omani Arabs, of Arab land alienation and of mainland African settlement made voting behavior in Pemba very different from that in Zanzibar. This difference in voting patterns, however, visibly decreased between June, 1961, and July, 1963, and there was an observable tendency for Pemba to become more and more like Zanzibar in its voting pattern. The ASP's percentage of the popular vote grew by more than twenty per cent during this period, and by the last election, the ASP's popular vote in Pemba was only about twenty per cent less than its vote in Zanzibar. This increase raises a serious question about the strength and permanency of anti-ASP feeling among the Pemba electorate, and calls attention to the need for a national theory of voting behavior which will explain transition and change in the pattern of party affiliation.

Changing voting patterns in Zanzibar can best be understood in terms of a cross-pressure theory of influence on political behavior. Cross-pressures shape the electorate's perception of the political parties, define the range of voting options available, and largely determine the final choice of party affiliation.

Ethnic identifications have been the strongest source of group unity in Zanzibar. The perception of party affiliation as a natural extension of racial community has been present among the supporters of all parties. This factor has been the principal determinant of voting support for the ASP: as initially and primarily perceived by the nation's electorate, the ASP had one powerful motivating appeal—its public identification as an African political party. The strength of communal solidarities largely accounts for the ASP's clear popular majority.

Socio-economic, historical and religious factors, however, also had strong political influence as cross-pressure influences on voting behavior in Zanzibar. These could be powerful alternatives to race as motivational factors shaping party preference. Indeed, even though racial identification was the strongest single psychological impetus to party affiliation, it could not overcome multiple combinations of these other factors when they functioned together as countervailing motivations. Thus, the coalition gained popular support from Shirazis because its appeal combined several attractive cross-pressures: the parties' identification with religiosity, national institutions (the Sultanate), historical relationships, and in the case of the Pemba Shirazis, a definite perception of mutual socio-economic interest. These Shirazis, though affiliated to the ASP by race, generally voted ZNP/ZPPP because of their Islamic, economic and other bonds of identity with the Arab population.

A delicate balance existed in Pemba between the attraction of ethnic identification on the one hand and these combined cross-pressures on the other. Where any one of these latter factors or any combination of them did not run counter to the instinctive projection of racial community into party membership, the natural forcefulness of an ethnic basis of political affiliation reasserted itself. Thus, in areas of Pemba where there are noticeable economic discrepancies between Pemba Shirazis and Arabs due to poor soil, an essential ingredient of the coalition's complex multi-motivational appeal was missing.[8] Here, Pemba Shirazis voted ASP.

This cross-pressure theory helps explain the steady shift of Pemba voters to the ASP. During the 1963 election the ASP radically varied the character of its election campaign in Pemba. It softened its strident anti-Arab tone and gave greater local emphasis to religious and patriotic themes designed to attract Shirazi sympathies. This, in effect, neutralized important dimensions of the coalition's appeal, since it enabled the Pemba electorate to perceive Islamic devotion and national loyalty as characteristics of the ASP as well as the ZNP/ZPPP. Once these characteristics were no longer exclusively associated with the coalition, the existing balance of cross-pressures was changed; ethnic identification became decisively important, and the ASP started to gain support.

By mid-1961, and especially by 1963, the ASP had begun to recover from the effects of the 1959 split. It was slowly rebuilding its electoral organization and was actively recruiting influential local leaders to replace the Pemba Shirazi leaders who had defected to form the ZPPP. These organizational improvements were important adjuncts to the party's new campaign style; they enabled the ASP to communicate effectively with a far

[8] These are the Micheweni-Kojani and Panza-Mkoani regions mentioned on page 249 of this chapter.

greater proportion of the Pemba electorate than it had in the past. Most of this increased popular support in Pemba came from the ranks of the ZPPP, which was suffering a gradual but persistent attrition of its membership. The ZPPP split after the January, 1961, election proved costly to the party. The defection of Ali Sharif alone shifted about five per cent of the Pemba electorate from the ZPPP to the ASP, and a number of village and district leaders also left the ZPPP at this time and each one carried his personal following with him.

The formation of an electoral and governmental coalition between the ZPPP and the ZNP was the chief impetus to a large-scale migration of ZPPP supporters to the ASP. The coalition undermined the entire basis of the ZPPP's popularity. Whereas the ZPPP had previously presented itself as an autonomous third force responsible to Shirazi interests alone, it could not do so after the coalition. The joint ZNP/ZPPP Government created a visible political identification between the two parties and thereby forced the ZPPP to make a public case for an identity of Shirazi and Arab interests. In this way the coalition prevented Pemba Shirazi voters from seeking a neutral middle-ground and forced them to make a clear choice between the ZNP and the ASP. Reacting to the ASP's new ability to make successful use of religious and patriotic campaign themes, most of these voters preferred that party, and the ASP vote in Pemba increased eight per cent after June, 1961.

The figures in Table 18 on page 239 make it appear that the decline in popular support for the coalition parties was experienced by the ZNP, not the ZPPP. This was not the case. The ZNP figure did drop ten per cent after June, 1961, but these percentage figures are not an accurate reflection of the distribution of coalition support between the two parties. The percentage changes for the ZNP and the ZPPP in Pemba were the result of an electoral strategy; in the 1963 election the ZNP "loaned" some of its popular support to the ZPPP in order to help replace ZPPP members who were leaving the party.

The rising popularity of the ASP among ZPPP voters forced ZNP and ZPPP leaders to devise a method whereby the coalition could retain as much ZPPP support as possible. Their problem was to take maximum advantage of the strong commitment of ZNP supporters and to place as little strain as possible on the weakening commitment of ZPPP voters. Since ZPPP members were reacting negatively to the partnership between the parties, the danger of a massive defection was greatest in the constituencies where ZPPP voters would be called upon to vote for a ZNP leader. On the other hand, wherever a ZPPP candidate represented the coalition, the symbolic obligation on ZPPP voters to remain loyal to the coalition was greater.

Therefore ZNP leaders agreed to allow the ZPPP to put up candidates in several constituencies where the ZNP was in fact the stronger of the two parties, but where ZPPP voters were essential to a coalition victory. This caused a sharp decrease in the vote registered for the ZNP since many more ZNP voters were called upon to support ZPPP candidates. This strategy explains the sharp drop in the ZNP's percentage of the Pemba vote in 1963, and why the ZPPP gained about three per cent over its June, 1961, figure. By giving the ZPPP a few extra constituencies where its voters could provide the coalition with the additional margin of support necessary for success, coalition leaders helped prevent a wholesale exodus of ZPPP members and rescued Pemba for the coalition parties. This technique may well have saved the election for the coalition.

The apparent decision of the ZPPP to continue its dependent relationship with the ZNP played into the hands of Arab ZNP leaders, for they were able to exert the same sort of influence over their coalition partner that they enjoyed within their own party (i.e. the domination of the political sophisticate over those with limited political experience). This influence extended over the entire range of public policy and even included such questions as recruitment into the higher civil service and redistribution of land—areas where drastic reform was necessary if Shirazis or Africans were to advance. It became the unspoken premise of all public policy that there must be no social or political change which threatened the position of Zanzibar's entrenched minority.

This explains the ZNP/ZPPP coalition's decision not to accept the ASP's offer to form a "national" government, for a "national" government would have meant that Africans independent of Arab influence could control important ministries. This decision, however, created a situation of ominous instability. Well over half the population voted against the ZNP/ZPPP coalition, and in Zanzibar, the seat of government, the figure approached two-thirds. The ASP was also supported by Zanzibar's most powerful trade unions, and the coalition's refusal strengthened the position of militant and extremist leaders within both the party and its trade union affiliates. These leaders believed that peaceful constitutional processes would never enable Zanzibar to be rid of its Arab rulers.

CONCLUSION

The African Revolution

The introduction of democratic political institutions could have led to a constitutional transfer of power from the Arab oligarchy to the African majority, but due to the unusual results of the 1963 election this failed to occur. Had Zanzibar's electoral districts been differently arranged or had proportional representation been employed instead of single member constituencies, the ASP's strong popular majority would have enabled it to assume power as the result of an orderly electoral process. The ZNP's electoral victories meant that the small Arab oligarchy had survived the introduction of representative majoritarian institutions. This was the immediate cause of the revolution—Africans overthrew the ZNP/ZPPP Government by force because there no longer seemed to be any way to create an African state by constitutional means.

The revolution took place on January 12, 1964, approximately one month after independence.[1] Armed African insurgents seized control of Zanzibar, overthrew the ZNP/ZPPP Government and installed in power a Revolutionary Council headed by leaders of the ASP. Among the earliest acts of the revolutionary government was the mass arrest and internment of thousands of Arabs and the confiscation or destruction of considerable Arab property. With the permanent banishment of the Sultan and the proscription of the ZNP and ZPPP, the new regime completed the political and economic destruction of the Arab oligarchy.

The revolution was not entirely unforeseen, for the

[1] Intensive press coverage of the Zanzibar revolution may be found in *The Tanganyika Standard*, *The East African Standard*, *The Daily Nation*, *The Observer* (London), *The Times* (London) and the *New York Times* during the two weeks or so after January 12, 1964.

strength and solidarity of extremist anti-Government groups had become the most conspicuous feature of Zanzibar politics during the months immediately prior to independence. The most significant of these was a new political party, *Umma* (The Masses), which was formed just before the July election. It was the creation of Abdul Rahman Mohammed (Babu) and two other defecting members of the ZNP Executive Committee.

Babu's split with the ZNP climaxed two years of increasing tension between himself and the moderate wing of the party led by Ali Muhsin. Until mid-1961 the two wings of the party had been willing to submerge their differences because of the major challenge being posed by the ASP, but the defeat of the ASP in the election of June, 1961, removed this important incentive to intra-party cooperation. Moreover, since an ultimate ZNP victory seemed assured, the ideological debate within the party took on added importance and became, in effect, a struggle over which political creed—Islam or Marxism—would predominate in a future ZNP-controlled independent state. The virtual disappearance of external pressure towards cooperation and the increased importance of the ideological conflict led the two wings of the party to move further and further apart between 1961 and 1963. Muhsin and the parliamentary group remained rigidly committed to the party's religiously derived theory of national community, despite its profoundly conservative social and political implications. Babu and the militant group were increasingly attracted by the revolutionary socialism of Communist China and Cuba. Their rejection of the Islamic concepts of Muhsin and the ZNP cabinet ministers was intensified by a conviction that such views were the product of a "bourgeois" class position.

The final break in the ZNP did not result directly from these ideological differences, but from a disagreement over electoral strategy and the sincerity of the party's efforts to achieve a multi-racial society.[2] Babu believed that the party ought to abandon its long-standing practice of running candidates of different racial communities in constituencies where ethnic factors would weigh in their favor. Specifically, he opposed the system of assigning Arab candidates to predominantly Arab constituencies and Asian candidates to predominantly Asian constituencies; he sought a distribution of candidates which would compel the party's Arab, Asian and Comorian supporters to vote for Shirazi African leaders, and which would therefore exemplify the ZNP's commitment to a policy of fostering closer ties between the races. Babu also wanted the party to give contemporary meaning to its origin as an African peasant movement by nominating at least one of the founder-members to a safe constituency. Only if these changes were made, he felt, would the concept of multi-racialism become an accurate description of the ZNP's relationship to Zanzibar society.

Muhsin felt that it was unwise to test the depth of multi-racial sentiments among the party's supporters at such a critical time; he believed it might jeopardize the ZNP's chances in the election. Muhsin rallied the party's branch and regional leadership to his support, and in a special meeting called to consider the party's nominations, Babu's proposals were rejected, and he resigned. His defection, however, did not appreciably affect the ZNP's popular support. The Umma party, which Babu formed immediately after his resignation, did not stand any candidates in the July election; even if it had done so, their chances of electoral success would have been slight. Umma was of the utmost importance as an anti-Government organization, although this did not appear

---

[2] See Zanzibar Nationalist Party, *Statement on Babu's Resignation* (Zanzibar, mimeograph, 1963).

until after the election, and even then the size of its membership was inconsequential. Umma's real significance lay in providing a center through which Babu and his close personal associates built a unified political movement out of the myriad groups opposed to the ZNP.

Umma drew its support from the entire range of anti-Government elements: some members of the ZNP executive who agreed with Babu and who had resigned with him, the ZPFL, ASP militants, the opposition press and most of the top leadership of the FPTU. Umma functioned as an organizational meeting-ground for all these groups during the six-month period between the July election and the revolution. Under Umma's influence, the feasibility of revolution was seriously considered not only by many leaders of the ASP who were deeply embittered by election defeat and by rejection of their demand for a "national" government, but by all those to whom the concept of violent political change was an integral part of an ethos of class warfare. These varied opposition elements were drawn to Umma because its ideological and political militancy endowed it with a singleness of purpose and determination for action which the ASP did not possess at the time.

Among the first official supporters of Umma were the vast majority of the leaders of the FPTU. Their massive defection from the ZNP reflected the degree to which Babu, as chief party organizer, had created within the party structure a substantial segment of leadership personally devoted to him and ideologically committed to the revolutionary Marxist views he expressed. Although the rank-and-file membership of the FPTU remained overwhelmingly loyal to Muhsin and the ZNP, the FPTU ceased, almost overnight, to function as a ZNP affiliate. For the defecting leaders not only constituted the FPTU's main body of skilled personnel—they also controlled its entire organizational resources, its financial reserves and its transportation, communication and propaganda facilities. This left the Government without effectively organized trade union support and, furthermore, cleared a path for the unification—under Umma's aegis—of the leadership of Zanzibar's two large trade union movements.

The FPTU and the ZPFL had in the past been deeply separated on political grounds. Some union leaders preferred to explain the disunity of Zanzibar's labor movement by asserting that the FPTU was an "industrial" union, whereas the ZPFL was a "craft" union. But the real difference between them was their party affiliation. The rank and file and the leadership of the ZPFL were predominantly mainland Africans, and their political sympathies were wholly with the ASP. The FPTU, however, had often mirrored the anti-mainland African prejudices of its parent body, the ZNP, and this was a major obstacle to any cooperation between the two unions. Once the FPTU leadership had disassociated itself from the ZNP, this obstacle was removed and common ideological sentiments began to draw the two movements together.

Umma leaders were able to play an important role in the unification process. They sponsored and organized a national labor committee composed of leaders of both unions. When this committee was formed, most top ZPFL leaders began to cooperate more closely with Umma than with the ASP. They had, in any case, become disillusioned with the internal disunity of the ASP and with its unwillingness to adopt a revolutionary socialist program.

Umma was also able to unify the opposition press. Party leaders formed a newspaper editors' association called the *All Zanzibar Journalists' Organization* (AZJO). This association brought numerous editors, journalists and newspaper owners into close working cooperation with the Umma party. Babu, who himself joined AZJO as editor of Zanews, was the association's most influential member. AZJO also included the editors of *Afrika Kwetu; Sauti ya Umma* (The Voice of Umma), Umma's official party newspaper; *Kibarua* (The Message), the journal of the FPTU; *Agope,* a new newspaper owned by Jamal Ramadhan; and *Jamhuri* (The Republic), edited by Abdulla Suleiman, a former leader of the ZPPP who had defected after the election of January, 1961, and joined the ASP. Through these newspapers, Umma's revolutionary ideas began to gain a direct and intensive penetration of the ASP's popular following.

Umma had developed by late 1963 into a fully organized shadow government. The party itself was highly disciplined and tightly integrated; it possessed a powerful, unifying marxist ideology and enjoyed considerable *esprit de corps.* Umma's activist element included several of Zanzibar's most effective propagandists and organizers; Babu himself was universally acknowledged as the organizational genius of Zanzibar politics, and in a very brief time had placed Umma at the head of practically all the militant opposition groups. Umma had strong working ties with the largest trade unions, the press, and even with several influential members of the ASP. Had Umma been an African political party rather than predominantly Arab and Comorian, it might well have completely undermined the ASP by recruiting substantial sectors of its leadership and its popular following.[3] In its ability to harass the Government, to unify and

[3] The essentially non-African composition of Umma was most clearly reflected in its leadership. Only two of the top Umma leaders were African; Abdul Razak Musa and Muhsin Abeid, who defected with Babu from the ZNP Executive Committee, are Hadimu Shirazi. Babu is of mixed Arab and Comorian descent. The remaining top Umma leaders—Salim Ahmed, Ali Sultan Issa, Ali Mafudh and Mohammed Ali Foum—are of either Arab or Comorian descent.

inspire the African population, and to gain international support for the opposition cause, Umma stood in marked contrast to the African party.

The ASP was almost wholly unable to provide a meaningful alternative to the revolutionary type of opposition represented by Umma. It had emerged from the election more disunited than ever, divided on political strategy, wracked by mutual recriminations over responsibility for the defeat, and consequently largely unable to maintain the enthusiasm of its regional and local leadership. There were several bodies of conflicting opinion within the party. One group of leaders believed that the ASP ought to pursue the possibility of a coalition government at all costs, and argued that the party could not continue indefinitely as an opposition without losing its popular support. This group was strong initially, but lost its strength within the party when the ZNP/ZPPP coalition's conditions for a "national" government became known. A second group of leaders, led by party President Karume, favored forming a strong but loyal parliamentary opposition. They felt that this would prevent the Government from using legal and police pressures against the party, and would thus enable the ASP to seek assistance from the parties of the East African countries. A third group wanted to cooperate openly with Umma and to consider tactics of resistance and civil disobedience. For want of an agreed plan of action, the ASP lost its political morale, became more and more enmeshed in its own internal difficulties, and was unable to act as an effective opposition force.

This divided and dispirited condition affected every phase of party activity, especially relations with the

---

Since both these communities were associated with the historic pattern of alien elite domination over Zanzibar's African majority, many ASP leaders were unwilling to embark on a full cooperative relationship with Umma.

Government. Party leaders had virtually no success in gaining definite constitutional guarantees against arbitrary or suppressive administrative activities. An ASP delegation attended a final constitutional conference held in England a few months before independence, but without a clearly articulated and broadly supported party policy the delegation was unable to make any concrete demands, even though pressure from the British colonial authorities might have had some influence on the ZNP/ZPPP coalition. The ASP's success in London was limited to an assurance that a Bill of Human Rights would be incorporated in the constitution of Zanzibar.[4] However, while this might protect the party and its supporters from gross abuses of their political freedoms, it could have little effect against the subtle economic and social pressures which the Government was in a position to apply.

Inability to undertake concerted action was also reflected in the ASP's endless absorption in matters of dubious political importance. Party leaders literally spent weeks in interminable debate over whether or not to oppose the Government's design for a national flag, and whether or not its supporters should participate in the Independence Day celebrations. Some leaders lost interest in party affairs and ceased altogether to attend meetings that dealt only with trivial issues. Under these conditions, it was practically inevitable that Umma, not the ASP, should become the spearhead of the movement to resist and eventually supersede the ZNP/ZPPP Government.

Umma's numerous propaganda and agitational activities forced the Government to initiate a series of measures to consolidate and stabilize its political position. The first of these was an effort to rebuild trade union

---

[4] Great Britain, *Minutes of the Meeting*, Zanzibar Independence Conference, 1963 (London, mimeograph, 1963).

support. The ZNP organized a new trade union federation, the *Zanzibar Trade Union Congress* (ZTUC), among the rank and file of the FPTU. Most of the FPTU members had not supported their union's defection to Umma, and the ZTUC had some initial success, especially among the seamen's, dockworkers' and agricultural workers' unions of the FPTU. These unions were composed largely of Tumbatu and Pemba Shirazis whose natural political sympathies lay with the coalition parties. Despite this good start, however, the Government's organized trade union support was extremely limited. The ZTUC was able to achieve only the barest beginnings of an organization before the revolution, and the former FPTU members were left without effective organized trade union ties to the ZNP. Since a few portions of the FPTU and the entire ZPFL remained in determined opposition, the Government had to seek additional means to ensure its stability.

During the months prior to the revolution, the ZNP/ZPPP regime undertook a series of measures designed to provide the maximum possible degree of social control. It passed or initiated legislation which imposed severe limitations on the activities of opposition groups and of the press, staffed politically strategic sectors of the bureaucracy with Arabs known to support the ZNP, and made party loyalty the primary consideration in a major reorganization of the Zanzibar police. The ultimate effect of these restrictive policies would have been to transform Zanzibar from a constitutional monarchy into a rigid authoritarian regime. None of these policies could be effectively implemented before the revolution occurred, however, and, in the short time left to the Government the repressive measures probably contributed to the vulnerability of the regime by absorbing the energy and attention of its top leaders. Incipient authoritarianism may, indirectly, have contributed to the effort to overthrow the Government; its policies created a pervasive atmosphere of fear and apprehension which further unified the opposition behind its militant leadership, and lent a sense of special urgency to the militants' belief in the necessity of revolutionary political change.

The Government's authoritarian measures included the imposition of crippling restrictions on the activities of both opposition parties. Travel to mainland and European countries was curtailed and arbitrary search and seizure was not uncommon. Just before independence, the Government introduced a law in the National Assembly which would have established strict censorship and political control of the press, but the harshest measure was a law passed during late August "to provide for the registration and control of societies." This law, which placed completely arbitrary power in the hands of the Minister for Internal Affairs (Ali Muhsin), merits quotation: "The Minister may . . . by order declare to be unlawful any society which *in his opinion* [italics mine] is being used for any purpose prejudicial to or incompatible with the maintenance of peace, order and good government."[5] ASP parliamentary leaders argued in vain that this law was a violation of the human rights provision of the Zanzibar constitution, and claimed that it was so broadly worded that it could be applied as easily to a peaceful opposition, such as their own, as to a more violently inclined group.

The Control of Societies law and other similar measures drove the ASP closer and closer to Umma; they undermined the position of those leaders who felt that the Bill of Rights would ensure the safety of a legitimate

[5] Bill Supplement to the *Official Gazette of the Zanzibar Government,* Vol. LXXII, No. 4292, of 17th August, 1963, "A Bill Entitled A Decree to Provide for the Registration and Control of Societies."

parliamentary political party. Within the ASP, numerous influential leaders disagreed with the view that the party ought to continue to function as a responsible opposition. In early January, only a week or two before the revolution, one group split openly with the party's top leadership and formed a separate intra-party faction under Othman Sharif.[6] This group, calling itself "The Progressives," was unwilling to commit the ASP to the ethos of total revolution espoused by Umma, but they did want the party to seek more aggressive means to resist the Government's suppressive measures.

The ZNP/ZPPP Government also aroused widespread fear by its willingness to treat the administration as an extension of its party apparatus. The ZNP began to staff top posts in the civil service, especially the District Administration, with Arabs of proven political loyalty. Since those officials of the District Administration serving as regional officers and district commissioners exercised combined police and judicial functions, full Arabization of this branch of the bureaucracy would eventually have given the ZNP a form of direct legal and police control over the rural population, independent of the established court system.

The ZNP became particularly concerned about ensuring the loyalty of the Zanzibar police force—the lower ranks were filled with a vast majority of mainland Africans who had been recruited by the British in Tanganyika, Kenya and Nyasaland. Officials in the Ministry of Home and Legal Affairs believed that these mainlanders were sympathetic to the ASP and therefore could not be depended upon to support the Government in a crisis. Muhsin initiated a program of repatriating the mainland African policemen to their countries of origin, and began to replace them with Arab or Asian youths or with carefully selected indigenous Africans. This pro-

[6] *Reporter* (East Africa), January 4, 1964.

gram had several consequences which, in fact, reduced the Government's political security. It demoralized the Zanzibar police force, removed many of its more experienced members, and led to the hasty recruitment of untrained personnel. Just after independence, a number of African policemen were discharged without being repatriated. This created a disaffected group in Zanzibar, experienced in the use of weapons and well versed in the operations and logistics of the Zanzibar police. The repatriation program also placed the ZNP/ZPPP in an awkward position in its relations with the mainland countries and it convinced many local Africans that the Government fully intended to create an Arab police state.

Thus, despite all its precautions, the ZNP/ZPPP regime remained extremely vulnerable to a coup. Not only had nearly all its policies failed to achieve their desired objectives, but they had forced the ASP into a desperate position, hardened the opposition, and thereby strengthened Umma. Moreover, Zanzibar in January, 1964, exhibited several other symptoms of a highly unstable political and social order.

1). *Political instability was a result of the extreme socio-economic discrepancies between competing ethnically defined political groups.*

The social structure of the country was ominous with revolutionary potential. The striking economic differences between the Arab elite and the African mass had long since created bitter social frustrations within the African community. Now, with the ZNP's final victory and the Government's increasing use of authoritarian controls, most Africans were convinced that, under the prevailing political arrangements, this situation would never be corrected and that they would remain a radically deprived community.

2). *The race-class division was so pronounced that it*

became the sole political issue in the nation. The emergence of a single overriding political issue which superseded and obscured all others was a basic cause of regime instability. With only one operative source of disagreement, political conflict divided the society into two polarized segments. No other sources of disagreement were important enough to create overlapping and crosscutting patterns of membership between the two opposed groups. Thus, there was no effective social pressure towards a politics of accommodation.

With the virtual merger of the ZNP and ZPPP, Zanzibar politics hardened into an almost evenly balanced two-party system, but there was little prospect of this system enduring. In the ferocity of their competition, the parties totally politicized Zanzibar society and everyday social relations became more and more segregated along party lines. There was no network of politically neutral clubs or activities which might have bound individuals to each other outside politics, and thereby provided a sort of social unity that transcended political divisions. Nor was there any sizeable social group, with the one possible exception of the Pemba Shirazis, which experienced political cross-pressures sufficient to make it attractive to the parties to bring their views into closer harmony. Individual Zanzibaris generally did not feel divided political loyalties. Instead, they misunderstood and misinterpreted each other's parties to a degree which made mutual accommodation impossible.

The parties were not separated in the final analysis by disparate attitudes towards foreign or domestic policies; they were separated by elemental and irreducible racial fears. ZNP members saw in the ASP disrespect for the Muslim faith, the unbridled use of political power to reverse the social structure of the country, and the ultimate political domination of Zanzibar by the African mainland. To ASP supporters, the ZNP symbolized perpetual economic servitude and political subjection to a racial minority; the ZNP victory of 1963 meant the end of their hope for a better life.

3). *The weakness of the parliamentary system resulted partially from the political fragility of the dominant elite. Colonial rule undermined and altered the political position and role of the traditional ethnic oligarchy. This oligarchy was no longer an inherently powerful political force and could not buttress representative institutions with autonomous powers of social control.*

Despite the persistence of considerable economic advantages, the political viability of the Arab oligarchy had been critically impaired during the seventy-three years of British protection. The elite segment of the Arab community had been steadily reduced in size and wealth and no longer possessed the decisive socio-economic paramountcy which it had enjoyed in the nineteenth century. This decline was a result of several factors: the indebtedness crisis, recurrent depression in the clove industry, and the Islamic system of inheritance which divided property among all eligible heirs. Partitive inheritance was especially harmful economically, as in two or three generations many of the largest estates often became fragmented into tiny units no larger than peasant farms. Many old Omani families had lost their property altogether and had become absorbed into various non-elite segments of the Arab population, while most of those who survived no longer had sufficient income to support a feudal style of life.

Loss of socio-economic paramountcy deprived the Arab oligarchy of its principal basis of social control and was indicative of the profound transformation which the oligarchy had undergone during colonial rule. The Arab elite was no longer a powerful baronial aristocracy with absolute political authority, based upon military supremacy over a culturally differentiated African popula-

tion and upon a system of administration which enforced African subordination. The politically active
members of the Arab elite were part of an urbanized
professional class whose disproportionate political influence was based largely upon their organizational
skills, their control over the administration, and their
status as the top leadership of a parliamentary political
movement. Whereas the Arabs' position in the past
rested upon their superior force as a caste of colonial invaders and upon an ability to use this force to dominate
the economy, their security now depended upon the intrinsic stability of a parliamentary system.

4). *Parliamentary institutions lacked inherent stability because they had not acquired popular consensual
validation. There was no widespread acceptance among
Zanzibaris of a basic political philosophy which might
have led to a commitment to democratic parliamentary
procedures. The symbolic political values of this society
were confined strictly to party goals, and for this reason,
the preservation of the representative system was treated
with broad indifference on both sides.*

The ZNP/ZPPP coalition had not acquired political
legitimacy even though it had come to power as the result of a basically fair and honest parliamentary process,
for most Africans did not regard this as a valid claim to
the possession and exercise of political authority. There
were two principal reasons why representative institutions failed to attain legitimate status and to confer it on
the coalition government.

First, many Africans were unable to understand how
their party had gained a majority vote and yet lost the
election. They felt that they had been cheated of victory and frequently believed that the coalition government had come to power through fraud and decep-
tion. Second, representative institutions had come to be
viewed in highly instrumental terms rather than as in-

tegral and essential features of Zanzibar's national political life. There was no sense that parliamentary institutions possessed an intrinsic functional and symbolic
merit; instead, they were accepted and adhered to only
insofar as they appeared to be directly relevant to the
achievement of other kinds of political and symbolic objectives. Six years of competitive electoral politics had
fostered an environment in which most political partici-
pants felt a far stronger attachment to the symbolic values of their political party than to the maintenance of
parliamentary structures and norms.

Instrumental attachment to parliamentary government was equally characteristic of both sides. For the
Arab oligarchy, the electoral system and even the ZNP itself merely furnished a convenient framework through
which a dominant socio-economic status might be preserved, and through which strict political controls might
operate. This was apparent in the ZNP's readiness to violate the basic principles of parliamentary behavior by
pursuing policies designed to consolidate permanently
its position as the ruling party. The ZNP's attempt to
politicize the entire administration, and to convert it
into an extension of the party organization by staffing
top bureaucratic posts with loyal party followers, would
have destroyed the distinction between State and Society. This, in turn, would have undermined the parliamentary system at a critical point—the need for an impartial civil service.

For the ASP, too, parliamentary structures had negligible intrinsic worth, especially after the July, 1963, election. These institutions had exhibited little usefulness
in the effort to bring about an African-ruled state and to
create an African social revolution. The ASP and the ZNP,
then, had one fundamental attitude in common: both
participated in the parliamentary process because the
presence of Great Britain required it, and because there

was some possibility that such participation would yield a total victory. Once the question of parliamentary victory was decided and the Colonial Government was removed, the two most impelling restraints against extra-parliamentary conduct were no longer effective.

5). *Economic stagnation was directly contributory to parliamentary instability and regime weakness. It reinforced the politically harmful socio-economic polarities by frustrating policies to achieve gradual economic integration of the society. This handicapped any governmental effort to achieve broad popular consensus.*

Financial difficulties severely impaired the political viability of the ZNP/ZPPP regime. The economic crisis in Zanzibar was so great that no government could easily have found a feasible solution, but the ZNP/ZPPP Government sought to meet the crisis by reducing social services. It closed schools, fired teachers, reduced hospital facilities and cut back welfare programs. Not only were these policies very unpopular among Africans, but they were wholly insufficient to place the administration on a sound financial footing.

6). *Geopolitical considerations are highly relevant to political stability. A Government's ability to deal with and overcome a crisis may depend upon the geographical distribution of its local support and upon its external relations with neighboring countries.*

The Zanzibar Government's geopolitical position was extremely precarious. Nearly all the ZNP/ZPPP coalition's popular support was in Pemba or in the remotest areas of Zanzibar. The Stonetown area (which contained the Sultan's palace, the Government office buildings and ministerial residences) is located on a peninsula and enclosed by massive areas of ASP followers. Stonetown had no police protection since all the police stations were in the African area of Zanzibar Town. ZNP/ZPPP leaders were thus geographically cut off from their popular following and were totally unprotected. Lacking defense arrangements with Great Britain or nearby mainland countries and without the support of a well-organized trade union movement in Zanzibar, they could rally no one to their assistance once internal police resistance had been overcome.

The greatest paradox of the Zanzibar revolution is that the initial seizure of power was not accomplished by either of the two principal opposition groups, the ASP or Umma, but by a third political force—an autonomous revolutionary army recruited and organized by a hitherto obscure political leader, John Okello.[7] Little is known in detail about Okello's past. He was born in Uganda about 1935 or 1936, but migrated to Pemba possibly in 1958 or 1959 and for a brief time was employed there in the Zanzibar police. For several years before the revolution he was an ASP branch leader in a small Pemba village. He left Pemba after the July, 1963, election and went to Zanzibar, possibly with the intention of overthrowing the coalition government.

Okello recruited the insurgents from two principal sources: policemen discharged by the government after independence and militant members of the *Afro-Shirazi Youth League* (ASYL). Initially the insurgent army was quite small, as the strategy of the coup depended upon surprise rather than superiority of force. Okello was able to plan on limited resistance; Zanzibar had no army, and the only significant internal resistance to be overcome was from the police force, which had been demoralized and critically weakened by the repatriation program.

The extreme vulnerability of the Zanzibar Government is most vividly illustrated by the ease with which

[7] For a detailed and well-informed account of the events of the revolution, see *The Spectator*, February 7, 1964, "Gideon's Voices," and February 14, 1964, "How it Happened."

the seizure of power was carried out. The police had only two armories, located fairly close to one another in the African quarter of Zanzibar Town. Neither was prepared to withstand a surprise attack since Government intelligence sources, preoccupied with the conspicuously subversive activities of Umma, were unaware of Okello. Okello's army staged quick Commando-like raids on both armories at about 3:00 A.M. Sunday morning. Capture of these two armories deprived the Government of virtually its entire capacity to resist or to retaliate, and placed full military power in the hands of the insurgents. The Zanzibar radio station, completely undefended, was also in the African quarter of the town and lay between the two armories. It was seized next. Mopping up Arab groups in the rural areas had to continue for several days, but the sporadic resistance never posed a serious threat to the new regime. The revolution was, for all practical purposes, completed within an hour or two.

The formal capitulation did not occur until Sunday afternoon. Okello was afraid that there might be a unified counterattack by a concerted force of armed Arabs from the fertile quadrangle, and was unwilling to despatch troops to seize Stonetown until it was certain that the revolution was secure. Though no attack materialized, many hours elapsed between the capture of the police stations and the seizure of the capital. This delay enabled the Sultan to escape and created an erroneous impression that the revolution was accompanied by a long and bitter pitched battle between the revolutionary army and the police.

The abruptness and decisiveness of Okello's seizure of power has led to several other misconceptions about the nature of the coup. One concerns the size and character of Okello's army. After capturing the armories, the insurgents distributed arms to known sympathizers in the

African quarter. When dawn broke, the revolutionary army therefore appeared to consist of hundreds of well-armed soldiers and was, for this reason, widely reported as having been organized and equipped outside Zanzibar. A second widely publicized report concerned the presence of Cuban militiamen among the revolutionaries. There is no concrete evidence at all that this was the case. It is most probable that the Cuban rumor was a result of the presence of several ZPFL and FPTU leaders who had joined the revolutionaries early on the first day. Many members of these groups had adopted the Cuban style of dress and appearance, and even employed the Cuban cry "Venceremos" (We Shall Conquer) as a political symbol. Their Cuban type of uniform set them off clearly from the ASYL members and were probably the basis of the report that the revolutionary army contained Cuban soldiers.

These rumors have obscured the most important feature of the Zanzibar revolution—that it was John Okello's own personal creation and that it was neither assisted by outside forces nor initiated by the two opposition parties in Zanzibar. This seizure of power by an autonomous military force independent of the existing political opposition had extreme significance: it did not result in an immediate and decisive transfer of power from the former government to the ASP. Instead, the collapse of the ZNP/ZPPP regime was followed by an interlude of political ambiguity during which the opposition groups competed to gain control of the state machinery. In this competition, the badly dispirited and internally divided ASP was at a singular disadvantage against the highly organized and tightly disciplined Umma party.

Okello, whose command of the revolutionary army placed him temporarily above the crisis, did not resolve the conflict in favor of his former party. He appointed a

Revolutionary Council which was predominantly under the control of the ASP, but which also included Babu and several other Umma leaders.[8] The ensuing distribution of top Government positions revealed that Okello's decision to create a combined regime had placed Umma in a position of influence nearly equal to that of the ASP. Abedi Karume, President of the ASP, assumed the position of President in the newly reconstituted "People's Republic of Zanzibar and Pemba"; Abdulla Hanga, Deputy General-Secretary of the ASP and one of the strongest supporters of Babu in the party, was named Vice-President; and Babu himself became Minister for Defense and External Affairs. The remaining ministerial positions were assumed by various parliamentary leaders of the ASP, but important Umma leaders were assigned to top-ranking administrative positions in several critical ministries.

The most striking feature of Zanzibar's revolutionary government has been the rapid consolidation of the diverse opposition groups and the formation of a highly unified regime. Within a short time after the coup, Umma merged with the ASP; the trade union affiliates of the two parties also joined in a single national trade union organization, *The Federation of Revolutionary Trade Unions*. The ASP-Umma merger has had enormous bearing on Zanzibar's present political development. It confirmed the close working relationship which had already grown up between Umma leaders and the

[8] Okello's decision not to hand all political power to the ASP probably stemmed from his personal disillusionment with the party, a result of its electoral defeat and lack of resolution during the period before independence. As a highly militant African nationalist, he was more sympathetic to the revolutionary ethos of Umma than to the moderate outlook of his own party. He was reluctant to hand full political power to Umma, however, possibly because of Umma's non-African character.

ASP militants, and thereby facilitated the emergence of militant leadership as the major force in post-revolutionary Zanzibar politics.

The unification of the opposition may, in part, be traced to pre-revolutionary political attitudes and events. All the opposition groups, for example, had shared an antipathy to Arab rule, and a pattern of close cooperation among them had been necessitated by the former Government's authoritarian policies and its refusal to differentiate between parliamentary and revolutionary opposition. Moreover, Babu himself had always enjoyed considerable popularity in the African community, despite his position as General-Secretary of the ZNP. His personal opposition to Muhsin and to the influence of the Arab oligarchy within the ZNP were widely known to Africans, as was his deep commitment to revolutionary social change. His final break with the ZNP and his bitter opposition to it before independence had demonstrated unequivocally the genuineness of his desire to create a more egalitarian social and political system. Even before the Arab government fell, these factors provided a viable basis for the ASP-Umma merger.

In at least two important ways, however, the revolution itself helped to facilitate the full unification of the opposition. First, the revolution resolved the political issue of alien racial domination. With the Arab community politically and economically dispossessed, and with African leaders at the head of the Revolutionary Council, non-African ethnic groups did not challenge the creation of an African state. Once this change had occurred, many African leaders were no longer reluctant to form a multi-racial national leadership body and were therefore prepared to accept a merger with Umma despite its predominantly non-African character.

The second important change brought about by the revolution was the creation of mass enthusiasm for militant leadership. The new legitimacy of the revolutionary leaders was reflected both in the powerful role played by those who had sought violent overthrow of the old regime, and in a decisive shift in power within the ASP from moderate to radical elements. This shift contributed directly to the ease and rapidity with which the ASP-Umma merger was carried out, for the ASP moderates who might have been disinclined to join with a radical movement such as Umma exercised no effective influence within the party after the revolution.

The puritanical socialist credo of the Umma party imbued the Revolutionary Council with a high degree of ideological militancy. The combined ASP-Umma regime was determined to complete the political revolution by bringing about a rapid restratification of the Zanzibar population. Its objective was to transform Zanzibar into a wholly egalitarian society, so that the African community would achieve full social and economic parity with other ethnic groups. Toward this end, the new government initiated a series of policies designed to ameliorate the social position of the African majority. It recruited African personnel into the administrative levels of the civil service and undertook measures to bring about a fairer distribution of the arable land. The Revolutionary Council also sought to eliminate from Zanzibar all symbolic vestiges of a racially divided society. It banned all racial clubs and organizations, and sought to infuse the society with a radical socialist ethos stressing class and national solidarity rather than race.

The revolutionary government began to face critical problems, however, in consummating the African social revolution. This was due in part to the depressed condition of Zanzibar's economy and the massive economic dislocation brought about by the revolution itself, and in part to the difficulty of maintaining political viability in so small a state. An additional and more subtle problem was that former Umma leaders, in informal co-alition with ASP militants, began to dominate the ASP parliamentary leaders in the Revolutionary Council. President Karume looked to the mainland countries for support. The ASP had traditionally held close ties with TANU, and the ASP's social reforms had the sympathy of Tanganyika's President, Julius Nyerere. Karume and Nyerere concluded a constitutional merger of their two countries in late April (1964), about three months after the revolution.

The new state was at first called the Republic of Tanganyika and Zanzibar and later was renamed Tanzania. President Nyerere became President of Tanzania and there are two vice-presidents, Karume and Rashidi Kawawa (former Vice-President of Tanganyika). The constitutional relationship between the two countries is, in basic principle, modeled on the relationship between England and Northern Ireland.[9] Most major areas of policy are the responsibility of the Tanzanian National Assembly. These include defense and foreign affairs, taxation, trade, citizenship and immigration. Zanzibar was allowed to retain separate legislative and administrative institutions, but these were, in theory, to have power only over limited local matters.[10]

Zanzibar has in actual practice resisted administrative and political integration, however, and continues to

[9] The author is indebted to Professor Thomas Franck of New York University, constitutional adviser to the Afro-Shirazi Party, for this view of the Tanzanian constitution.

[10] Tanganyika Government, Special Supplement to *The Tanganyika Gazette,* Vol. XLV, No. 28, 24th April, 1964, "A Bill for an Act to ratify the Articles of Union between the Republic of Tanganyika and the People's Republic of Zanzibar, to provide for the government of the United Republic and of Zanzibar, to make provision for the Modification and Amendment of the Constitution and Laws of Tanganyika for the purpose of giving effect to the Union and the said Articles and for matters connected therewith and incidental thereto" (Dar es Salaam: Government Printer, 1964).

practice considerable independence both in domestic and international affairs. The Zanzibar Government unofficially maintains an almost exclusive jurisdiction over several areas of policy which, by the terms of the constitution, were assigned to the Tanzanian Government. To some extent, this separatism is related to the distribution of power in the Revolutionary Council. The tendency for an informal coalition of Umma leaders and ASP ideological militants to become the controlling force in internal Zanzibar politics has accelerated since the merger with Tanganyika. Many of the ASP moderates, who had gradually begun to regain a certain degree of influence in the two or three months after the revolution, left Zanzibar to take up positions in the Tanzanian Government. Their exodus has left the militants virtually unopposed in Zanzibar.

The leadership of the Tanzanian Republic must still face the critical problems of achieving full integration of the two countries, of completing the African social revolution, and of fostering an atmosphere of mutual trust between all Zanzibaris. There is little doubt, however, that if the constitution can be fully implemented, the chances for political stability, racial harmony and economic recovery will be far greater than when Zanzibar stood alone.

APPENDIX
BIBLIOGRAPHY
INDEX

Appendix

THE ARTICLES OF UNION
between
THE REPUBLIC OF TANGANYIKA AND THE PEOPLES' REPUBLIC OF ZANZIBAR

WHEREAS the Governments of the Republic of Tanganyika and of the Peoples' Republic of Zanzibar, being mindful of the long association of the peoples of these lands and of their ties of kinship and amity, and being desirous of furthering that association and strengthening of these ties and of furthering the unity of African peoples, have met and considered the union of the Republic of Tanganyika with the Peoples' Republic of Zanzibar:

AND WHEREAS the Governments of the Republic of Tanganyika and of the Peoples' Republic of Zanzibar are desirous that the two Republics shall be united in one Sovereign Republic in accordance with the Articles hereinafter contained:—

(i) The Republic of Tanganyika and the Peoples' Republic of Zanzibar shall be united in one Sovereign Republic.

(ii) During the period from the commencement of the union until the Constituent Assembly provided for in Article (vii) shall have met and adopted a Constitution for the united Republic (hereinafter referred to as the interim period), the united Republic shall be governed in accordance with the provisions of Articles (iii) to (vi).

(iii) During the interim period the Constitution of the united Republic shall be the Constitution of Tanganyika so modified as to provide for—

(a) a separate legislature and executive in and for Zanzibar from time to time constituted in accordance with the existing law of Zanzibar and having exclusive authority within Zanzibar for matters other than those reserved to the Parliament and Executive of the united Republic;

(b) the offices of two Vice-Presidents one of whom (being a person normally resident in Zanzibar) shall be the head of the aforesaid executive in and for Zanzibar and shall be the principal assistant of the President of the united Republic in the discharge of his executive functions in relation to Zanzibar;

(c) the representation of Zanzibar in the Parliament of the united Republic;

(d) such other matters as may be expedient or desirable to give effect to the united Republic and to these Articles.

(iv) There shall reserved [sic] to the Parliament and Executive of the united Republic the following matters—

(a) The Constitution and Government of the united Republic.

(b) External Affairs.

(c) Defence.

(d) Police.

(e) Emergency Powers.

(f) Citizenship.

(g) Immigration.

(h) External Trade and Borrowing.

(i) The Public Service of the united Republic.

(j) Income Tax, Corporation Tax, Customs and Excise.

(k) Harbours, Civil Aviation, Posts and Telegraphs.

And the said Parliament and Executive shall have exclusive authority in such matters throughout and for the purposes of the united Republic and in addition exclusive authority in respect of all other matters in and for Tanganyika.

(v) The existing laws of Tanganyika and of Zanzibar shall remain in force in their respective territories subject—

(a) to any provision made hereafter by a competent legislature;

(b) to such provision as may be made by order of the President of the united Republic for the extension to Zanzibar of any law relating to any of the matters set out in Article (iv), and the revocation of any corresponding law of Zanzibar;

(c) to such amendments as may be expedient or desirable to give effect to the union and to these Articles.

(vi) (a) The first President of the united Republic shall be Mwalimu Julius K. Nyerere and he shall carry on the Government of the united Republic in accordance with the provisions of these Articles and with the assistance of the Vice-Presidents aforesaid and of such other ministers and officers as he may appoint from Tanganyika and Zanzibar and their respective public services.

(b) The first Vice-President from Zanzibar to be appointed in accordance with the modifications provided for in Article (iii) shall be Sheikh Abeid Karume.

(vii) The President of the united Republic in agreement with the Vice-President who is head of the Executive in Zanzibar shall—

(a) Appoint a Commission to make proposals for a Constitution for the united Republic.

(b) Summon a Constituent Assembly composed of Representatives from Tanganyika and from Zanzibar in such numbers as they may determine to meet within one year of the commencement of the union for the purpose of considering the proposals of the Commission aforesaid and to adopt a Constitution for the united Republic.

(viii) These Articles shall be subject to the enactment of laws by the Parliament of Tanganyika and by the Revolutionary Council of the Peoples' Republic of Zanzibar in conjunction with the Cabinet of Ministers thereof, ratifying the same and providing for the Government of the united Republic and of Zanzibar in accordance therewith.

IN WITNESS WHEREOF Julius K. Nyerere, the President of the Republic of Tanganyika and Abeid Karume, the President of the Peoples' Republic of Zanzibar, have signed these Articles, in duplicate, at Zanzibar, on this twenty-second day of April, 1964.

Bibliography

BOOKS

GENERAL WORKS

Almond, Gabriel A. and Coleman, James S. *The Politics of the Developing Areas*. Princeton: Princeton University Press, 1960.

Apter, David E. *The Gold Coast in Transition*. Princeton: Princeton University Press, 1955.

――――. *The Political Kingdom in Uganda: A Study in Bureaucratic Nationalism*. Princeton: Princeton University Press, 1961.

Coleman, James S. "The Emergence of African Political Parties," in C. Grove Haines (ed.), *Africa Today*. Baltimore: Johns Hopkins Press, 1955.

――――. *Nigeria: Background to Nationalism*. Berkeley and Los Angeles: University of California Press, 1958.

Coser, Lewis. *The Functions of Social Conflict*. Glencoe: The Free Press, 1956.

Deutsch, Karl W. *Nationalism and Social Communication*. New York: John Wiley and Sons, 1953.

Duverger, Maurice. *Political Parties: Their Organization and Activity in the Modern State*. London: Methuen and Co., Ltd., 1961.

Furnivall, John Sydenham. *Colonial Policy and Practice*. New York: New York University Press, 1956.

Geertz, Clifford (ed.). *Old Societies and New States*. Glencoe: The Free Press, 1963.

Hodgkin, Thomas. *Nationalism in Colonial Africa*. London: Frederick Muller, 1956.

Levy, Marion J. *The Structure of Society*. Princeton: Princeton University Press, 1952.

Liebenow, J. Gus. "Liberia," in Gwendolen M. Carter (ed.), *African One-Party States*. Ithaca: Cornell University Press, 1962.

Lipset, Seymour Martin, Trow, Martin and Coleman, James. *Union Democracy: The Internal Politics of the I.T.U.* Glencoe: The Free Press, 1956.

Michels, Robert. *Political Parties: A Sociological Study of the Oligarchical Tendencies of Modern Democracy.* Translated from the 1915 edition by Eden and Cedar Paul. New York: Dover Publications, Inc., 1959.

Plamenatz, John. *On Alien Rule and Self-Government.* London: Longmans, 1960.

Sklar, Richard L. *Nigerian Political Parties: Power in an Emergent African Nation.* Princeton: Princeton University Press, 1963.

ISLAM

Anderson, J. N. D. *Islamic Law in Africa.* London: Her Majesty's Stationery Office, 1954.

Baulin, Jacques. *The Arab Role in Africa.* London: Penguin Books, 1962.

Gibb, Sir Hamilton, A. R. *Mohammedanism, an Historical Survey.* New York: Mentor Books, 1955.

Guillaume, Alfred. *Islam.* Edinburgh: Penguin Books, 1956.

Harries, Lyndon P. *Islam in East Africa.* London: Universities Mission to Central Africa, 1954.

Kerekes, Tibor (ed.). *The Arab Middle East and Muslim Africa.* New York: Frederick A. Praeger, 1961.

Levy, Reuben. *The Social Structure of Islam.* Cambridge: Cambridge University Press, 1957.

Smith, Wilfred Cantwell. *Islam in Modern History.* New York: Mentor Books, 1959.

HISTORY AND ETHNOGRAPHY

Coupland, R. *East Africa and Its Invaders.* Oxford: The Clarendon Press, 1961.

————. *The Exploitation of East Africa, 1856-1890.* London: Faber and Faber Ltd., 1939.

Gray, Sir John. *History of Zanzibar From the Middle Ages to 1856.* London: Oxford University Press, 1962.

Hailey, Lord Malcolm. *Native Administration in the British African Territories.* London: His Majesty's Stationery Office, 1950. Part II.

Hamilton, Genesta. *Princes of Zinj: The Rulers of Zanzibar.* London: Hutchinson & Co., 1957.

Bibliography

Hollingsworth, L. W. *Zanzibar Under the Foreign Office, 1890-1913*. London: Macmillan & Co. Ltd., 1953.

Ingham, Kenneth. *A History of East Africa*. London: Longmans, 1962.

Ingrams, W. H. *Chronology & Genealogies of Zanzibar Rulers*. Zanzibar: Government Printer, 1926.

——. *Zanzibar, Its History and Its People*. London: H. F. & G. Witherby, 1931.

Lanchester, H. V. *Zanzibar, A Study in Tropical Town Planning*. Cheltenham: Ed. J. Burrow & Co. Ltd., 1923.

Marsh, Zoe and Kingsworth, G. W. *An Introduction to the History of East Africa*. Cambridge: The University Press, 1961.

Marsh, Zoe. *East Africa Through Contemporary Records*. Cambridge: The University Press, 1961.

Middleton, John. *Land Tenure in Zanzibar*. London: Her Majesty's Stationery Office, 1961.

Oliver, Roland and Mathew, Gervase (eds.). *History of East Africa*. Oxford: The Clarendon Press, 1963.

Ommaney, F. D. *Isle of Cloves*. London: Longmans, Green and Co., 1955.

Pearce, Major F. B. *Zanzibar, The Island Metropolis of Eastern Africa*. London: T. Fisher Unwin Ltd., 1920.

Prins, A. H. J. *The Swahili Speaking Peoples of Zanzibar and the East African Coast*. London: International African Institute, 1961.

Reusch, Richard. *History of East Africa*. New York: Frederick Ungar Publishing Co., 1961.

Saleh, Ibuni. *A Short History of the Comorians in Zanzibar*. Dar es Salaam: The Tanganyika Standard Press, 1936.

ARTICLES AND PERIODICALS

Africa Report. 1961-1964.

Cave, Basil S. "The End of Slavery in Zanzibar and British East Africa," reprinted from the *Journal of the African Society* (1909), pp. 19-30.

Coleman, James S. "Nationalism in Tropical Africa," *American Political Science Review*, XLVIII (June, 1954), pp. 404-426.

Kyle, Keith. "Gideon's Voices," *The Spectator* (February 7, 1964), p. 175.
―――. "How It Happened," *The Spectator* (February 14, 1964), pp. 202-203.
Lofchie, Michael. "Party Conflict in Zanzibar," *The Journal of Modern African Studies,* Vol. I, No. 2, (June, 1963), pp. 185-207.
―――. "Zanzibar, Problems and Prospects," *Commonwealth Journal,* Vol. VI, No. 6, pp. 247-251.
Reporter (East Africa). 1962-1964.
Rotberg, Robert. "The Political Outlook in Zanzibar," *Africa Report* (October, 1961), pp. 5, 6, and 12.
Sanger, Clyde. "Zanzibar Revisited," *Africa Report* (June, 1963), pp. 19-22.
Smith, M. G. "Social and Cultural Pluralism," *Annals of the New York Academy of Sciences,* Vol. 83, Art. 5, pp. 763-777.
Spearhead. 1962-1963.

PUBLIC DOCUMENTS

GREAT BRITAIN

Great Britain. *Colonial Annual Reports: Zanzibar, 1948.* London: His Majesty's Stationery Office, 1949.
Great Britain. *Colonial Reports, Zanzibar 1949 & 1950.* London: Her Majesty's Stationery Office, 1952.
Great Britain. *East Africa Royal Commission 1953-1955 Report.* London: Her Majesty's Stationery Office, Cmnd. 9475.
Great Britain. *The Kenya Coastal Strip: Report of the Commissioner.* London: Her Majesty's Stationery Office, 1962. Cmnd. 1585.
Great Britain. *Report of a Commission of Inquiry into Disturbances in Zanzibar during June, 1961.* London: Her Majesty's Stationery Office, 1961. Colonial No. 353.
Great Britain. *Report of the Kenya Coastal Strip Conference, 1962.* London: Her Majesty's Stationery Office, 1962. Cmnd. 1701.
Great Britain. *Report on Zanzibar.* London: Her Majesty's Stationery Office, 1962.
Great Britain. *Report of the Zanzibar Constitutional Confer-*

ence, 1962. London: Her Majesty's Stationery Office, 1962. Cmnd. 1699.

Great Britain. *Zanzibar, 1955 and 1956.* London: Her Majesty's Stationery Office, 1957.

ZANZIBAR

Agricultural Indebtedness

Bartlett, C. A. and Last, J. S. *Report on the Indebtedness of the Agricultural Classes, 1933.* Zanzibar: Government Printer, 1934.

Binder, B. H., F.C.A. *Report on the Clove Industry.* Zanzibar: Government Printer, 1936.

Dowson, Sir Ernest M., K.B.E. *A Note on Agricultural Indebtedness in the Zanzibar Protectorate.* Zanzibar: Government Printer, 1936.

Kirkham, V. H. *Memorandum on the Functions of a Department of Agriculture with Special Reference to Zanzibar.* Zanzibar: Government Printer, 1931.

Strickland, C. F. *Report on Co-operation and Certain Aspects of the Economic Condition of Agriculture in Zanzibar.* London: Crown Agents for the Colonies, 1932.

Troup, R. S. *Report on Clove Cultivation in the Zanzibar Protectorate.* Zanzibar: Government Printer, 1932.

Zanzibar Protectorate. *Memorandum on Certain Aspects of the Zanzibar Clove Industry.* London: Waterlow and Sons, Ltd., 1926.

Zanzibar Protectorate. *Report of the Commission on Agricultural Indebtedness and Memorandum thereon by the Government of Zanzibar.* Zanzibar: Government Printer, 1935.

Zanzibar Protectorate. *Report of the Retrenchment Committee.* Zanzibar: Government Printer, 1927.

Zanzibar Protectorate. *Zanzibar, The Land and Its Mortgage Debt.* London: Waterlow and Sons, Ltd., 1932.

Constitutional and Electoral

Arundell, Sir Robert. *Report of the Delimitation Commissioner, Zanzibar, 1962.* Zanzibar: Government Printer, 1962.

Blood, Sir Hilary. *Report of the Constitutional Commissioner,*

Zanzibar, 1960. Zanzibar: Government Printer, 1960.

Coutts, W. F. *Methods of Choosing Unofficial Members of the Legislative Council.* Zanzibar: Government Printer, 1956.

Zanzibar Protectorate. "Constitutional Development, Zanzibar: Exchange of Despatches between the British Resident, Zanzibar and the Secretary of State for the Colonies," Sessional Paper No. 9 of *Papers Laid before the Legislative Council, 1955.* Zanzibar: Government Printer, 1956, pp. 75-80.

Zanzibar Protectorate. "Constitutional Reforms 1960," Sessional Paper No. 14 of *Papers Laid before the Legislative Council, 1960.* Zanzibar: Government Printer, 1961, pp. 40-48.

Zanzibar Protectorate. *Debates of the Legislative Council, 1926-1938 and 1945-1961.* Zanzibar: Government Printer.

Zanzibar Protectorate. *Papers Laid before the Legislative Council, 1935-1939, 1945-1962.* Zanzibar: Government Printer.

Zanzibar Protectorate. *Report of the Committee on the Extension of the Franchise to Women.* Zanzibar: Government Printer, 1959.

Zanzibar Protectorate. "Report of Select Committee of the Legislative Council Appointed on 16th February, 1957, to Consider the Legislative Council (Elections) Bill, 1957," Sessional Paper No. 3 of *Papers Laid before the Legislative Council, 1957.* Zanzibar: Government Printer, 1958, pp. 8-11.

Zanzibar Protectorate. *The Report of the Supervisor of Elections on the Elections in Zanzibar, 1957.* Zanzibar: Government Printer, 1958.

Zanzibar Protectorate. *Report of the Supervisors of Elections on the Registration of Voters and the Elections held in January, 1961.* Zanzibar: Government Printer, 1961.

Zanzibar Protectorate. *Report of the Supervisor of Elections, June, 1961.* Zanzibar: Government Printer, 1961.

Zanzibar Protectorate. *Selection of Appointed Representative Members of the Legislative Council.* Zanzibar: Government Printer, n.d.

Miscellaneous

Bartlett, C. A. *Statistics of the Zanzibar Protectorate, 1890-1935.* Zanzibar: Government Printer, 1936.

Bibliography

Batson, Edward. *Report on Proposals for a Social Survey of Zanzibar.* Zanzibar: Government Printer, 1948.

Crofts, R. A. *Zanzibar Clove Industry: Statement of Government Policy and Report.* Zanzibar: Government Printer, 1959.

Gray, Sir John. *Report of the Arbitrator to Enquire into a Trade Dispute at the Wharf Area at Zanzibar.* Zanzibar: Government Printer, n.d.

————. *Report on the Inquiry into Claims to Certain Land at or Near Ngezi, Vitongoji, in the Mudiria of Chake Chake in the District of Pemba.* Zanzibar: Government Printer, 1956.

Kerr, A. J. *Report on an Investigation into the Possibilities of Co-operative Development in the Zanzibar Protectorate and Ancillary Subjects.* Zanzibar: Government Printer, 1950.

Selwyn, P. and Watson, T. Y. *Report on the Economic Development of the Zanzibar Protectorate.* Zanzibar: Government Printer, 1962.

Vasey, E. A. *Report on Local Government Advancement in Zanzibar Township.* n.p., n.d.

Wilson, F. B. *A Note on Adult Literacy Amongst the Rural Population of the Zanzibar Protectorate.* Zanzibar: Government Printer, 1939.

Zanzibar Protectorate. *Annual Report of the Department of Education for the Year 1955.* Zanzibar: Government Printer, 1956.

Zanzibar Protectorate. *Annual Report of the Department of Education for the Year 1962.* Zanzibar: Government Printer, 1963.

Zanzibar Protectorate. *Annual Reports of the Provincial Administration, 1950-1963.* Zanzibar: Government Printer.

Zanzibar Protectorate. *Annual Report on the Treatment of Offenders for the Year ended 31st December, 1961.* Zanzibar: Government Printer, 1962.

Zanzibar Protectorate. *Annual Report of the Zanzibar Police for the year 1961.* Zanzibar: Government Printer, 1962.

Zanzibar Protectorate. *East African Common Services Organization: The Gross Domestic Product of the Protectorate of Zanzibar, 1957-1961.* East African Statistical Department, n.d.

Zanzibar Protectorate. *Estimates of Revenue and Expenditure for the Zanzibar Protectorate, 1955-1963.* Zanzibar: Government Printer, n.d.

Zanzibar Protectorate. *The Gazetteer of Zanzibar Islands.* Zanzibar: Government Printer, 1962.

Zanzibar Protectorate. *General Statement of the Aims and Policies of His Highness's Government, 1961.* Zanzibar: Government Printer, 1962.

Zanzibar Protectorate. *A Guide to Zanzibar.* Zanzibar, Government Printer, 1952.

Zanzibar Protectorate. *A Guide to Zanzibar.* Nairobi: East African Printers Ltd., n.d.

Zanzibar Protectorate. *Labour Report for the year 1955.* Zanzibar: Government Printer, 1956.

Zanzibar Protectorate. *Memorandum on Economic and Social Development, 1943.* Zanzibar: Government Printer, 1943.

Zanzibar Protectorate. *Memorandum on Native Organization and Administration in Zanzibar.* Zanzibar: Government Printer, 1926.

Zanzibar Protectorate. *Notes on the Census of the Zanzibar Protectorate, 1948.* Zanzibar: Government Printer, 1953.

Zanzibar Protectorate. *Notes on Contributions and Subventions to Inter-Territorial Organizations.* Zanzibar: Government Printer, n.d.

Zanzibar Protectorate. *Report on the Census Enumeration of the Whole Population, 1931.* Zanzibar: Government Printer, 1931.

Zanzibar Protectorate. *Report on the Census of the Population of Zanzibar Protectorate, 1958.* Zanzibar: Government Printer, 1960.

Zanzibar Protectorate. *Report on the Civil Disturbances in Zanzibar on July 30, 1951.* Zanzibar: Government Printer, 1952.

Zanzibar Protectorate. *Report of the Commission of Enquiry Concerning the Riot in Zanzibar on the 7th of February, 1936.* Zanzibar: Government Printer, 1936. Also printed as Sessional Paper No. 4 of *Papers Laid before the Legislative Council, 1936.*

Zanzibar Protectorate. *Report of the Commission of Inquiry* on the Conditions of Service of Government Primary School Teachers. Zanzibar: Government Printer, 1962.

Zanzibar Protectorate. *Report of the Committee on Education, 1959.* Zanzibar: Government Printer, n.d.

Zanzibar Protectorate. *Report of the Committee on Immigration, 1959.* Zanzibar: Government Printer, 1960.

Zanzibar Protectorate. *Report of the Committee on Wages of Muster Roll Employees of the Government, 1961.* Zanzibar: Government Printer, 1961.

Zanzibar Protectorate. *Report on the Native Census, 1924.* Zanzibar: Government Printer, 1924.

Zanzibar Protectorate. *Report on the non-Native Census, 1921.* Zanzibar: Government Printer, 1921.

Zanzibar Protectorate. *Report on the Progress of the Development Programme for the years 1946-1951.* Zanzibar: Government Printer, 1951.

Zanzibar Protectorate. *Report and Recommendations on the Present Position and Future Prospects of Agriculture in the Zanzibar Protectorate.* Zanzibar: Government Printer, 1959.

Zanzibar Protectorate. "Report of the Select Committee Appointed to Enquire into the Public Order Bill," Sessional Paper No. 7 of *Papers Laid before the Legislative Council, 1959.* Zanzibar: Government Printer, 1960.

Zanzibar Protectorate. *Review of the Systems of Land Tenure in the Islands of Zanzibar and Pemba.* Zanzibar: Government Printer, 1945.

Zanzibar Protectorate. *Staff Lists, 1955-1963.* Zanzibar: Government Printer.

Zanzibar Protectorate. *Summary Digest of Useful Statistics.* Zanzibar: Government Printer, n.d.

Zanzibar Protectorate. *Trade Report (Annual) 1956-1962.* Zanzibar: Government Printer.

NEWSPAPERS

GREAT BRITAIN

The Guardian (Manchester). 1957-1964.
The Observer (London). 1957-1964.
The Times (London). 1957-1964.

EAST AFRICA

Daily Nation. 1962-1964.
East African Standard. 1957-1964.
Sunday Nation (Weekly). 1962-1964.
Tanganyika Standard. 1957-1964.

ZANZIBAR

Adal Insaf. 1948-1963. Independent 1948-1956; ZNP 1956-1960; Independent 1960-1963.
Afrika Kwetu. 1947-1963. ASP.
Agope. 1963. ASP.
Agozi. 1959-1962. ZAYM, ASP.
Al Falaq. 1929-1963. Arab Association.
Al Nahadha. 1951-1954. Independent.
Jasho Letu. 1961. ZPFL.
Kibarua. 1961-1963. FPTU.
Kipanga. 1961. ASP.
Kwacha. 1963. Umma Party.
Mkombozi. 1961. ASP.
Mwangaza. Published irregularly between 1954 and 1960. Independent.
Mwiba. 1963. ASP.
Mwongozi. 1942-1963. Independent, but affiliated with the Arab Association from 1942 to 1956; ZNP, from 1956 to 1963.
Samachar. 1902-1963. Independent.
Sauti ya Afro-Shirazi. 1959-1961. ASP.
Sauti ya Jogoo. 1961-1963. ZNP.
Sauti ya Umma. 1963-1964. Umma Party.
Sauti ya Wanachi. 1960-1963. ZPPP.
Umma. 1960-1963. ZNP.
The Worker. 1962-1963. FPTU.
Zanews. 1961-1964. ZNP, from 1961-1963; Umma, 1963 to 1964.
Zanzibar Voice. 1922-1963. Independent.

UNPUBLISHED MATERIAL

Batson, Edward. *The Social Survey of Zanzibar.* Department of Social Studies, University of Capetown. Capetown: by the direction of the Zanzibar Government, n.d. 21 volumes.

Bibliography

BBC Radio Monitoring Service. *Zanzibar Radio Broadcasts January 10 through February 25, 1964.* (mimeograph.)

Clove Growers Association, Board of Management. *Minutes of Board Meetings, 1935-1938.* (typescript.)

Great Britain. *Minutes of the Proceedings, Zanzibar Constitutional Conference, March-April, 1962.* London, 1962.

——. *Minutes of the Proceedings, Zanzibar Independence Conference, October, 1963.* London, 1963.

Institute of Current World Affairs. *Zanzibar Arabs.* (mimeograph, 1954.)

——. *The Zanzibar Elections.* (mimeograph, 1957.)

Pan African Freedom Movement of East and Central Africa. *Minutes of the Meetings of the PAFMECA Conference held at Mwanza, Tanganyika, October, 1958.* (mimeograph, n.p. n.d.)

——. *Minutes of the Meetings of the PAFMECA Conference held at Zanzibar, April, 1959.* (mimeograph, n.p. n.d.)

Zanzibar Government. *Proceedings of the Commission of Inquiry into the Civil Disturbances of June, 1961.* Zanzibar, 1961.

——. *Minutes of the Meetings of the Round Table Conference held in Zanzibar, October, 1958.* Zanzibar, 1958.

Zanzibar Information Office. *Press Release on the Results of the July, 1963 Election.* (mimeograph, 1963.)

Zanzibar Protectorate. *The Crown, Prosecutor, versus Abdulla Suleiman el Harthi et al.,* Criminal Case #1805 (1954).

Zanzibar Protectorate. *The Crown, Prosecutor, versus Mohammed Hamoud,* Criminal Case #3585 (1955).

DOCUMENTS, STATEMENTS AND PUBLICATIONS OF THE POLITICAL PARTIES

AFRO-SHIRAZI PARTY

The Analysis of the New Constitution to be Enacted by the People of Zanzibar.

ASP Draft Constitution Presented to the Second Annual Conference, August, 1962.

ASP Letter to His Excellency, the British Resident, August 27, 1962.

298

ASP Resolutions passed at the Second Annual Conference, August, 1962.

ASP Statement to the Moshi Afro-Asian People's Solidarity Conference, February, 1963.

The Committee of Seventeen: The Question of Zanzibar. Statement made before the Committee at the United Nations, New York, on behalf of the Afro-Shirazi Party, by A. A. Karume, Party President, and O. Sharif, Leader of the Opposition in Legislative Council, July 13, 1962.

Interviews with Party Officials.

Memorandum by the Afro-Shirazi Party to the Secretary of State for the Colonies during his visit to Zanzibar.

Memorandum Presented to the United Nations Committee of Seventeen, by Abdulla Kassim Hanga, Deputy General Secretary, Afro-Shirazi Party; Saleh Sadalla M.L.C.; Aboud Jumbe, Opposition Chief Whip; the President of ASY League, Seif Bakar, representing the Afro-Shirazi Party, and Messrs. Soud Othman and Abdulla Mwinyi, representing the Zanzibar Association.

Mimeographed Speeches, ASP Second Annual Conference, August, 1962.

Speeches made at party meetings.

ZPFL. Memorandum Submitted by Comrades Muhammed Mfaume and Diria Hassan, the President and the Deputy Secretary General respectively of the Zanzibar and Pemba Federation of Labour.

ZPFL. Resolutions Passed at the Second Annual Conference of the Zanzibar and Pemba Federation of Labor, October, 1963.

ZANZIBAR NATIONALIST PARTY

Mohammed, Abdul Rahman (Babu). *Utawala wa Kibeberu (Colonial Government)*. Political Education Series Pamphlet No. 1. Zanzibar: Zanzibar Nationalist Party, 1959.

Mohammed, Ali Mafudh and Foum, Mohammed Ali. *Forge Ahead to Emancipation*. Havana: Zanzibar Nationalist Party, 1963.

FPTU. *Memorandum of the Federation of Progressive Trade Unions to Mr. Duncan Sandys, Secretary of State for the*

Bibliography

Colonies and Commonwealth Relations, 23rd. February,
1963. Zanzibar: FPTU, 1963.

FPTU Political Bureau. The Brief History of International
Working Class Struggle. Zanzibar: FPTU, 1962.

Zanzibar Nationalist Party. Dawn in Zanzibar. Cairo: intermittent periodical published by the Foreign Mission of the
Zanzibar Nationalist Party.

Zanzibar Nationalist Party. Whither Zanzibar? The Growth
and Policy of Zanzibar Nationalism. Cairo: Zanzibar Nationalist Party, n.d.

Interviews with party officials.

Manifesto for the General Election of 17th January, 1961.

Memorandum of the Youths Own Union to Mr. Duncan
Sandys, Commonwealth and Colonial Secretary, 23rd February, 1963.

Miscellaneous press communiqués.

Party Regulations.

Speeches made at party meetings.

Statement on Party Organization.

Statement by the Youths Own Union on the Arrest of the
General Secretary, ZNP, President of Y.O.U. and Other Nine
Militant Members.

Zanzibar Nationalist Party Memorandum to Sir Hilary Blood,
Constitutional Commissioner, 1960.

Zanzibar Nationalist Party Statement on the Situation in the
Comoro Islands.

ZANZIBAR AND PEMBA PEOPLE'S PARTY

Interviews with party officials.

List of Officers.

Party Constitution.

Party Manifesto.

Speeches made at party meetings.

ZNP/ZPPP COALITION

United Nations General Assembly. Special Committee on the
Situation with regard to the Implementation of the Declaration on the Granting of Independence to Colonial Countries
and Peoples. The Question of Zanzibar, Memorandum Sub-

Bibliography

mitted to the Special Committee of Seventeen by Ali Muhsin.
United Nations: mimeograph, 1962.

Restatement of Policy. Zanzibar, December 1, 1961.

Statement by the ZNP/ZPPP Alliance Following Discussions with
Mr. Duncan Sandys, Commonwealth and Colonial Secretary.

Statement by ZNP and ZPPP on the conviction of Babu. 1962.

"Why You Should Vote ZNP/ZPPP." 1963.

ZNP/ZPPP Comments on Disturbances Report. 1961.

The Zanzibar Nationalist Party and Zanzibar and Pemba People's Party's Observations on the British Resident's Statement.

ZNP/ZPPP Statement on the Arrest of Members.

ZNP/ZPPP Statement on Colonial Secretary's Announcement Re-
garding Constitutional Development for Zanzibar.

ZNP/ZPPP Statement on the Party's International Policy.

The ZNP/ZPPP Statement on the Robertson Report on the
Coastal Strip.

INDEX

abolition: as impetus for British colonialism, 53; used to consolidate power, 58; emancipation process, 60-61; failures of, 61; compensation, 61, 99-100; as cause of indebtedness, 105-06; and squatter farming, 184. *See also* slave trade

African Association: origin, 99, 168; YAU in, 160; in nationalist movement, 160-61, 164; effect of civil service restrictions, 163-65; position on Rankine Plan, 166; in ASU merger, 171, 180; in 1957 election, 178-79. *See also* African nationalism, ASU

African community: under communal representation, 18, 65n, 99, 102-03, 139, 161-62, 168; bourgeoisie, 81; occupations, 81, 89; land ownership, 85, 87-88, 249; agriculturalists, 88; middle class, 88, 90; in pre-war politics, 102-03; as an underlying population, 103; role in ZNU, 142; lack of elite, 156, 159; squatters, 184-85. *See also* African nationalism, Afro-Shirazi disunity, Mainland community, Shirazi community, social stratification, traditional societies

African nationalism
  conservatism, 156-57; objectives, 156, 165-66; cause of, 158-59; position on Rankine Plan, 166; fear of common roll elections, 166-67
  phases defined, 158
  effect of British policy on, 159, 165-66
  militant phase: role of YAU, 160; role of African Associa-

tion, 160-61; methodology, 160; grievances, 160-63; decline, 163-64

Afrika Kwetu, 160, 168, 262

Afro-Shirazi disunity, 81-83, 155-56, 168; factors of, 82-83, 169-71, 250-51; British influence on, 162-63; 168; significance, 168; economic tensions, 187. *See also* ASU, communal identification, *Ittihad ul'Umma,* Shirazi community, ZPPP

Afro-Shirazi Party
  1957-1960: origin, 9-10; motivation, 10; trade union affiliates, 186-87, 233-34; consumer boycotts, 188, 192; and PAFMECSA, 189-92; in Freedom Committee, 190-92; internal conflict, 192-96, 231-34; policy, 194; consequences of split, 196, 230-31; relationship with Tanganyika, 199, 207-08, 216; effect of Freedom Committee, 199-200; structure and organization, 222-23; executive committee, 223, 231-33; organizational weaknesses, 230-34; recruitment, 230, 234; party funds, 231-32; objectives, 234; ideology, 235; Asian support, 235
  1961-1963: objectives, 198, 208-09; appeals, 198-99, 206-07; at Constitutional Conference, 212-17, 220; post-election fears, 213-14; strategy, 214-15, 253; campaign issues, 215-17; factors of defeat, 222; support, 243, 251; organization, 253-54
  post-election: hopes for "national" government, 219-20, 263; relationship with *Umma,* 262-63, 266-67; internal con-

lence in policy, 143-44; consolidation of support, 144-45; *Al Falaq* sedition trial, 144-45
multi-racial phase: formation of the NPSS, 147-48; demand for common roll election, 151-52; formation of the ZNP, 153-56. *See also* Arab Association, Seif Hamoud, Lemke, nationalism, NPSS, ZNP

Arab oligarchy
maintenance of political hegemony: in competitive representative democracy, 11; Islamic theory of obedience, 13; Shirazi support, 16, 47, 68; as leisured aristocracy, 27; importance of British policy, 52, 59; legitimacy, 68; social mobility, 76-77
decline, 102, 257, 270-71. *See also* British colonial policy Articles of Union, 285-87

Asian community: as a middle class, 14, 79; economic domination, 27, 79; under communal representation, 65n, 139; in civil service, 77; religious diversity, 79-80; isolationism, 80; political non-involvement, 80-81, 127-28; elite, 89, 94; money-lenders, 107, 109n; in franchise dispute, 131-32, 134-36. *See also* indebtedness, immigration

authoritarianism, 265-67

Babu, *see* Abdul Rahman Mohammed

Barghash, Sultan Seyyid, 55

Barnabas, Herbert, 165

Bartlett, C. A., 105n, 107n, 109n, 111n

Batson, Edward, 50n, 72n, 85ff, 89n, 91n-92n, 248n. *See also* Social Survey of Zanzibar

Bill of Human Rights, 344, 347

Binder, B. H., 105n, 107n, 110n, 115n, 119n

Blood, Sir Hilary, *see* Blood Report

Blood Report, 197, 213

boycotts: Legislative Council, 9, 146-47, 152; clove, 119-24; party consumer, 188-89

British colonialism after 1914, *see* British colonial policy, constitutional development

British colonialism to 1914, 18-20, 52; cooperation with Oman, 30-31, 53-54; abolition as impetus, 53-54; Busaidi dependency, 54-55; Protectorate Treaty, 55-56; dual mandate, 57-58; consolidation of power, 57-58. *See also* abolition, slave trade

British colonial policy: political tutelage, 20; abolition, 54, 60-61; concept of dual mandate, 57-58; phases defined, 59-60; pre-war/post-war compared, 127; effect on emergent nationalism, 131-33, 145-46
maintenance of Arab supremacy, 18-20, 52, 128; concept of Protectorate Treaty, 18, 59, 113-14; consequences of policy, 52, 66, 68, 101, 114, 129; preference shown, 59, 62-63, 90; impact on other policies, 60-61, 65-66, 113-14; non-Arab reaction to, 118, 161
civil service: reorganization of bureaucracy, 62; concept of role, 62n; recruitment, 62-63, 90; ban on political activity, 159; consequences of ban, 142, 159-60, 163-65
introduction of parliamentary institutions: Protectorate Council, 63; Executive Council, 63; Legislative Council, 63-67
communal representation: in

Index

Index

Index

Zanzibar Trade Union Congress, 265

Zanzibar and Pemba Federation of Labor: role in ASP, 233; support of *Umma,* 260; in national labor committee, 261; in revolution, 276

Zanzibar and Pemba People's Party: origin, 10, 192, 195; effect of coalition, 11, 236-37, 254-56; motivation, 173, 195; organization, 195, 236; support, 195, 235-36; objectives, 199; appeals, 199, 206-07; party split, 201; electoral coalition, 201-02; campaign issues, 216-17; consequences of split, 235-36; recruitment, 236. *See also* elections, *Ittihad ul'Umma,* voting behavior, ZNP-ZPPP coalition

Zanzibari Association, 141. *See also* ZNU

Zanzibarization, 90; as a political issue, 215-18

ZAYM, *see* Zanzibar African Youth Movement

ZNP-ZPPP coalition

1961-1963: origin, 10, 68, 200-03; significance, 10; appeals, 207; position on constitutional advance, 212; at Constitutional Conference, 213-14; structure, 214-15; campaign issues, 216-17; factors of electoral success, 221-22, 238; commitment, 237-38; Shirazi support, 252; strategy, 255

post-election: position on "national" government, 220; coalition stability, 221; authoritarian measures, 265-68; political legitimacy, 271. *See also* elections, voting behavior, ZNP, ZPPP

ZNU, *see* Zanzibar National Union

ZPFL, *see* Zanzibar and Pemba Federation of Labor

ZPPP, *see* Zanzibar and Pemba People's Party

ZTUC, *see* Zanzibar Trade Union Congress